Cli-Fi and Class

Under the Sign of Nature: Explorations in Environmental Humanities
Serenella Iovino, Kate Rigby, and John Tallmadge, Editors
Michael P. Branch and SueEllen Campbell, Senior Advisory Editors

Cli-Fi and Class

SOCIOECONOMIC JUSTICE IN CONTEMPORARY
AMERICAN CLIMATE FICTION

Edited by Debra J. Rosenthal
and Jason de Lara Molesky

UNIVERSITY OF VIRGINIA PRESS
CHARLOTTESVILLE AND LONDON

University of Virginia Press
© 2023 by the Rector and Visitors of the University of Virginia
All rights reserved
Printed in the United States of America on acid-free paper

First published 2023

9 8 7 6 5 4 3 2 1

Library of Congress Cataloging-in-Publication Data

Names: Rosenthal, Debra J., editor. | Molesky, Jason de Lara, editor.
Title: Cli-fi and class : socioeconomic justice in contemporary American climate fiction / edited by Debra J. Rosenthal and Jason de Lara Molesky.
Description: Charlottesville : University of Virginia Press, 2023. | Includes bibliographical references and index.
Identifiers: LCCN 2023018067 (print) | LCCN 2023018068 (ebook) | ISBN 9780813950242 (hardcover) | ISBN 9780813950259 (paperback) | ISBN 9780813950266 (ebook)
Subjects: LCSH: Climatic changes in literature. | Social justice in literature. | American fiction—21st century—History and criticism.
Classification: LCC PS374.C555 C55 2023 (print) | LCC PS374.C555 (ebook) | DDC 813.60905—dc23/eng/20230620
LC record available at https://lccn.loc.gov/2023018067
LC ebook record available at https://lccn.loc.gov/2023018068

Cover art: Buildings estherpoon/istock.com; wave Ig0rZh/istock.com

Contents

Acknowledgments vii

Introduction 1

Part I. Class Structure and Resource Extraction

Hadestown and Other Myths for the Anthropocene: Company Towns and Proletarian Traditions in US Climate Fiction 15
   Jason de Lara Molesky

Burnout: Cli-Fi and Exhaustion 32
   Lisa Ottum

Resource Utopia and Dystopia: Excavating Class in Afrofuturist Cli-Fi Film 47
   Martín Premoli and B. Jamieson Stanley

Dreaming a Decolonized Climate: Indigenous Technologies and Relations of Class and Kinship in Cherie Dimaline's *The Marrow Thieves* 63
   Jessica Cory

Part II. Class Differentiation and Climate Risk

Climate-Change Fiction and Poverty Studies: Kingsolver's *Flight Behavior*, Diaz's "Monstro," and Bacigalupi's "The Tamarisk Hunter" 81
   Debra J. Rosenthal

Learning to Survive: Place-Based Education in *Strange as This Weather Has Been* and *Parable of the Sower* 101
   Jennifer Horwitz

Settler Apocalypses: Race, Class, and the Erasure of Indigenous Resilience in Alaskan Cli-Fi   117
  Jennifer Schell

Black: A Speculative Almanac for the End of the World   133
  Kimberly Bain

Part III. Class Privilege and Climate Anxiety

Class and Revolution in the Climate Fictions of Kim Stanley Robinson: Transition to Postcapitalism   151
  Andrew Milner

Heartland of Darkness: Nostalgia and Class in the Climate Fiction of Paolo Bacigalupi   167
  Jeffrey M. Brown

Whose Odds? The Absence of Climate Justice in American Climate Fiction of the 2000s and 2010s   184
  Matthew Schneider-Mayerson

Cli-Fi and the Crisis of the Middle Class   205
  Magdalena Mączyńska

Homelessness in Lauren Groff's Florida Fiction: Climate Change and Displacement   221
  Teresa A. Goddu

Epilogue: What Has Changed since *Anthropocene Fictions*?   235
  Adam Trexler

Notes on Contributors   245

Index   249

Acknowledgments

Debra J. Rosenthal is grateful for support from a Grauel Faculty Fellowship at John Carroll University, from King's College London where she served as a Visiting Scholar, and from Tea House Theatre in London.

Jason de Lara Molesky was supported in this work by a Porter Ogden Jacobus Fellowship at Princeton University and a residency at the Blue Mountain Center. He would like to express his deep thanks to both institutions.

Debra J. Rosenthal's essay in this volume first appeared as "Climate-Change Fiction and Poverty Studies: Kingsolver's *Flight Behavior*, Diaz's 'Monstro,' and Bacigalupi's 'The Tamarisk Hunter'" in *ISLE: Interdisciplinary Studies in Literature and the Environment,* vol. 27, no. 2, 2020, pp. 268–86. A shortened version of Matthew Schneider-Mayerson's essay appeared as "Whose Odds? The Absence of Climate Justice in American Climate Fiction Novels" in *ISLE: Interdisciplinary Studies in Literature and the Environment,* vol. 26, no. 4, 2019, pp. 944–67. Both essays are included here courtesy of Oxford University Press.

Cli-Fi and Class

Introduction

Since its inception in the late twentieth century, climate fiction has concerned itself as much with class struggle and popular revolt as with rising seas. Indeed, the focus on redressing disparities in this corpus is salient enough that one might reasonably consider cli-fi a form of protest literature. This collection of essays aims to invigorate the literary imagination's engagement with planetary heating by focusing on representations of socioeconomic justice in climate-change narratives. In its exploration of cli-fi and class, the collection draws attention to the ways that descriptors of climate change such as "anthropogenic" and "human-caused" tend to conflate all people as equally complicit in the climate crisis. Such designations flatten humanity into a general category, implying that every person, culture, and socioeconomic system holds the same degree of relative responsibility for altering the biosphere (Karera 39). A central goal of this volume, then, is to tease out the issue of class from the broader, species-level frameworks usually invoked, and in this way to analyze the complex interplays between climate change and inequalities of wealth and power.

The contributors recognize that low-wage, low-status workers and those unable to work, especially in the Global South, will suffer the ravages of our imploding carbon-based economy sooner and more severely than will the rich. These groups are responsible for comparatively little greenhouse pollution, yet they are already bearing the brunt of its socioecological harms. "The gulf between the responsibility for and suffering from climate change is staggering," Matthew Schneider-Mayerson notes in this volume in reference to international differences, going on to explain that "approximately 20 percent of the global population has been responsible for 75–80 percent of historical greenhouse gas emissions since the Industrial Revolution." Similar dynamics apply within any given nation-state: poverty begets vulnerability, as the poor have fewer resources to ameliorate their difficulties. Within nations or among them, class inequalities tend to precipitate cruel cascades of disproportionate hardship in response to climate impacts. To take just one example, people of sufficient economic means can recover more readily from severe weather events and better insulate themselves, at least for the moment, from related societal impacts. Focusing on the structures of socioeconomic differentiation laid bare in such disparities, this collection of essays operates at the intersection of the economic and the ecological to foster new perspectives on the art and literature of climate change.

During the same decades that witnessed the rise of climate fiction (and its equivalents in other media), scholars in the social sciences and environmental history began generating urgent, sophisticated Marxian analyses of ecological crisis and fossil fuel extraction. This work takes off from Marx's and Engel's deep engagements with the environmental problems of their era, and its key insights—particularly the view of nature and the poor as simultaneous objects of exploitation—continue to influence climate activists worldwide.[1] Despite its relevance to cli-fi texts, however, this line of Marxian thought has not yet made significant inroads in literary criticism about climate fiction, which has tended to focus on more abstract issues like multiscalar complexity and distributed agency in relation to narrative form.[2] Another major goal of this volume, therefore, is to illuminate some of the crucial questions about class and crisis that Marxian frameworks offer to the study of cli-fi. What might it mean to read climate fiction not as an artifact of the Anthropocene but of the Capitalocene?[3]

If Marx penetrated the everyday illusions of free market exchange, many contemporary Marxian scholars turn their sights on what Nancy Fraser, repurposing Marx's well-known phrase, calls the "hidden abode" of production itself ("Behind Marx's Hidden Abode" 60). This entails a conceptual shift from the exploitation of citizen-workers through alienated wage labor within the nation-state to the violent expropriation of nonwage labor and ecological commons, such as the atmosphere, from marginalized populations around the globe. Scholars like David Harvey contend that expropriation is not confined to capitalism's garish origins in land enclosure and plantation slavery, as Marx theorized, but remains the foundational element of the system. Building on this idea, Fraser argues that capital mobilizes racialization and other technologies of social othering to differentiate the merely exploitable areas of the capitalist core from the "expropriable" ecosystems of the peripheries, including the peripheries within the core—for example, the distressed North American urban centers and extraction zones addressed in several of this volume's essays (Fraser, "Expropriation and Exploitation"). Expropriation, then, which Fraser calls "the back-story" of capitalist production, expands prevailing ideas of class conflict in critical ways. Boundary struggles over what can and cannot be expropriated into the productive process come to the fore, such that mass protests against mines, power plants, pipelines, and other fossil fuel infrastructure, spearheaded by the frontline communities John Bellamy Foster identifies as an emerging "environmental proletariat" (398–99), are now understood to entail the same solidarities as labor strikes (440–41).

Assertive labor actions also feature prominently in Marxian climate theory. Matthew Huber, among others, holds that workplace militancy in the core industrialized areas must drive any effective climate movement. Expanding on Timothy Mitchell's writings about the centrality of coal miners' unions in achieving mass democracy, Huber calls for a global "working-class climate politics" that would eschew what he views as the austere, professional-class rhetoric of sustainability, and instead focus on "linking climate solutions to practical improvements in workers' everyday lives" and "recovering workers' militant capacity to strike," especially in high-emitting industries (40). From an adjacent perspective, Ashley Dawson advocates going beyond green capitalism and placing the energy and electric utility sectors under participatory democratic control. Looking to popular struggles for mass electrification in the 1920s and 1930s, as well as to worker-led uprisings for energy nationalization, Dawson imagines a "global energy commons," in which energy is treated not as a privately owned commodity but as a public good shared among all people (17). Such arguments suggest that the powerful interests Andreas Malm terms "fossil capital" are unlikely to cede influence unless compelled to do so by a class-based justice movement springing from the world's billions of proletarianized workers, particularly those living at the frontlines of fossil energy development projects.

Ecological Marxian visions of class struggle, whether centered upon sites of production or zones of expropriation, offer powerful tools for scholars of art and literature seeking to address their work to the climate emergency. Seen through the lens of class, climate fiction comes to seem less an imagined story of the future and more the refracted "back-story" of the present. Many have argued that cli-fi can help us to imagine a way beyond the crisis. From the ecological Marxian perspective, which understands class stratification as a geophysical process as much as a socioeconomic one, cli-fi instead helps us to imagine a way deeper into the crisis, to a place of convergence where rising seas and rising inequalities can be simultaneously combated by popular groundswells.

Class, of course, involves factors beyond income and wealth. As scholars since E. P. Thompson have argued, class might best be conceived as an embodied set of group relations based on histories of economic production but also encompassing many other intersecting cultural elements, notably race and racialization. Theories of racial capitalism, as initially developed by Cedric Robinson from earlier work on Black radicalism and the imperial world system, offer robust models for understanding how the imbrications of race and class have evolved over time.[4] Perhaps the key insight emerging from this corpus is that the term "racial capitalism" is effectively tautological; since the early modern period, when one discusses the logic of race or the logic of capital, one is also necessarily discussing the other. Race does not influence class systems from the outside, as an external force, nor is it entirely an artifact of cynical antilabor strategies; rather, ideas of race act as formative elements in the development of modern capitalism and its characteristic modes of socioeconomic differentiation.

Robinson posits that, from feudal antecedents in colonized Ireland and elsewhere, European racial thought was transplanted into the Atlantic world, where it ripened in the strange soils of the plantation-genocide-industrial complex and gave rise to a "new racism" that continues to structure global economies and ecosystems, not least in the United States and its spheres of influence (189). Race, then, as Stuart Hall notes, is often "the medium through which class relations are experienced" (216). Many of the essays in this volume frame the climate crisis not only as the result of these commingled historical forces but as the quotidian apocalypse that reveals the inextricable, mutually constitutive links binding them in the here and now. In this regard, the collection aims to contribute to burgeoning theoretical efforts by Kathryn Yusoff and others to establish racial capitalism as a fundamentally socioecological process, one that impacts natural and social worlds alike and must deeply inform any class-centered account of Anthropocene cultural production.[5]

Operating within these and related analytics, several contributors also focus on the crucial role that whiteness plays in constituting class systems. Indeed, as Nancy Tuana argues, extractive networks of corporate wealth are "grounded in both racism and environmental exploitation" (14). *Cli-Fi and Class* emphasizes a sort of economic geology, a framework in which the same systems of socioeconomic stratification that privilege white access to the middle classes also drive the extreme weather events disproportionately affecting the poor. While it would be inaccurate to claim that a phenomenon as overarching as climate change could be caused primarily by ideas of whiteness, it would likewise be wrong to ignore the affinities between fossil capitalism and the structural legacies of white supremacy.

The systemic dynamics favoring white identity have also created popular desires for the symbols of upward class mobility that drive outsize carbon emissions and other forms of environmental degradation. For example, a class-based analysis of Italian, Irish, Polish, and Jewish immigrants, who were originally excluded from "Nordic" American opportunities due to the eugenic beliefs of the early twentieth century, reveals an intricate connection between the attainment of a fully white racial identity and an anxious move into the middle and upper strata of the postwar class system.[6] By accessing whiteness, such immigrants were able to assimilate into environments that frequently excluded African Americans, Asian Americans, tribal nations, and "white trash." The petroleum-drenched Fordist economy, with its emphasis on creating mass markets for standardized manufactured goods, encouraged such workers to embrace a consumerist model of white identity that contributed mightily to escalating greenhouse pollution during the post-1945 period of parabolic growth often referred to as the Great Acceleration. To liberate notions of collective prosperity from this ideological fusion of whiteness and fossil fuels remains one of the most urgent challenges facing climate politics today.

More concretely, ideas of whiteness have permitted white-owned American companies to exploit the lands and labor of racially marginalized peoples in order to extract and refine fossil resources. For example, citing slavery's evolution into other modes of legalized compulsion, Tuana shows that "Alabama's convict lease program fueled the [state's] coal industry" well into the twentieth century, and that the descendants of the enslaved people who had been made to mine coal for the Confederacy were later compelled to power the industrialization of the region (16). Andrew Needham reveals that similar extractive dynamics held sway over the lands of the Diné (Navajo), noting that the explosive growth of Sunbelt cities such as Phoenix and Las Vegas "relied overwhelmingly on coal that was both mined and transformed into electricity on Indian land" (10). The lived reality of racialized vagrancy laws and the disproportionate number of minorities who have lived near polluting fossil-fuel infrastructure form the foundation of many environmental justice movements, but the social phenomenon of whiteness allows corporations to deploy such practices and for governments to endorse them.

Even the poorest whites benefit from racial privilege insofar as they are distanced from such harmful scenarios. Nonetheless, whiteness studies can be faulted for sometimes homogenizing white-identified people in ways that can elide not only historical disparities but also the vast inequalities of the neoliberal order. Further, the term "white trash" is complicated, particularly on former plantation zones in the South, as Du Bois shows in *Black Reconstruction* and Faulkner portrays in his novels, and in rural areas, where inhabitants were constructed as archaic primitives by local color writers in the late nineteenth century to justify the expropriation of land for extractive projects. This legacy, too, continues today, facilitating the regional uptake of extreme extraction technologies, such as shale hydrofracking and mountaintop-removal coal mining, as discussed in several contributors' essays.

In attempting to tease out, and productively re-entangle, the intersecting elements of class, community, and ecological health, this volume's approach to climate vulnerability complements the important scholarship on environmental justice that has come out of American and postcolonial studies in recent decades. Indeed, the two fields—the climate humanities on one hand and environmental justice on the other—inhabit increasingly adjacent academic spaces. While their origins are very different, their trajectories are rapidly converging around the urgent question of how our socioeconomic system externalizes the harms of fossil-fueled hypergrowth and viscerally imposes them on the bodies and ecosystems of the marginalized poor. Concerns over climate change began as abstract projections in academic journals and are only now—as theorized droughts become actual droughts, and hurricanes leap from spreadsheets to flood actual cities—taking shape as movements for meaningful climate action. The story of environmental justice, on the other hand, can almost be seen as following the opposite path. Emerging as a series of grassroots movements against toxic pollution in poor, minority, and working-class districts, it is only now pervading the academy, which still often retains the tendency to think beyond the pain of others rather than striving to think through it.[7]

Much humanities scholarship has suggested that the vast scales at stake in the climate crisis, and the ways it seems to diffuse causality across epochs and continents, render it insuperable to human cognition and beyond any possibility of narrative representation. Environmental justice activists demonstrate what is perhaps a more pragmatic way of thinking. They have often been made to breathe and drink the toxic effluents of causal chains that are no less complex than those involved in climate change—that are, indeed, downstream from the same systemic forces, often impacting the same communities. In response, environmental justice pioneers like Robert and Linda Bullard in rural Georgia, Lois Gibbs in Love Canal, and Hazel Johnson in the South Side of Chicago, forged coalitions to protest harms that were both enormously complex and simply obvious—much like the impacts of the climate crisis on poor and underserved communities today. In trying to strike a similar balance, the contributors to *Cli-Fi and Class* often draw influence from the adjacent sphere of environmental justice scholarship, which, in spite of its distinct evolution and unique discursive through lines, is a forceful ally in this volume's examinations of the climate emergency.

The importance of socioeconomics to climate change literature crosses many genres. Our contributors discuss the intersection of cli-fi and class in best-selling popular novels, science fiction titles, literary novels that have been recognized by awards juries, Hollywood films, and Broadway plays, among other forms. If, as Gary Saul Morson observes, "*genre* does not belong to texts alone, but to the interaction between texts and a classifier" (x; emphasis original), then as we readers become more accustomed to the reality of climate catastrophe, our position as "classifiers" renormalizes cli-fi to the realm of realism and not "genre" fiction or sci-fi. Perhaps this current expansiveness of genre redresses Amitav Ghosh's point that cli-fi themes often predetermine generic contours and prevent a work from being considered high-brow literary fiction. Ghosh posits that "fiction that deals with climate change is almost by definition not of the kind that is taken seriously by serious literary journals: the mere mention of the subject is often enough to relegate a novel or a short story to the genre of science fiction" (7). As an example, Ghosh points to climate change–induced extreme weather as something that seems "improbable" from the perspective of "the regularity of bourgeois life"; therefore, for a writer to include such a happening in a novel is "to court eviction from the mansion in which serious fiction has long been in residence; it is to risk banishment to . . . those generic outhouses that were once known by names such as 'the Gothic,' 'the romance,' or 'the melodrama,' and have now come to be called 'fantasy,' 'horror,' and 'science fiction'" (24). Ghosh's architectural metaphor and the provocative language in which it is couched strongly imply that his generic distinctions are also, or even primarily, class distinctions (and perhaps racialized ones, given the implicit imagery of the plantation). The element of class also comes to the fore in Ghosh's understanding of literary realism as coextensive with the bourgeois realism of James and Flaubert, a mode of writing defined in part by its aversion to the lifeworlds of the poor. By these lights, climate impacts seem like another in the long line of insults the poor have borne that are considered too vulgar for inclusion in high realist novels. What is "improbable," in other words, depends on one's class position. Underlying the regularity on which this kind of literary realism depends is the chaos of the slums and extraction zones most vulnerable to climate impacts.

The fourteen essays in *Cli-Fi and Class* fit together in many interlocking possibilities. To clarify some compelling ways to think about the intersection of ecology and economy, we have organized the volume into three sections. The first, "Class Structure and Resource Extraction," comprises four essays on the imbrication of class, capitalism, and resource removal in narratives of fossil fuel extraction. Jason Molesky's essay attends to the frequent appearance of the company coal town, the originary site of climate change, in speculative climate fiction. Through a reading of *Hadestown*, Molesky argues that the binary class structures in the speculative portrayals at once clarify and obscure the means of contesting climate chaos. Lisa Ottum examines how "regimes of bioderegulation" exhaust lands and poor communities for the benefit of global finance in Jennifer Haigh's hydrofracking novel, *Heat and Light*. Ottum argues, more broadly, that realist fiction concerned with class and resource extraction can illuminate the everyday workings of climate crisis and encourage ameliorative action at least as well as speculative texts. Martín Premoli and B. Jamieson Stanley's essay examines the blockbuster film *Black Panther* through a decolonial lens by attending to the non-Western, Afrofuturist imaginary manifest in Wakanda. Drawing out the implications of vibranium mining and the clean, high-tech culture it enables, Premoli and Stanley analyze the film's vexed attempts to envision alternatives to imperial structures of class that may help us to navigate a climate-changed world. Jessica Cory's essay on Cherie Dimaline's novel *The Marrow Thieves* examines ideas of technology as vectors of racial and class power. By addressing the complex metaphors at work in the novel's figures of extraction and expropriation, Cory draws attention to how postapocalyptic scenarios, for Indigenous peoples, can refract already existing forms of settler violence.

The essays in the second section, "Class Differentiation and Climate Risk," attend to the way socioeconomic stratification affects how climate change is experienced. Debra J. Rosenthal's essay provides an "ecopoverty" analysis of Barbara Kingsolver's *Flight Behavior* by reading wealth inequality through climate change to understand the impossible dilemma faced by the low-income Turnbow family in Appalachia as they must make terrible decisions about their home and livelihood. At the same time, their lives intersect with those of the Delgado family, climate migrants who had to flee their home in Mexico due to climate-induced flooding and landslides. Jennifer Horwitz's essay considers the ways that historical class position can mediate one's relationship to home and futurity. Focusing on Ann Pancake's novel *Strange as This Weather Has Been*, Horwitz raises increasingly important local questions about how we might best care for "places that prove deadly" in the age of climate impacts. Jennifer Schell's essay explores similar class dynamics in fiction dealing with Indigenous lifeways on the frontlines of climate change in Alaska. Schell suggests that whereas realist novels situated here often present class structures in the starkly binary terms laid out by settlers, Don Rearden's speculative novel *The Raven's Gift* is better situated to "highlight the thorny contradictions and complexities of life in the Arctic" as the climate rapidly shifts, which may open avenues for moving beyond present disparities. Kim Bain's essay asserts that "an attention to climate and capitalism is by necessity preoccupied with anti-Blackness and anti-Black speculative forms." To that end, Bain probes the intersection of climatic extremes, digital racism, and surveillance capitalism by discussing the final episode of Terence Nance's *Random Acts of Flyness*.

In the third section, "Class Privilege and Climate Anxiety," five essays assess the potential of climate narratives to imagine and emplot novel forms of social organization. Andrew Milner's essay takes up the surprising absence of labor politics from cli-fi texts, even those authored by avowed socialists. In a provocative reading of Kim Stanley Robinson, Milner investigates the forms of postcapitalist society that could become possible if scientists recognize themselves as "employees, what Marx would have termed proletarians." Jeffrey M. Brown's essay argues that the work of another major cli-fi author, Paolo Bacigalupi, evinces the "relentless pull of literary history and narrative form" on climate fiction's attempts to envision alternate modes of social organization. Situating Bacigalupi alongside Joseph Conrad, Brown draws out the ways that the plots of the past can insinuate themselves into efforts to reimagine the anxiety of climate impacts.

Matthew Schneider-Mayerson asks: whose perspectives are emphasized and whose are left out as cli-fi becomes popular? He argues that cli-fi prioritizes the experiences of wealthy, white, educated Americans, and thus frames climate catastrophe to shape our actions in a way that benefits the privileged. Magdalena Mączyńska's essay also addresses class mobility and mobilization. In what she calls "the crisis of the middle-class spatial imaginary," Mączyńska discusses cli-fi's futuristic scenarios of bifurcated societies that displace a sense of home: the superrich live in protected compounds, while the extreme poor scavenge for scraps amidst the destruction. The anxiety of middle-class life eroding matches ambivalence about the role of the novel's traditional loci of the suburban home or the city. Finally, Teresa Goddu argues that Lauren Groff uses the "psychogeography" of Florida—the state's paradoxical role as the sunny symbol and gothic underbelly of the nation—to puncture the American fairy tale of upward mobility and white middle-class stability. Groff uses ecological crisis to expose the economic insecurity that already stalks America's homes and city streets even as she critiques the class privilege that undergirds her own climate dread. Goddu argues that in Groff's rendering, Florida is full of "human flotsam"—the evicted, the abandoned, the homeless—who portend America's climate future.

Finally, Adam Trexler's seminal 2015 study, *Anthropocene Fictions*, opened the door for many literary scholars of climate fiction and made possible many of the essays in this volume. As an epilogue to *Cli-Fi and Class*, Trexler reflects back to survey how much the field has changed since the publication of *Anthropocene Fictions*, particularly with regard to the attention paid to issues of socioeconomics. Trexler's epilogue casts backwards as it propels us forward for future considerations of the embeddedness of class structure in climate change.

NOTES

1. Andreas Malm points to the salubrious influence of ecological Marxist ideas on climate activism, in particular as discussed in the work of Naomi Klein; for his arguments, see *The Progress of This Storm*, especially p. 175n40.

2. For two excellent overviews of climate fiction and its criticism, see Johns-Putra, "Climate Change in Literature and Literary Studies," and Craps and Crenshaw, "Introduction: The Rising Tide of Climate Change Fiction."

3. The starting point of the Capitalocene not surprisingly remains an object of contention. Jason W. Moore, who seems to have coined the term, posits the late

fifteenth century, while many others support later moments, such as Watt's invention of efficient steam engines in the late eighteenth century. For the term as Moore uses it, see Moore, *Capitalism in the Web of Life*.

    4. Principally, Robinson draws on the signal contributions of scholars such as C. L. R. James, W. E. B. Du Bois, Eric Williams, and Oliver Cox.

    5. See Yusoff, *A Billion Black Anthropocenes or None*. Interdisciplinary work around concepts like the Plantationocene also plays a key role in this effort.

    6. See Noel Ignatiev's *How the Irish Became White*, Jennifer Guglielmo's *Are Italians White?*, and David Roediger's *Working toward Whiteness: How America's Immigrants Became White; The Strange Journey from Ellis Island to the Suburbs*.

    7. For an important early document in the environmental justice movement, see Bullard, *Dumping in Dixie*, which presents his and Linda Bullard's research into toxic waste sites in the American South. The Bullards' work has given rise to other frameworks that inform the essays in *Cli-Fi and Class*. For example, Andrew Hurley and Julie Sze, respectively, extend theories of classed, racialized toxicity to the industrial city and the postindustrial metropolis, paying special attention to the multiracial coalitions that have formed in response to environmental threats not dissimilar to those in cli-fi texts. See Hurley, *Environmental Inequalities*, and Sze, *Noxious New York*.

WORKS CITED

Bellamy Foster, John, Brett Clark, and Richard York. *The Ecological Rift*. Monthly Review, 2010.

Bullard, Robert. *Dumping in Dixie: Race, Class, and Environmental Quality*. 1990. Routledge, 2000.

Craps, Stef, and Rick Crenshaw. "Introduction: The Rising Tide of Climate Change Fiction." *Studies in the Novel*, vol. 50, no. 1, 2018, pp. 1–8.

Dawson, Ashley. *People's Power: Reclaiming the Energy Commons*. Verso, 2020.

Fraser, Nancy. "Behind Marx's Hidden Abode: For an Expanded Conception of Capitalism." *New Left Review*, no. 86, 2014, pp. 55–72.

———. "Expropriation and Exploitation in Racialized Capitalism: A Reply to Michael Dawson." *Critical Historical Studies*, vol. 3, no. 1, 2016, pp. 163–78.

Ghosh, Amitav. *The Great Derangement: Climate Change and the Unthinkable*. U of Chicago P, 2016.

Hall, Stuart. "Race, Articulation, and Societies Structured in Dominance." *Essential Essays*. Edited by David Morely, vol. 1, Duke UP, 2019, pp. 172–221.

Harvey, David. "The 'New' Imperialism: Accumulation by Dispossession." *Socialist Register*, no. 40, 2014, pp. 63–87.

Huber, Matthew T. *Climate Change as Class War: Building Socialism on a Warming Planet*. Verso, 2022.

Hurley, Andrew. *Environmental Inequalities: Class, Race, and Industrial Pollution in Gary, Indiana, 1945–1980*. U of North Carolina P, 2009.

Johns-Putra, Adeline. "Climate Change in Literature and Literary Studies." *WIREs Climate Change*, no. 7, 2016, pp. 266–82.

Karera, Axelle. "Blackness and the Pitfalls of Anthropocene Ethics." *Critical Philosophy of Race*, vol. 7, no. 1, 2019, pp. 32–56.

Malm, Andreas. *The Progress of This Storm*. Verso, 2018.

Moore, Jason W. *Capitalism in the Web of Life: Ecology and the Accumulation of Capital*. Verso, 2015.

Morson, Gary Saul. *The Boundaries of Genre*. U of Texas P, 1981.

Needham, Andrew. *Power Lines: Phoenix and the Making of the Modern Southwest*. Princeton UP, 2014.

Robinson, Cedric J. "White Signs in Black Times: The Politics of Representation in Dominant Texts." *Cedric J. Robinson: On Racial Capitalism, Black Internationalism, and Cultures of Resistance*. Edited by H. L. T. Quan, Pluto Press, 2019, pp. 185–94.

Sze, Julie. *Noxious New York: The Racial Politics of Urban Health and Environmental Justice*. MIT Press, 2007.

Tuana, Nancy. "Climate Apartheid: The Forgetting of Race in the Anthropocene." *Critical Philosophy of Race*, vol. 7, no. 1, 2019, pp. 1–31.

Yusoff, Kathryn. *A Billion Black Anthropocenes or None*. Minnesota UP, 2019.

PART I

Class Structure and Resource Extraction

Hadestown and Other Myths for the Anthropocene
Company Towns and Proletarian Traditions in US Climate Fiction

JASON DE LARA MOLESKY

American climate fiction attends more intensely to socioeconomic disparities and corporate power than perhaps any coherent body of US writing since the height of the proletarian movement in the 1930s. Everywhere in the cli-fi corpus, one encounters instances of oppression based on class or caste and the concomitant drive for systemic transformation. Yet most criticism on the subject still focuses on relatively abstract concerns such as multiscalar complexity, distributed agency, and the question of whether the novel as a form can adequately comprehend the ineffable hyperobjects said to be at the root of the climate crisis. Such approaches to climate texts have proven enormously impactful in illuminating emergent political assemblages and highlighting art's imaginative potential. Nonetheless, the time seems ripe for an expansion of our critical vision in regards to cli-fi, one that would account not only for vibrant matter but also for the violent hierarchies at the center of so many of these texts. If we conceptualize cli-fi as a form of protest literature oriented around social justice—that is, a contemporary analog to abolitionist, proletarian, or anti-colonial writing—new kinds of questions begin to arise, and cli-fi assumes its place within longer histories of class-based resistance and activism.

It seems far from incidental that many important works of climate fiction, a category in which I include films, stage plays, and other kinds of narratives, situate action within company towns, corporate enclaves, and similar sites controlled by capital as such. This apparently minor or atmospheric detail, when repositioned at the core of the interpretive matrix, compels contemporary artworks about climate change into a stranger and more complex relation to genre and tradition, while animating a series of urgent questions about class, capital, and environmental harm in the Anthropocene. One could argue that climate change emerges, in large part, from US company towns like Ludlow, Homestead, and Pullman—not to mention Ciénaga, Colombia; Dhahran, Saudi Arabia; Harbel, Liberia; and other international outposts of America's corporate imperium.[1] But why should speculative cli-fi texts as varied as *Parable of the Sower*, *Snowpiercer*, *Cyberpunk 2077*, and *The Hunger Games* all feature company towns or derivative settlements? In what ways, and to what effects, do such texts draw upon American literary and cultural traditions like naturalism or cyberpunk, which deploy the figure of the company town to contest unjust class arrangements and to counter the hegemony of capital over societies and environments? What half-shorn taproots of popular memory are their creators remixing here, and to what artistic and social purposes?

My way into these questions is deeply personal, arising from my years as an underground coal miner, as well as from my familial experiences in the diverse, military-industrial regions of Appalachia and the Sonoran borderlands. The company towns in cli-fi texts have haunted me since I first encountered the genre. For example, the impunity with which the CorpSeCorp private security forces in Margaret Atwood's *Oryx and Crake* surveil and harass even the relatively privileged residents of the novel's corporate-owned Compounds brings forth images of my great-uncle, who, at age fifteen, lost his right eye to a mercenary's tear gas canister while visiting his striking father on the picket line. The coal town in which this happened, Ellsworth, still bears the name of its initial owner, a board member of the 1893 Columbian Exposition who would later use the "stupendous profit" from the sale of the town to purchase Villa Palmieri in Florence, where Boccaccio wrote the *Decameron*, as well as other literary artifacts such as a Gutenberg Bible and several of the earliest incunabula ("J.W. Ellsworth").

Company towns in climate fiction, to whatever extent they might intend it, take inspiration from deep histories of class like this one. They do so primarily by incorporating tropes, generic markers, and other representational elements derived from artworks about company towns, especially the archetypal coal towns authors draw from most often. In other words, we are dealing with a phenomenon of cultural mythology—one that arguably originated, like the term "company town," in literary reportage from nineteenth-century mining camps and has subsequently evolved across multiple genres and mediums to become a powerful vehicle for chronicling the Anthropocene.[2]

In what follows, I discuss several cli-fi texts that marshal the figure of the company town in this way. Principally, I focus on a narrative that has evolved across several mediums since its 2006 debut as a bare-bones, folk-opera adaptation of the Orpheus and Eurydice myth for an age of climate crisis and socioeconomic precarity. Most, no doubt, will know Anaïs Mitchell's *Hadestown* as a multiple-Tony-award-winning musical, and it is in that guise that I first encountered it in late 2019, just before the pandemic shuttered Broadway. Mitchell, who got her start as a folk singer, adapted the musical from the project's second iteration, her 2010 album of the same name, which features a cast of indie standouts alongside her own performance of a working-class Eurydice imperiled by climate fallout.

Unless otherwise noted, I am referring here to the Broadway production. But all versions of *Hadestown* employ the same rollicking fusion of jazz, ragtime, blues, roots, country, and other Americana. All begin in a fantastic nightclub suggestive of New Orleans, where Eurydice works as a waitress and Orpheus as a busboy. Outside, the world is riddled with famine and other climatic impacts. As a harried Eurydice sings in the opening number, "Weather ain't the way it was before / Ain't no spring or fall at all anymore / It's either blazing hot or freezing cold" (Mitchell, *Working* 21).[3] Crucially, the song's refrain—"Any way the wind blows / Wind comes up, ooooh"—features the same powerful wind imagery that saturates the opening sequence of Émile Zola's coal mining epic, *Germinal*. And indeed, Étienne, Zola's central figure, wanders the wastes in search of food and a job, precisely as Eurydice does here. That this refrain is delivered by a chorus consisting of the three Fates only further reflects the strategies *Hadestown* will use to dynamically interweave mythic and proletarian forms around its core interest in bringing what Matthew Huber refers to, in another context, as a "working-class politics of climate" to the unlikely environs of a Broadway stage (39).

Given Mitchell's allusive register, it is perhaps not surprising that the second half of the musical shifts to the subterranean industrial zone of Hadestown, where Hades, "king of oil and coal," owns everything, including the souls of his workers (Mitchell, *Working* 96). The plot unfolds with the elegant logic of myth. Hades's manic expansion projects, including a border wall along the river Styx, have disillusioned his wife, Persephone, disrupted the climate, and driven the workers into abjection and amnesia. Eurydice, on the verge of starving, gives herself over to become one of them, and Orpheus steals into the underworld to reclaim her with a song. Once there, he rouses the workers and appeals to Persephone, hoping to restore balance to the seasons. This collective effort nearly succeeds, but, as in the ancient story, Orpheus is undone by doubt and fatally looks back just as he and the group approach daylight.

Hadestown, I want to suggest, synthesizes classical poetry, proletarian zeal, and environmental urgency to propose the outlines of a myth for the Anthropocene. Like many radical women writers before her, Mitchell uses the figure of the company town to animate the possibility of moving beyond ossified power arrangements. In an era when the fabulous Orphic claim that human desires can sway the natural world has become a banal truth, Mitchell's musical examines the links between social and climatic ills, while underscoring the ways in which precarity can lead the desperate to ally themselves with the selfsame systems that dispossessed them of a livable environment in the first place. Drawing at once on the Orpheus story and on histories of class-based collective action in America's coal towns, *Hadestown* encourages us to reflect not only on nonhuman animacy but on political agency, and to consider how art might recollect lively traditions of dissent in order to shape our responses to the crises of the present.

THE GIFT OF ORPHEUS

Mitchell describes *Hadestown*'s setting as "this kind of post-apocalyptic, American Depression-era company town style of place" ("Anaïs Mitchell"). The qualifiers she uses—"kind of," "style of place," "type of thing"—serve to highlight the impressionistic character of her vision, the mélange of inputs and echoes that inform the play's unique conjuncture of class struggle and climate crisis. But Mitchell's is far from the only cli-fi company town animated by multiple intertexts. In general, the company towns featured in climate fiction show influences ranging from the brutal coal villages of *Germinal* to the high-tech arcologies of William Gibson's *Neuromancer*, eliding disparate eras and styles of corporate governance into a single figure.

One of Octavia Butler's characters in *Parable of the Sower* knowingly nods to this eclecticism when a new company town called Olivar emerges to profit from climate change in the novel's near-future California. "This business sounds half antebellum revival and half science fiction," he says (122). Yet Olivar also reflects perhaps the most important way that cli-fi company towns tend to differ from their precursors in adjacent sci-fi genres like cyberpunk; namely, many characters are desperate to reside there in corporate vassalage rather than to struggle for freedom.

Lauren, the novel's central figure and narrator, reflects on this curiosity using a register that is at once grounded and metatextual: "Maybe Olivar is the future—one face of it. Cities controlled by companies are old hat in science fiction. My grandmother left a whole bookcase of old science fiction novels. The company-city subgenre always seemed to star a hero who outsmarted, overthrew, or escaped 'the company.' I've never seen one where the hero fought like hell to get taken in and underpaid by the company. In real life, that's the way it will be. That's the way it is" (123–24). Sea-level rise, drought, disease, and crime ravage Butler's climate-changed United States, just as, in *Oryx and Crake*, they ravage the so-called pleeblands beyond the Compounds' armed perimeters. Within the walls, workers find a modicum of safety but quickly end up "in debt to the company . . . an old company town trick" (121). Aptly, then, Lauren says of Olivar, "Something new is beginning—or perhaps something old and nasty is reviving" (118). In each of these texts, climatic breakdown has rendered existence short and brutish enough that even skilled, educated workers clamor to surrender their rights as citizens in exchange for the dubious security of peonage.

Atwood's and Butler's Hobbesian visions have much in common with, and may even have influenced, the speculations of some social scientists who write on climate, class, and geopolitics. Michael Klare predicts that an aggressive Pentagon will attempt "what are termed 'stability operations'" in a world of "civil unrest, ethnic strife, and state collapse" (12). Likewise, Christian Parenti warns of a "politics of the armed lifeboat" as climate chaos intensifies (20). "Developed economies," he writes, could "transform themselves into fortress societies while the rest of the world slips into collapse," a scenario redolent of these two fictional worlds.[4]

Such vicious futures, however credible one finds them, are far from inevitable. The pitfall of salutary dystopias like *Parable* and *Oryx* is that they offer relatively little space to consider alternatives to collapse. Unlike real historical company towns, many of which evolved into generative matrices of radical politics and collective action, places like Olivar and the OrganInc Compound give rise to no formidable popular movements against social and ecological exploitation—or, as Lauren puts it, no internal force that "outsmarted, overthrew, or escaped the company." Though *Parable* ultimately presents a kind of communal alternative in Lauren's Earthseed group, neither novel offers any serious prospect of confronting the corporate neofeudalism which, itself, plays the foremost role in incubating the crises it then purports to solve.

If Lauren considers desperate acquiescence simply "real life" and "the way it is" for most who live under climatic stress and corporate rule, *Hadestown*'s narrator, Hermes (played by André De Shields), describes a more hopeful set of possibilities. The musical's story, Hermes admits, is "a sad tale, it's a tragedy," but the "gift" of Orpheus, and the production itself, inheres in the ability to imagine otherwise, to "make you see how the world could be / in spite of the way it is" (Mitchell, *Working* 247). Addressing the audience in the penultimate number, he continues, "Can you see it? / Can you hear it? / Can you feel it like a train?" Hermes's pointed inquiries assume an air of hopefulness here, but also one of challenge toward the audience. "Is it coming this way?" he sings, almost rhetorically. In a venue where a pair of decent seats likely costs more than the custodians earn in a month, these lines might even be said to evince a kind of "spite" at "the way it is," not only in American society, but also in terms of theater access and economic privilege on Broadway.[5]

"Understated" may seem an odd descriptor for a highly capitalized production teeming with spectacular effects suggestive of nineteenth-century melodramatic stagecraft—brilliant floodlights, riotous dance numbers, a spellbinding interlude lit only by miner's cap lights and swinging electric torches.[6] Yet Hermes's trespasses of the fourth wall, during which he frequently insists that we are watching an acting troupe perform an "old song . . . an old tale from way back when" (15–16), always keep us at an artful remove from the spectacle, inviting us to place ourselves within the theater's embodied class dynamics on the one hand and within the longue durée of myth and climate on the other.

Interestingly, *Hadestown* debuted in 2006 at the Old Socialist Labor Party Hall in Barre, Vermont, once the foremost granite town in the world and a hotbed of anarcho-syndicalism. Even when staged on Broadway, techniques like Hermes's direct address achieve a distancing effect that allow the play to retain some of the class-centered energies that such origins would suggest. Moreover, the conviction with which its plot embraces the radical spirit of historical American company towns sets it apart from the instructive fatalism of cli-fi texts like *Parable* and *Oryx*. In gesturing toward a sustainable future, as well as toward the kind of politics that may further the same, *Hadestown* concurs with writer-activists like Ashley Dawson and Naomi Klein that the health and stability of the climate reflects the health and stability of working-class communities, and that collective action may promise a way forward on both fronts.[7]

MYTHS FOR THE ANTHROPOCENE

Many works of climate theater have successfully incorporated mythological themes as a means of navigating the spatiotemporal horizons of the crisis, while also calling on the cultural resources of the past in response to the novel artistic challenges it poses. Chantal Bilodeau's *Sila* features the Inuit goddess of the sea and draws heavily on traditional tribal myths, while its sequel, *Forward,* uses the mythical character of Ice. Also an activist and critic, Bilodeau argues that the climate crisis demands a "new consciousness," which, in turn, "requires new artistic constructs" ("In Search"). For her as for Mitchell, pursuing the new seems to involve reimagining the ancient, perhaps after the familiar manner of modernism or the Renaissance. *Gaïa Global Circus,* a series of surreal vignettes conceived by the philosopher Bruno Latour, includes mythic characters ranging from the titular earth goddess to Cassandra and the Biblical Noah.[8] If we seek, following the drama scholar Theresa J. May, "the stories that will inspire a new understanding of, and sense of responsibility for, humanity as a geologic force" (239), our inquiries increasingly seem to land in the realm of myth. Timothy Clark, in an adjacent context, warns of the dangers of "scale framing," that is, rendering superbly complex ecological problems comprehensible in ways that risk evasion (22). However, these playwrights, in invoking the mythic, do not reduce the complexity of the climate crisis but rather embody it using stories that transcend, or collapse, conventional realist ideas of time and space, opening outwards toward the inconceivable.[9]

Hadestown's major ensemble song, "Chant," clarifies how Mitchell repurposes the myths of Eurydice and Orpheus, and Persephone and Hades, into a proletarian environmental technology. An oscillating call-and-response spectacle of dance and color that involves the entire cast, "Chant," like most ensembles, delivers necessary exposition and links previously disparate dramaturgic elements prior to the acceleration of the plot in the second act. Accordingly, we see the musical's two couples onstage together for the first time here, as Persephone's cyclical transit to Hadestown has brought the surface and subterranean worlds into contact. At this point, the couples do not yet directly interact; instead, they run complementary scenes that outline the play's parallel, interlocking problems. Around them, Hades's workers march, the Fates croon, the jazz band riffs. Hermes stands apart from the clamor, modeling the engaged attitude of the ideal audience.

Given the importance of "Chant" to the dramatic structure, it is highly significant that the workers, seven men and women comprising several racial groups, begin the number. Wearing mechanic's overalls fit for the mine or perhaps the foundry, they tramp in a circle about Hades and Persephone, intoning what Mitchell reveals to be the "chant" in the song's title: "Oh, you gotta keep your head low (kkh!) / If you wanna keep your head (huh! kkh!)" (107, 100). Whether the plosives signify the clangor of machines, the snap of a guillotine, or simply the grunts of an industrial army, they set the tone and control the pace. The workers' chant recurs in other numbers throughout the rest of the play before disintegrating near the climax, suggesting that the class dynamics of the company town hold the key to the play's dramatic infrastructure—and possibly, by extension, the infrastructure of global climate change.

Mitchell, perhaps not surprisingly, has cited Brecht as a major influence on her dramaturgy. Like him, she seems to understand character not in the sense of individual depths but as a means to condense broad social or natural forces into discrete agents for the illumination of the audience. Myth, of course, functions in much the same way. One risks no oversimplification, then, in recognizing that Hades, in the play, represents a modern variant of what he has always represented; in effect, he is the brute, paranoid impulse of capital for expansion and control, the quintessence of the company town to which he has given his name. Dressed in a pinstripe vest and sharkskin boots, Hades appears half mafioso, half oil magnate. His works, he brags, are fueled by "fossils of the dead," a phrase that refers in this context not only to fossil fuels but to his exploited workforce of underworld shades. With this line, which Hades rumbles while the workers pantomime exertion, the play intimates that the extraction of fossil energy involves also the coerced extraction of labor, yet again linking climate chaos to the unjust class arrangements exemplified in the figure of the company town.

Persephone, generatrix of the seasons, wearing a bright, sequined green dress and frequently drawing wine or laudanum from a flask, embodies and speaks for a natural world pushed beyond the stability of the Holocene. "Lover, what have you become?" she responds, her tone mixing pity, rage, and despair. She then supplies an ironic, metonymic answer that speaks to the material bases of capital's hegemony: "Coal cars and oil drums" (105). Exasperated, she continues,

> And in the meantime up above
> The harvest dies and people starve
> Oceans rise and overflow
> It ain't right and it ain't natural

The brilliant pair of near rhymes in this, Persephone's closing quatrain, heightens the dominant sense of "Chant," that skewness is grasping for balance on multiple fronts—social, environmental, interpersonal—but that all parties remain mired in the chaos of isolation, unmoored from their own histories and from any chance at collective purpose.

Eurydice, more than any other character, exemplifies this species of precarity. Though technically a nymph, she suffers hunger and want, whereas the archetypal forces with whom she shares a stage, including Orpheus, seem impervious to climate impacts. Buffeted constantly by harsh winds, accosted by bandits, pining for the simple dignities of food and shelter, Eurydice, played by Eva Maria Noblezada, also typifies many aspects of the contemporary global working class: young, female, a person of color, a climate migrant, initially working not in the traditional proletarian occupations but as a waitress, a seasonal service job at the margins of the economy.

Perhaps the play's most crucial deviation from the classical myth and its many previous operatic adaptations lies in the fact that, rather than dying from a snakebite, Eurydice chooses to enter Hadestown.[10] Far from being a maiden in need of rescue or some token of masculine exchange, she, not Orpheus, drives the play's action. *Hadestown*, incredibly, is the first winner of the Tony Award for Best Musical to have been written and directed entirely by women: Mitchell and the director, Rachel Chavkin, who together transformed the figure of Eurydice from a passive victim to an active force. Her resilience suggests the strength of the global working classes she seems to typify, but also their lack of good options within a neoliberal system in which constraint passes for free choice. Indeed, in "Chant," we see Eurydice pushed to the extremes that will lead her to embrace the ghastly security of Hadestown, just as certain figures in other cli-fi texts choose Olivar or the Compounds.

Fittingly, then, "Chant" culminates in discord, as each character desperately shouts to the other over the howling wind and the workers' chant—which itself, at this point in the action, reflects not solidarity but uniform dismay. At the heart of this tempest lies the question of amnesia, of lost knowledge. Orpheus observes that "the reason we're on this road / And the seasons are wrong" is "because of the gods / The gods have forgotten the song of their love!" (103). Ironically, even as he criticizes Hades and Persephone, he fails to notice Eurydice's plight or the storm that will subsume her. Orpheus's monomania, his quest for individual heroism, has rendered him as amnesiac as Hades. These kinds of forgetting, however, are nothing compared to that which assails Eurydice. Having joined the workers' corps in Hadestown, she soon learns that residing there will plunge her into Lethean "oblivion" and cause her "to forget / Who you are / And everything that came before" (150–51). Before long, she can no longer recall even her own name. "No one has a name down here," the Fates rasp, as the workers once more intone their familiar chant (149).

Clearly, the musical is working hard to assemble a scenario in which an awakening to previously forgotten knowledge will hold the key to restoring, or perhaps inaugurating, some species of harmony among the binaries it navigates—capital and labor, climate and industry, nature and culture, and so on. Concerning Hades and Persephone, this structure may seem to reify the early environmentalist canard, ultimately deriving from Christian myths by way of Rousseau, that (masculine) humanity and (feminine) nature once existed in a state of prelapsarian harmony that civilization somehow disrupted. Yet on another level the call for recollection in *Hadestown* has much to do with what Amitav Ghosh pointedly calls "recognition," a harking back to "something prior, an already existing awareness that makes possible the passage from ignorance to knowledge" (4).

Ghosh writes that in the Anthropocene, "the uncanny and improbable events that are beating at our doors" have compelled many of us to "recognize something we had turned away from: that is to say, the presence and proximity of nonhuman interlocutors" (30). For him, the literary modes most suited to encouraging moments of recognition are "epic or myth," which, more open to nonhuman agency than modern genres, can help us to "approach the world in a subjunctive mode, to conceive of it *as if* it were other than it is . . . to envision what it might be" (128). We have seen that Hermes attributes precisely this subjunctive capacity to *Hadestown*. And while the play teems with uncanny, nonhuman agencies—the hound dogs patrolling the Styx; the trees and rivers that Orpheus promises will sing at his and Eurydice's wedding—Mitchell is arguably more interested in another mode of lost knowledge that Ghosh briefly discusses, the transformative potential of collective *human* agency. However, while Ghosh refers vaguely to an "aggregate" and an "idea of the collective" (80), Mitchell's work extends a particular, proletarian artistic tradition that sees such matters in terms of workers' collective opposition to the forces of fossil capital.

It is crucial in this regard that the play's diegesis, possibly alone among the many adaptations of the Orpheus and Eurydice myth, never shows Orpheus exercising his characteristic gift to sway the forces of nature in sympathy with his songs. Pointedly, though, "the workers heard him" and echo his calls (174). In other words, while Orpheus—that is, the power of art—may not possess the capacity to move the trees, rivers, or rocks in Hadestown, his songs do rouse the sap within the workers, as it were, springing them from enforced stupor to the liveliness of common purpose.

Mitchell writes of having studied John Sayles's historically faithful strike film, *Matewan*, when drafting the songs that would become the play, "to get ideas about poverty, company towns, [coal] mining, etc." ("History"). And while this proletarian influence pervades the entirety of the production, it emerges with particular vigor after Orpheus follows Hermes's directions on "how to get to Hadestown," steals past the gate, and begins to gain his bearings in the underworld (126). The loss of Eurydice appears to have disabused him of his obsession with individual exceptionalism. The second half of the play turns with him and chronicles the awakening of the workers of Hadestown as Orpheus's singing startles them from their malaise.

At the start of the sustained underworld sequence, the stage is dark, the scene lit only by roving beams from the workers' mining headlamps. They apprehend Orpheus and beat him at Hades's behest, but soon they attentively listen as he assumes a role akin to that of the union agitator in Sayles's film. "I believe there is a way," Orpheus sings, as the workers lie disheveled about the stage (176). "I believe in us together / More than anyone alone." Such lines may seem like stale bromides, but for those without memories of an era when labor enjoyed some modicum of hard-won dignity—like Hades's amnesiac workers, or anyone born in the West after the fall of the Berlin Wall—they could easily sound more inspired than insipid. If neoliberalism in its corporate, media, and academic guises has crushed class-based justice movements and expunged their ghosts from the culture at large, it has also, even in this victory, freed their characteristic slogans and imagery from the musty, excessively masculine associations of the postwar era and cleared the ground for their resurgence in an age of ecological upheaval and class stratification the likes of which we have not witnessed since the droughts, floods, and cascading economic collapses of the proletarian 1930s. Mitchell's musical stands at the forefront of this effort to recollect and re-purpose the spirit of texts like *Matewan* for the emerging age of climate chaos and popular dissent.

Slowly, one by one, the workers stand. What Mitchell calls "the rising rebellion of the Workers" continues to progress for a few more numbers (191), until, in "Chant (Reprise)," their chant, which has recurred throughout the play, disintegrates in fits and starts and then re-forms into expressions of solidarity:

> If I raised, If I raised, if I raised—
> Keep your head low . . .
> Why do we turn away instead of standing with him?
> Oh, keep your head . . .
> We can stand with our fellow man
> Keep your head! (189–90)

The dramatic movement encapsulated in "Chant (Reprise)"—from "Keep your head low" to "Keep your head!"—not only marks the achievement of class-based awareness among Hadestown's marginalized, multiracial workforce, it also leads directly to the final confrontation, in which Orpheus sings to Hades and Persephone and incites in them a renewed consciousness of the love they had forgotten. Only the workers' resolve threatens Hades sufficiently to allow this chance. That is to say, the possibility of social and environmental regeneration arises in the play not as a result of Orpheus's legendary ability to move the natural world but through the power of his songs to reopen assertive channels of worker agency like those that once held sway in places like the Old Socialist Labor Hall in Barre, Vermont, or certain illegal taverns in Ellsworth, Pennsylvania. In this amalgamation of proletarian culture and classical poetry, *Hadestown* forges a myth for the Anthropocene that encompasses but goes beyond nonhuman animacy to account also for collective human agency and the affective power of art.

AN OLD SONG

Hadestown's worker-centered vision distinguishes it from most other cli-fi texts, including those that feature company towns. Yet the play's circular, recursive ending exchanges the Brechtian drama of stylized revolt for an ambiguity that is at once faithful to its classical sources and self-reflective about the legacies of working-class art and activism. In short, Mitchell rejects rote formulas of the sort typically associated with proletarian texts, and, through the leveraging of repetition, closes the action on a note of nuanced possibility that also pays homage to the traditions in which she works.

This shift begins when Orpheus, leading Eurydice and the train of workers to the surface, turns back at the threshold, as he does in mythic accounts. "Is this a trap that's being laid for me?" he sings, evincing the vexations that undo him (238). Immediately, darkness subsumes the workers. Eurydice descends back to Hadestown via hydraulic platform as Orpheus reaches for her in a slow, tortuous sequence. Hope, until now palpable in the audience, deflates. "It's an old song / And that is how it ends," Hermes reminds us (246). How could we have thought otherwise?

But then, as we await the curtain, the play does something extraordinary: it begins again. Eurydice swaggers onstage and shouts, "Anybody got a match?" just as she does at the outset. The band segues into the first notes of the opening number. Hermes sings that although he and the rest of the company "know how [the story] ends," they will "sing it again / As if it might turn out this time." This hope, he says, is "the thing," the reason they continue performing. We are left with the sense that the saga we have just witnessed may repeat interminably, or at least until it "turn[s] out" in accord with "how the world could be" (246–47).

Certainly, myths are forever retold, and plays often run nightly for many seasons. But Mitchell operates beyond such puerile autoreferentiality; more is at stake here. It would have been tempting and arguably logical to end the play in the usual fashion of proletarian texts like Upton Sinclair's *The Jungle*—or, for that matter, Sayles's *Matewan* or Zola's *Germinal*—which tend to close just after the spirit of dissent has taken hold but before it has triumphed, the idea being that the awakened audience will continue the drama's work in the world outside. For example, Hermes could have interrupted the narrative just before Orpheus turns back, and *Hadestown* could have closed on the march. Instead, the musical carries the myth to its tragic conclusion but then reopens the matter, insisting that someday things may "turn out" for the principals and, by extension, for the exploited workers and damaged ecologies they seem to typify.

Hadestown, that is, attempts to reconcile its classical and proletarian influences by pursuing an ending that melds both traditions—the eternal recurrence of myth, the progressive telos of activist art. One could argue, from the latter position, that the play thereby enacts failure on an endless loop, desperately embracing Sisyphean futility. Rather than the commitment of Sayles or early Sinclair—which, after all, has pervaded the play to this point—we end with the ludic defiance of Camus. This pioneering cli-fi drama about collective politics, in this understanding, would become something akin to a sonata played on a sinking ship, a meditation on stoicism, beauty, and doom.

Such an argument no doubt has its merits, particularly given the absurdity of imagining that most in a Broadway audience will take to the barricades for radical climate solutions. Yet I would suggest, on the contrary, that Mitchell's ending further articulates the spirit of social justice that the play consistently advances. Saidiya Hartman, in embracing "the task of writing the impossible," asks, "How can a narrative of defeat enable a place for the living or envision an alternative future?" (14). As though in answer, the joyful pertinacity of *Hadestown*'s final scenes encapsulates the recurrent and perhaps interminable struggle that characterizes working-class art, much of it authored by radical women interested in company towns and similar sites of coercion. Mitchell, by artfully employing repetition, locates *Hadestown* at the contemporary vanguard of this cultural tradition.

The play is indeed an "old song," as Hermes sings, but in ways that go beyond classical myth. Critics often focus on urban agglomerations as the primary sites of Anthropocene fossil capitalism, but its true origins and most intense iterations were always in the extraction and industrial zones, the subterranean fundaments of modernity; areas often likened to Hell or the underworld and governed, then as now, by corporations. These capital frontiers again and again gave rise to dissent as adamant as the initial violence, such that Timothy Mitchell, among others, claims that modern mass democracy—the idea that all stations should enjoy material dignity and political voice—sprang, like steam power or ready electricity, from coal towns, from coal miners' bodies.[11]

Picket lines and tear gas bombs—and even, near Matewan, surplus warplanes strafing workers—spawned an activist lineage of song and story out of which *Hadestown* ultimately emerges. In the US, women disproportionately spearheaded this effort, perhaps because, as Tillie Olsen argues of Rebecca Harding Davis, they understood an adjacent breed of oppression. From Agnes Smedley in the 1920s to Denise Giardina in the 1990s, many in this line of company town writing have sung their versions of the "old song" at issue in *Hadestown*.¹² Seen from this perspective, the musical's closing note of repetition celebrates the tenacity of radical art and the resolve of diverse working-class people like Mitchell's Eurydice, who, together, might once again alter the geological future, this time for the better and of their own accord.

Art, too, has become, like Orpheus, a geophysical force. Artists and scholars who envision their work on the Anthropocene as a praxis of dissent might join Mitchell in seeking provocations in company towns, the foremost sites where workers have contested the paranoid corporate logics that wrenched the epoch from the earth. Mitchell sets herself apart as perhaps the first cli-fi writer to draw upon this cultural tradition in something like its original, proletarian spirit, pressing beyond the dystopias of Butler and Atwood to fashion a contemporary myth of collective action and artistic dynamism. Largely forgotten in an age of neoliberal ascendancy, class consciousness reemerges in *Hadestown* to take aim at the socioeconomic infrastructures subtending climate chaos. Eurydice's framing question, "Anybody got a match?" thus situates the musical itself as kindling. In a world on fire, *Hadestown* epitomizes the hope that old songs, raised up and reformulated, can move us to keep our heads and ignite a countervailing flame, a torch constant enough to light the path as we labor towards the threshold.

NOTES

1. US company towns remain prevalent in the developing world even today. For example, the Firestone Tire and Rubber Company (now a subsidiary of the Bridgestone Corporation) still owns and operates the Liberian rubber town of Harbel—named for the company's founder, Harvey, and his wife, Isabelle—including all houses, roads, schools, the hospital, the airport, and the like. Not incidentally, capital derived in part from Harbel endowed Princeton University's Firestone Library, where I did much of the research that informs this essay.

2. As the architectural historian John Garner writes, "The term *company town* is of recent origin. It was coined in America in the late nineteenth century and applied first to mining camps and smelters in Appalachia and the Monongahela Valley" (3). For a good example of the kind of literary reportage that shaped the cultural perception of such places, see Stephen Crane's "In the Depths of a Coal Mine," published in *McClure's* in August, 1894.

3. The album's opening is fiercer still, as the chorus of Fates croons, "In the fever of a world in flames / In the season of the hurricane / Flood'll get ya if the fire don't" (Mitchell, *Working* 25).

4. Giving actuality to Parenti's vision, Douglas Rushkoff recalls talking with a few ultrarich survivalists about their underground bunkers. Rushkoff writes, "The billionaires considered using special combination locks on the food supply that only they knew. Or making guards wear disciplinary collars of some kind." Curiously, pantry locks and shock collars play major roles in Butler's frequently horrific sequel, *Parable of the Talents*.

5. I received a complimentary ticket to the performance through a university program, which of course reflects an adjacent kind of privilege.

6. The relationship between sensational early theater and modern, electrified energy regimes in the context of the Anthropocene has been artfully pursued by the critic Devin Griffiths.

7. Dawson, in *People's Power*, argues that collective movements to secure "democratic control over energy production, distribution, and use" have become crucially important for the planet's future, calling this struggle "the key front in the fight for a better, sustainable world" (9). Similarly, Klein, in *This Changes Everything*, applauds what she calls "Blockadia": "a global, grassroots, and broad-based network" of everyday people resisting extractive industries in a manner "alive and unpredictable and very much in the streets" (293–94).

8. For an intriguing reflection on Latour's play in the context of experimental environmental art and climate politics, see Al Coppola's essay, "Latour and Balloons."

9. Working-class dramatists, particularly those concerned with coal mining, have also used mythic forms. To take two prominent examples, Tony Harrison's *Prometheus* casts the god as a retired British miner suffering black lung, while Robert Schenkkan's nine-part *The Kentucky Cycle* models several plays on the *Oresteia* of Aeschylus.

10. Many of the first operas were based on the Orpheus and Eurydice myth. These include the oldest surviving opera, *Eurydice*, composed by Jacopo Peri in 1600, and the earliest opera still regularly performed today, Claudio Monteverdi's *L'Orfeo*, from 1607.

11. Mitchell, in his important study *Carbon Democracy*, points to examples from around to globe to show that during the twentieth century, "coal miners led campaigns not just for improved pay and working conditions, but for more extensive changes to the way prosperity and well-being were distributed" among social classes (28).

12. Olsen argues that Davis composed *Life in the Iron Mills* "in absolute identification" with the novella's central figure, an iron puddler with a fantastic talent for sculpture, noting that the "circumstances that denied use of capacities" in the novella were also "her own . . . however differently embodied" (69).

WORKS CITED

Bilodeau, Chantal. "In Search of a New Aesthetic." *Howlround Theater Commons*, 19 April 2015, howlround.com/search-new-aesthetic. Accessed 1 Aug. 2021. Theater in the Age of Climate Change section.

Butler, Octavia. *Parable of the Sower*. 1993. Grand Central, 2019.

Clark, Timothy. *Ecocriticism on the Edge: The Anthropocene as a Threshold Concept*. Bloomsbury, 2015.

Coppola, Al. "Latour and Balloons: *Gaïa Global Circus* and the Theater of Climate Change." *Configurations*, vol. 28, no. 1, 2020, pp. 29–49.

Crane, Stephen. "In the Depths of a Coal Mine." *McClure's,* Aug. 1894, pp. 195–209.

Dawson, Ashley. *People's Power: Reclaiming the Energy Commons*. OR Books, 2020.

Garner, John. Introduction. *The Company Town: Architecture and Society in the Early Industrial Age*, edited by Garner, Oxford UP, 1992, pp. 3–16.

Ghosh, Amitav. *The Great Derangement: Climate Change and the Unthinkable*. U of Chicago P, 2016.

Griffiths, Devin. "Petrodrama: Melodrama and Energic Modernity," *Victorian Studies*, vol. 60, no. 4, 2018, pp. 611–38.

Hartman, Saidiya. "Venus in Two Acts." *Small Axe*, vol. 12, no. 2, 2008, pp. 1–14.

Huber, Matthew. *Climate Change as Class War: Building Socialism on a Warming Planet*. Verso, 2022.

"J.W. Ellsworth Dies in Florence Villa," *New York Times*, 4 June 1925, p. 21.

Klare, Michael T. *All Hell Breaking Loose: The Pentagon's Perspective on Climate Change*. Metropolitan, 2019.

Klein, Naomi. *This Changes Everything: Capitalism vs. the Climate*. Simon and Schuster, 2014.

May, Theresa J. *Earth Matters on Stage: Ecology and Environment in American Theater*. Routledge, 2021.

Mitchell, Anaïs. "Anaïs Mitchell—Backstage at Mountain Stage." Interview by Larry Groce. *NPR*, 3 Jan. 2011, youtube.com/watch?v=pzJtUU-opkE. Accessed 1 Aug. 2021.

———. "History." *Hadestown: A Folk Opera*. http://hadestown.anaismitchell.com/hadestown/history. Accessed 1 Aug. 2021.

———. *Working on a Song: The Lyrics of Hadestown*. Plume, 2020.

Mitchell, Timothy. *Carbon Democracy: Political Power in the Age of Oil*. Verso, 2011.

Olsen, Tillie, editor. "A Biographical Interpretation." *Life in the Iron Mills and Other Stories*. 1861. By Rebecca Harding Davis, Feminist Press, 1985, pp. 67–174.

Parenti, Christian. *Tropic of Chaos: Climate Change and the New Geography of Violence*. Nation Books, 2011.

Rushkoff, Douglass. "How Tech's Richest Plan to Save Themselves after the Apocalypse." *The Guardian*, 24 July 2018. theguardian.com/technology/2018/jul/23/tech-industry-wealth-futurism-transhumanism-singularity. Accessed 1 Aug. 2021.

Burnout
Cli-Fi and Exhaustion

LISA OTTUM

An iconic image of 2020 is the exhausted health care worker, head in hands, face imprinted with the outline of a protective mask. Thousands of such images circulate online and in the news media, accompanied by a now-familiar discourse of frontline worker burnout. "Doctors and nurses on the front lines are running on empty," a November 2020 *New York Times* headline declares, echoing similar stories about fatigue, depression, and trauma among ER personnel (Wu). The adjective *frontline* originated in the 1600s as a military term, acquiring its more quotidian meaning only in the second half of the twentieth century ("Frontline"). During the COVID-19 pandemic, the wartime origins of *frontline* resurfaced as hospitals morphed into battlefield-like environments. Equally prevalent was a use of *frontline* derived from firefighting.[1] Alongside war metaphors, politicians repeatedly invoked wildfire metaphors to describe COVID-19, referring to the disease as "burning out of control," and lamenting the difficulty of disease "containment." Meanwhile, public health departments and news outlets tracked virus "hotspots" and "flare-ups," color-coding maps in fiery shades of yellow, orange, and red. The migration of firefighting terminology to the domain of public health is notable given that 2020 saw record-setting wildfires in the US West. Between July and December, over ten million acres of land burned. California, Colorado, and Washington experienced the largest wildfires in their respective state histories (Masters).[2] Not coincidentally, 2020 was also the second-hottest year on record, just two-hundredths of a degree cooler than 2016 (NOAA).

How should we read in an era of burnout—of fire-ravaged landscapes and exhausted workers? The question of whether critique itself is exhausted—whether it has, in Bruno Latour's famous formulation, "run out of steam"—predates the pandemic by some years yet is newly relevant in its wake. It is especially relevant in the domain of climate fiction, where genre foregrounds the matter of how art relates, or should relate, to structural change. At first glance, the heat and death of the 2020s might seem to call for cli-fi, and a cli-fi criticism, trained squarely on pernicious systems, including the neoliberal capitalism responsible for decades of economic and environmental deregulation. Such methods—characterized as "paranoid" by their detractors—have lately fallen out of favor, due in part to burnout among critics, a condition often articulated in terms of "exhaustion" by proponents of weak theory and other reparative modes.[3] In the face of unabating climate change and social injustice, Wai Chee Dimock suggests that we embrace more tentative and open-ended critical frameworks, "damage-responsive" approaches to reading that avow their own shakiness and refuse grand conclusions (8). For Dimock, the power of literature lies not in its power to explode hegemonic structures; literary history, she writes, "offers one the best examples of redress as an incremental process, never finished because never without new input" (8). If this vision enables, it may likewise disappoint in a moment marked by both urgency and exhaustion: after all, the sense that one's professional efforts yield ever-smaller gains is the very definition of burnout, at least according to the World Health Organization ("Burn-Out").

This essay focuses on Jennifer Haigh's *Heat and Light* (2016), a novel that tests the limits of both "strong" and "weak" reading. On one hand, *Heat and Light* courts strong, Marxist modes of critique. Focused on the effects of fracking in a fictional Pennsylvania town already scarred by coal production, the novel uses multiple, intersecting narratives and narrative points of view spread across many decades; these techniques link energy extraction to globalized capitalism's ever-expanding reach. On the other hand, *Heat and Light* resists neat conclusions about causality and agency in the context of energy production. Haigh engages with climate change obliquely; a subplot involving the toxicity of fracking remains unresolved at the end of the book. There is no clear denouement: "Instead," the narrator muses, gas drilling in Bakerton, Pennsylvania, "ends the way everything ends, inscrutably" (405). In this and other ways, the experience of reading *Heat and Light* is one of what Donna Haraway calls "staying with the trouble." With its focus not on how damage might be prevented but on how people navigate settings already corrupted by decades of economic and environmental deregulation, *Heat and Light* prompts us to read with an eye toward the present and its "myriad unfinished configurations of places, times, matters, [and] meanings" (Haraway 1). It also invites us to reflect on the ethical and practical status of weak—that is, tentative, self-consciously imperfect, or even accidental—environmentalisms, including criticism itself. At issue, I argue, is not whether critique has run out of steam but rather the modes of deliberation available amid emergent conditions.

In some respects, *Heat and Light* can be seen as a novel of the Anthropocene, an emerging subgenre that "understands itself within epochal, geologic time and includes that form of time within its larger formal operations" (Marshall 524). A brief prefatory chapter invokes Pennsylvania's geologic past. "More than most places," the narrator intones, "Pennsylvania is what lies beneath": oil, first extracted in a boom that "no one is old enough to have witnessed personally," coal mined in the twentieth century, and natural gas (4). The book's final paragraphs return to Paleolithic times, referencing the "accidents of geology, larger than history, older than scripture" that "booby-trapped" the region with fossil fuel resources (426). Despite these fleeting references, however, *Heat and Light* is less concerned with a self-reflexive staging of fiction's relationship to deep time than it is with more recent events. Most of the novel is set in 2010 and 2012; subplots yoke the Three Mile Island disaster and the Gulf War to Pennsylvania's role in powering twentieth-century America.

In contrast to cli-fi that imagines life in the post-Anthropocene, or in a world decimated by climate change, *Heat and Light* maps the interlinked timescales and geographies of fossil fuel extraction in the present. At the beginning of the main narrative, energy company Dark Elephant (Darco, for short) is prospecting in Bakerton, hoping to secure drilling rights from local residents before other energy companies arrive. Some of the plot therefore takes place in Texas, where corporate executives anticipate a rush to develop the Marcellus Shale formation. Events in the novel extend far beyond the US, though: through the characters of Clifford "Kip" Oliphant—an oil company executive—and Rich Devlin—a Gulf War veteran—Haigh situates fracking within a decades-long global effort by US companies to secure oil resources, both in the US and abroad. She also foregrounds the role of hyperaccelerated financial markets in propelling rapid cycles of boom-and-bust drilling. When gas prices crater near the end of the novel and Darco abruptly departs from Bakerton, Kip finds himself in millions of dollars of debt, only to emerge weeks later with millions in financing for a new drilling venture. For Kip, such spectacular cycles of indebtedness and profit are something of a game: a former football player, he thinks in terms of "the Next Big Play," a phrase threaded throughout his storyline.

For the workers depicted in *Heat and Light,* the consequences of hyper-fast capitalism are more profound. Because capitalism wrings profit from speed, waiting for human and natural resources to replenish themselves in a given area is unprofitable; essentially, the pace of production "outstrips the ability of nature to reproduce or sustain itself," while also "press[ing] human beings to their limit" (Brennan 22). Thus, deregulation in the legal sense abets what Teresa Brennan refers to as *bio*deregulation, the process by which humans as well as the rest of the biosphere are debilitated by the unmooring of production from natural patterns of exertion and renewal.[4] As Brennan explains, "deregulation of trade, labor, and environmental legislation . . . seek[s] to remove the constraints which human time, and natural time, impose" (20). For workers, bioderegulation involves working longer hours; it often involves traveling farther to work, or "going the extra mile, literally and figuratively" (20). Fracking is uniquely bioderegulated: as depicted in *Heat and Light,* "the drilling literally never stops" (98), with workers pushing their bodies to accommodate the relentless pace and intensity of continuous drilling. As the narrator explains, rig workers for the fictional Darco Energy work twelve-hour shifts, seven days a week, for two-week stretches at a time, traveling around the country as drilling operations expand and contract. They live in dormitories assembled by subcontractors; in contrast to the deafening sound of the drilling itself, the dorms are quiet, because shifts start "at noon, at midnight, at 4:00 PM, at dawn," and so "always someone is sleeping" (96). The cafeteria, which never closes, serves bacon and eggs at all hours because "it's always breakfast time for someone" (96). Moreover, drilling is "backbreaking work, punishing to the body." Workers "yank and drag and push and pull" enormous pieces of equipment, with some "work[ing] injured, numbed by painkillers." For "twelve hours a day they hump and heave"; by the end of shift, "they'd rather sleep than drink or eat or talk to their families" (98).

As depicted in *Heat and Light,* drilling exemplifies what Jonathan Crary calls "24/7" capitalism and its "generalized inscription of human life into duration without breaks, defined by a principle of continuous functioning" (8). In a 24/7 world, the "fragility of human life" and humans' natural need for rest "is increasingly inadequate" compared to the continuous labor of machines (10). Unlike its human operators, drilling equipment can run around the clock. Furthermore, its sheer size emphasizes workers' physical vulnerability: "A drill rig isn't scaled for humans," the narrator remarks, noting that "from above, the men [on a rig] are larger than birds and bugs, but only a bit larger" (100).[5] As if to emphasize this point, Haigh often personifies machinery, subtracting human agents from scenes of perpetual mechanic motion. For example, there is the following scene in which Rich Devlin—exasperated by the "epic and surprisingly complex" noise of drilling—approaches the rig situated on his property: "The rig is lit, around the clock, with klieg lights. From a distance it radiates a sulfurous glow, like a football stadium at night. Several trucks idle loudly. Up close the diesel smell is overpowering. The engine noise makes [Rich's] entire body vibrate. He sees no sign of human presence. It's as though the giant machines are running themselves" (259). Here, "giant machines" obscure the human labor that keeps them running. On one hand, this representational strategy might seem like simple synecdoche, with machines standing in for the workers, or possibly for Darco. Yet the workers are easily separable from the drilling operation, laid off "as always . . . out of nowhere" when Darco abruptly shuts down drilling at the end of the novel (405).

Heat and Light also gestures—indirectly—toward the environmental costs of globalized 24/7 capitalism. The most obvious form of environmental destruction in the novel is the degradation of landscapes in Bakerton: similar to other works of hydrofracking literature, *Heat and Light* depicts the initial stages of drilling rigs vibrantly.[6] On Rich's property, century-old forest yields to "a Chisholm 600, the industry standard. From a distance it [the massive machine] resembles a giant's power sander. It severs each trunk at ground level, with a blade the size of a merry-go-round" (120). Less overtly rhetorical, though equally significant, is the novel's narrative structure, which links the cyclical exploitation of fossil fuel resources to the problem of heating and lighting America from the mid-twentieth century to the 2010s. Part of the novel takes place during 1979, against the backdrop of the Iranian Revolution and the Three Mile Island disaster. For several characters in the book, these events mark a personal turning point: to cite one example, Wesley Peacock, who later dies from thyroid cancer, is exposed to fallout during the nuclear accident. Haigh also situates the events of 1979 within the long arc of American imperialism in the Middle East. In *Heat and Light*'s closing paragraph, Rich Devlin recalls "turning nineteen aboard the SS *Roosevelt* . . . a ship so massive it seemed to be standing still as it carried six thousand men, three times the population of Bakerton, to the Persian Gulf, a distant and desolate place that mattered for one reason only" (427). Haigh does not need to specify this reason to readers, who will, by this point, see how Rich's personal history fits into a regional history and, beyond that, a national history shaped by globalized competition for fossil fuels.

Thus far, much of the scholarship on climate fiction has focused on whether the novel form is up to the task of capturing climate change as slow violence—that is, as an event unfolding across multiple timescales and geographies.[7] The Anthropocene is central to this discussion: many critics wonder whether, or how, the novel form registers geologic time and the peculiar notion of posterity entailed in an "age of humans" as viewed from the distant future.[8] Unlike most cli-fi, *Heat and Light* is not set in a climate-changed future, nor does it aspire to solve the formal challenges presented by a posthuman setting. Still, Haigh manipulates narrative form in the service of an equally important goal: apprehending that massive economic forces have created, and sustain, carbon-based prosperity for the few at the expense of the many. In this way, the novel points toward a new mode of reading cli-fi, one oriented more toward the Capitalocene than the Anthropocene. As detractors of the *Anthropocene* label point out, it is not "humankind" that is responsible for anthropogenic climate change, but rather a particular subset of humans, acting under particular economic relations that have created our warming climate. Thus, in addition to climate fiction that imagines a postapocalyptic future, there is room for cli-fi, and for a cli-fi criticism, focused on historical causality. In his analysis of the "toxic Gothic" in hydrofracking texts, including *Heat and Light,* Jason Molesky notes that this position is at odds with ascendant modes of ecocriticism, particularly material ecocriticism, which has increasingly eschewed distinctions between human and nonhuman forces, focusing instead on assemblages of material actants (62). With its emphasis on—to quote Stacy Alaimo—"incalculable, interconnected agencies" (20)—rather than the clear and powerful agency exercised by fossil fuel companies, such criticism may unwittingly abet the pro-fracking lobby, which routinely obscures causal links between fracking and problems including illness, pollution, and earthquakes. Molesky thus calls for modes of reading that "addres[s] toxic agents as they exist within and are dispersed by occulted regimes of hydrocarbon extraction" while also acknowledging the "framework of complex, posthuman bodies and emotions" that can still "offe[r] a potentially transformative vision of self and environment" (65).

Stephanie LeMenager proposes something similar in an essay on narratives of the "everyday Anthropocene," by which she means "both a feeling-state and its underlying socioecological conditions, characterized by enduring crises that never quite come to a head" (224). Whereas the notion of the Anthropocene as a geological epoch "displace[s]" the present "onto an elsewhere in which narrative significance resides," the everyday Anthropocene focuses on the day-to-day experience of living through climate change in vulnerable bodies (225). At its best, LeMenager argues, the everyday Anthropocene mode "is a project of reinventing the everyday as a means of paying attention and preparing, collectively, a project of staying home and, in a sense distant from settler-colonialist mentalities, *making home of a broken world*" (225–26). This vision of cli-fi invites us to read for both the somatic and the structural. It also invites critics to read weakly—to embrace the ongoing and experimental nature of "making a life" amidst shifting conditions.

Some theories of how ordinary life unfolds under globalized capitalism move toward this goal in the sense that they engage with affective routines associated with "getting by." For example, Lauren Berlant has explored capitalism as a biopolitical regime in which life for many people, especially the poor and people of color, feels exhausting—like a constant act of "doggy paddling" (779). Under such circumstances, people embrace "lateral agency," or forms of "exhausted practical sovereignty" that resist the temporal imperatives of bioderegulated capitalism. In contrast to the sovereign agency associated with the neoliberal subject, lateral agency manifests in activities "like sex or eating, oriented toward the pleasure of self-abeyance that do not occupy time, decision, or consequentiality in anything like the registers of autonomous self-assertion," but that nonetheless resist the relentless pace of capitalist production (757). Notably, many of Haigh's characters quell anxiety with repetitive behaviors: addiction and compulsion are a prominent theme in *Heat and Light*. Reading for lateral agency can recast seemingly aimless actions as coping mechanisms; under exhausting conditions, the day-to-day motions of survival can be their own act of resistance.

Still, the concept of lateral agency offers readers little in the way of imagining a better future: it is, after all, a form of what Berlant terms "slow death" at the hands of bioderegulated capitalism. Moreover, reading for acts of lateral agency cannot account for the problem that events in *Heat and Light* sometimes evade strongly determined explanatory frameworks. Indeed, although the novel can—as I have demonstrated—be subjected to readings that emphasize historical causality, it also raises the possibility that critical analysis and the putatively objective vantage point it affords are not automatically liberating. We might focus, for example, on the character Wesley Peacock, who searches obsessively for information that would definitively link his thyroid cancer to the Three Mile Island disaster. Enraged to be dying at thirty-seven, Wes amasses "hundreds of photocopied pages, studies of studies" about cancer and about the disaster (308); maddeningly, no source confirms what seems intuitively obvious to Wes (and to readers): that his illness is almost certainly a result of childhood exposure to radiation. Wes realizes that his fanatical research is not unlike devotional reading; a former pastor, he "recognizes the ridiculousness of the impulse" to probe numbers for meaning and yet cannot stop himself from believing that "numbers . . . are fraught with subtext" that he must uncover (305, 306). Meanwhile, official accounts of the nuclear disaster forestall close reading of any kind, by Wes or anyone else, obscuring causal links in bureaucratic doublespeak. Experts, Wes learns, explain Three Mile Island using the "Theory of Normal Accidents: an unanticipated interaction of multiple failures in a complex system" (308) (The narrator adds, with irony: "The disaster was unexpected, incomprehensible, uncontrollable, and unavoidable, according to people who know" [308]). In twenty-first-century parlance, Wes finds himself gaslighted; in turn, he grows ever more cynical, his anger "invigorating" but ultimately worthless (311).

Wes's storyline raises a theme worth lingering over, which is the usefulness of critique for confronting "complex systems" in an already damaged world. As Rob Nixon argues, a hallmark of slow violence is the disarticulation of causes from effects, such that those harmed by toxic pollution and other forms of slow violence are seldom acknowledged as victims (13). It follows that if slow violence can be apprehended, it can be redressed; to read for slow violence is to read for justice. But what of the time between the harm and its triumphant exposure? *Heat and Light* refuses to indict those responsible for human health and environmental harms; however, the novel does explore how people navigate the exhausting space between harm and the arrival of some possible future justice. In the novel, justice—if it can even be called that—takes forms that fall far short of the satisfying resolution imagined by critics of fracking. In the end, "strong" narratives of the type embraced by mainstream environmentalism fail to account for many of the ethical dilemmas faced by Haigh's characters, including the matter of what constitutes *caring for* versus *caring about* a community already scarred by years of environmental injustice.

This issue emerges explicitly in a subplot involving Lorne Trexler, a fast-talking academic and activist from upstate New York, and Rena Koval, a local resident who becomes briefly infatuated with him. A part-time nurse at the local hospital, Rena manages an organic dairy farm with her gender nonconforming partner, Susan "Mack" Mackey. When Trexler shows up in town, Rena is only faintly aware of environmental and health concerns surrounding fracking. Avowedly "not very political" (87), she is dazzled by Trexler: the narrator comments that Rena "had never met, or even imagined, a man like Lorne," a voluble academic who seems utterly unlike the "gruff coal miners she'd known all her life" (335). In contrast to these figures—and to Mack, who is also "self-conscious as a teenager"—Trexler is authoritative and confident, "an effortless talker" who seems, to Rena, to know everything about process, potential harms, and politics of fracking (221, 222). Despite her hesitancy to get involved in public life, Rena is flattered by Trexler's attention toward her; he soon convinces her to launch a local anti-fracking campaign. Initially, Trexler's opposition to fracking in Bakerton makes sense to Rena, who begins to feel that Darco may indeed be guilty of the harmful practices Trexler insists they will inevitably engage in, such as contaminating the drinking water. The threat of methane pollution appears to materialize when Shelby Devlin repeatedly brings her young daughter with nonspecific digestive symptoms, Olivia, to the hospital where Rena works. Trexler seizes on Shelby as "a godsend": "The DEP doesn't care about our rivers," he explains, "but even those idiots can't ignore a sick kid" (228).

As it turns out, Trexler himself can ignore a sick kid when Olivia's illness no longer supports his activist agenda. Rena notices suspicious patterns in Shelby's behavior, and in Olivia's lab results, irregularities that strongly suggest that Shelby may suffer from Munchausen syndrome by proxy, even as they do not conclusively prove this diagnosis. As with Wes's illness, Haigh invites readers to read between the lines, doling out troubling details about Shelby; if clues in the plot do not add up to interconvertible proof,[9] they nevertheless amount to something that encourages moral deliberation. Relevant here is Kathleen Stewart's advocacy for "weak theory" that "comes unstuck from its own line of thought to follow objects it encounters, or becomes undone by attention to things that don't just *add up* but take on a life of their own as problems for thought" (72). Shelby's behavior complicates the narrative that a more conventional anti-fracking text would entail: while there are numerous clues to suggest that perhaps Olivia *is* sick from methane exposure, indeterminacy precludes a confrontation between Rena or the Devlins and the drilling company. Where a "strong" interpretive paradigm might prove unhelpful is precisely this sort of situation, one in which a toxin or some other harm is already on the loose. In Olivia's case, a provisional narrative of events must be intuited rather than systematically deduced in order for ethical action of any kind to transpire; an attitude that would insist on static lines of causality not only fails to land the energy tycoons in jail, but also leads to a little girl who is still sick.

Rena's attraction to Trexler—and to activism—eventually falters when she accompanies him to an anti-fracking rally at a college campus. On a chaotic quad mobbed by groups whose "connections to gas drilling are strategic, or metaphysical, or perhaps imaginary," Trexler "moves through the crowd like an impresario," oblivious to Rena's discomfort (368). He sees the scene as an example of "what can happen when we speak truth to power" (369); Rena, meanwhile, is baffled by the event's lack of coherence and, further, annoyed by Trexler's casual dismissal of rural Pennsylvanians' "fatalism." "It's like they *expect* to have their land and water polluted," he tells Rena, "like they're just *waiting* to be screwed" (369). Months later, when Darco leaves Bakerton, Trexler still insists on the efficacy of activism, even though the company's sudden departure actually belies the importance of "democracy, the role of an informed citizenry, [and] the awesome power of collective action": Darco leaves town and "nobody, not even Lorne Trexler, knows why" (405).

On one hand, this plot might seem to suggest that only something much more ambitious than regional organizing can address climate change; on the other, it might suggest that a revolution against climate change is impossible. These interpretations overlook a key point, though. While conventional activism fails in the novel, Rena points to weaker, yet potentially effective, forms that ethical action could, and perhaps must, take in an increasingly exhausted, toxified world. Although she cannot prove that Shelby is poisoning her daughter, Rena nonetheless quits her job so that she can anonymously report Shelby to child protective services. This act of courageousness is the opposite of Trexler's activism: it is anonymous, risky, and based on intuition rather than proof. It is moral agency of a type more attainable for most people than the kinds of "strong" environmentalism often glorified by environmentalists and by the media.

What ultimately makes Trexler so unlikable is not only his narcissism but also the rigidity of his worldview. In a pivotal scene toward the end of the novel, when Rena reveals to Trexler her suspicion that Shelby might be poisoning Olivia, Rena suddenly realizes that Trexler *"doesn't care"* about Olivia, or any of the people in Bakerton—he admits that his concerns lies with "Darco. The DEP. The huge fucking propaganda machine that's telling the world that fracking is safe" (394). "Trust me, Rena," he adds, "You have no idea what we're up against" (394). Of course, in his focus on giant systems, Trexler has no idea what *he* is up against: convinced that "people are idiots," he is a "famous populist, [and] champion of the working classes until they dare to disagree with him" (375). In his unyielding dogmatism, Trexler typifies the figure of the paranoid reader; notably, he is also the only character in the book—other than Kip Oliphant—who "believes in his own power, his ability to affect outcomes" (376). In contrast, for example, Rich is reconciled to his own "basic and inescapable smallness" (427). If there is a lesson to be learned from the Trexler character, it may be the limitations of an inflexible worldview. Besides the fact that his ideology cannot imagine forms of causality that elude "huge fucking propaganda machine[s]," it cannot imagine strategies of resistance besides, as he tells Rena, "sounding the alarm . . . loudly and with great conviction" (394).

Addressing literary critics, Paul Saint-Amour warns that there are pitfalls to opposing neoliberal capitalism with "an equally totalizing theory of anti-capitalism" ("Weak Theory"). There are, he continues, "oppositions that bear repeating and disseminating. But when what you oppose has a death-grip on repetition and dissemination, you may need to shift registers: you may need not only different ways of speaking your opposition, but different scales and intensities at which to speak it." Following Saint-Amour's logic, we might reexamine how literature "speaks" opposition to climate change. To the extent that novels can apprehend the dynamics of bioregulation and other systemic socioecological phenomena, they are also able to illuminate facets of life in the Anthropocene that evade strongly theorized frameworks. Equally important, fiction can imagine as-yet-untried remedies, including forms of repair that are imperfect or based on incomplete information. In contrast to Hollywood depictions of fracking in which a community rallies to defeat a giant corporation, *Heat and Light* offers no reassurance that plucky heroes will triumph or any assurance that climate change can be halted. By rejecting a David-and-Goliath narrative, however, Haigh makes room for serious questions to emerge, such as: What forms of resolution *are* available to a community after energy jobs disappear? What are some ways of enduring with the knowledge that one's land, or water, or even one's body, is likely poisoned? The thought exercise Haigh asks readers to engage in is *not* how we might summon the courage to take down a giant energy corporation; it is, rather, how we—readers—would move forward in the absence of a grand showdown or even the promise of a sequel.

We will need this capacity to imagine livable futures amid emergent conditions. As Elizabeth Kolbert explains in *Under a White Sky*, the pace of global environmental change means that we face "no-analog climates, no-analog ecosystems, a whole no-analog future" (7–8). In this context, there are few, if any, universally applicable principles for action in the domain of climate change or any other environmental dilemma: in the words of Paul Kingsnorth, "Sometimes doing nothing is better than doing something. Sometimes it is the other way around" ("Life Versus"). We would be wise in this "no-analog predicament" to cultivate ways of reading that are adaptive and open to revision as conditions inevitably shift (Kolbert 8). To paraphrase Kingsnorth, sometimes that will mean drawing on paradigms that have worked well in the past to expose systemic environmental injustices. Sometimes it will mean improvising entirely new analytic frameworks. Perhaps our most important critical priority should be insisting upon the time needed to engage in deep moral imagining. Brennan asserts that "social justice means giving back to human beings the time and means they need to replenish themselves": in a more just world, telling and listening to stories would be considered a necessity instead of a luxury, a form of rejuvenation that, in its very pausing of capitalism's frenetic pace, served vital environmentalist ends (16). In an exhausted, burnt-out world, reading and creating cli-fi is its own sort of resistance—a reminder that there are alternative temporalities outside the warming, unequal world we inhabit now.

NOTES

1. In a wildfire, the "front" is the leading edge of the fire perimeter, where combustion flames rather than glows.

2. For more on the 2020 wildfire season in the US, see the National Interagency Fire Center, www.nifc.gov/fire-information/nfn.

3. "Weak reading" is among a cluster of related critical methods to emerge since 2000, including postcritique, surface reading, distant reading, and the new formalism. Broadly, these approaches are united by their resistance to "symptomatic reading"; unlike earlier modes of criticism, which claimed to expose the ruses of ideology or to demystify the hidden layers of texts, the so-called modest modes of reading to emerge in recent years make more tentative, circumspect claims about their own efficacy and about the functions of criticism in general. Some important landmarks in the development of "the new modesty in literary criticism" (Williams) include Rita Felski's *Uses of Literature* (2008) and *The Limits of Critique* (2015), Sharon Marcus's *Between Women* (2007) and a special issue of *Representations* coedited with Stephen Best (2009), and Caroline Levine's *Forms* (2015). Eve Kosofsky Sedgwick's *Touching Feeling* (2003) is also an important touchstone for reparative forms of reading, particularly within queer studies. Predictably, detractors have accused postcritique methods of political quietism; for an accessible overview of this debate see Williams, "The New Modesty"; see also Menely and Taylor, "Introduction" (10–14), and Saint-Amour, "Weak Theory." I borrow the insight about postcritique and its discourse of exhaustion from Patricia Stuelke's *The Ruse of Repair* (4–5, 29), a more recent response to the reparative turn.

4. See Brennan, *Globalization and Its Terrors*. For other perspectives on the disarticulation of production from biological constraints, see Crary, *24/7: Late Capitalism and the Ends of Sleep;* see also Barca, *Forces of Reproduction*.

5. Haigh gestures briefly to the potential for catastrophic injuries at drilling sites. Although rig manager Marshall "Herc" Bonner is irritated by Darco's prominent worksite safety signage, he also realizes that various "calamities . . . can happen on a drill rig," the likeliest of which is a "close to three-story fall" (101). The narrator acknowledges that drillers "are well paid" and that "a high school dropout can earn six figures if he is strong and willing. If nothing goes wrong" (98). If and when something *does* go wrong, the results can be fatal: "It's a truth most people never have to learn," Herc muses to himself, "that the human body is simply a bag of blood" (102).

6. See, for example, the opening chapter of John Sayles's *Yellow Earth*.

7. See Ghosh, *The Great Derangement*.

8. See, for example, Mertens and Craps, "Contemporary Fiction vs. the Challenge of Imagining the Timescale of Climate Change." Mertens and Craps observe that "climate change is characterized by a complex temporality that the linear idea of time and the limited duration usually found in novels fail to capture" (150). Their survey of recent cli-fi concludes, rather tepidly, that "some of the [formal] innovations" they analyze "see[m] to suggest that it might actually be possible to write 'the great climate change novel,'" although they also concede that "perhaps . . . other or hybrid art forms might be a way forward" (151).

9. As an example, Rena suspects that Shelby may be slipping Olivia ipecac, which "has kind of a weird smell, like grape candy" (393); although Rena tells Mack she has "never smelled that on Olivia," (393) elsewhere in the novel, we learn that Rich

Devlin's truck "still smells faintly of grape candy" (214) from a time Olivia vomited in it.

WORKS CITED

Alaimo, Stacy. *Bodily Natures: Science, Environment, and the Material Self.* Indiana UP, 2010.
Barca, Stefania. *Forces of Reproduction: Notes for a Counter-Hegemonic Anthropocene.* Cambridge UP, 2020.
Berlant, Lauren. "Slow Death (Sovereignty, Obesity, Lateral Agency)." *Critical Inquiry,* vol. 33, no. 4, 2007, pp. 754–80.
Brennan, Teresa. *Globalization and Its Terrors.* Routledge, 2003.
"Burn-Out an 'Occupational Phenomenon': International Classification of Diseases." World Health Organization, May 28, 2019. who.int/news/item/28-05-2019-burn-out-an-occupational-phenomenon-international-classification-of-diseases. Accessed 8 June 2022.
Crary, Jonathan. *24/7: Late Capitalism and the Ends of Sleep.* Verso, 2013.
Dimock, Wai Chee. *Weak Planet: Literature and Assisted Survival.* U of Chicago P, 2020.
"Front line, N. and Adj." *OED Online,* Oxford UP, 2021. www.oed.com/view/Entry/414623. Accessed 21 June 2021.
Ghosh, Amitav. *The Great Derangement: Climate Change and the Unthinkable.* U of Chicago P, 2016.
Haigh, Jennifer. *Heat and Light.* HarperCollins, 2016.
Haraway, Donna J. *Staying with the Trouble: Making Kin in the Chtulucene.* Duke UP, 2016.
Kingsnorth, Paul. "Life Versus the Machine." *Orion,* Winter 2018. orionmagazine.org/article/life-versus-the-machine/. Accessed 20 Sept. 2021.
Kolbert, Elizabeth. *Under a White Sky: The Nature of the Future.* Random House, 2021.
Latour, Bruno. "Why Has Critique Run Out of Steam? From Matters of Fact to Matters of Concern." *Critical Inquiry,* vol. 30, no. 2, 2004, pp. 225–48.
LeMenager, Stephanie. "Climate Change and the Struggle for Genre." *Anthropocene Reading: Literary History in Geologic Times,* edited by Tobias Menely and Jesse Oak Taylor, Pennsylvania State UP, 2017, pp. 220–38.
Marshall, Kate. "What Are the Novels of the Anthropocene? American Fiction in Geological Time." *American Literary History,* vol. 27, no. 3, 2015, pp. 523–38.
Masters, Jeff. "Reviewing the Horrid Global 2020 Wildfire Season." *Yale Climate Connections,* 4 Jan. 2021. yaleclimateconnections.org/2021/01/reviewing-the-horrid-global-2020-wildfire-season/. Accessed 20 Sept. 2021.
Menely, Tobias, and Jesse Oak Taylor. Introduction. *Anthropocene Reading: Literary History in Geologic Times,* edited by Menely and Taylor, Penn State UP, 2017, pp. 1–24.
Mertens, Mahlu, and Stef Craps. "Contemporary Fiction vs. the Challenge of Imagining the Timescale of Climate Change." *Studies in the Novel,* vol. 50, no. 1, 2018, pp. 134–53.

Molesky, Jason. "Gothic Toxicity and the Mysteries of Nondisclosure in American Hydrofracking Literature." *Modern Fiction Studies*, vol. 66, no. 1, 2020, pp. 52–77.

National Oceanic and Atmospheric Administration (NOAA). "Global Climate Report—Annual 2020." July 9, 2021. www.ncdc.noaa.gov/sotc/global/202013. Accessed 20 Sept. 2021.

Nixon, Rob. *Slow Violence and the Environmentalism of the Poor.* Harvard UP, 2011.

Saint-Amour, Paul. "Weak Theory, Weak Modernisms." *Modernism/Modernity*, vol. 3, no. 3, 2018. modernismmodernity.org/articles/weak-theory-weak-modernism#_edn41. Accessed 20 Sept. 2021.

Sayles, John. *Yellow Earth.* Haymarket Books, 2020.

Stewart, Kathleen. "Weak Theory in an Unfinished World." *Journal of Folklore Research*, vol. 45, no. 1, 2008, pp. 71–82. www.jstor.org/stable/40206966. Accessed 20 Sept. 2021.

Stuelke, Patricia. *The Ruse of Repair: US Neoliberal Empire and the Turn from Critique.* Duke UP, 2021.

Williams, Jeffery J. "The New Modesty in Literary Studies." *Chronicle of Higher Education*, 5 Jan. 2015. www.chronicle.com/article/The-New-Modesty-in-Literary/150993. Accessed 20 Sept. 2021.

Wu, Katherine J. "Covid Combat Fatigue: 'I Would Come Home with Tears in My Eyes.'" *New York Times*, 25 Nov. 2020. www.nytimes.com/2020/11/25/health/doctors-nurses-covid-stress.html. Accessed 20 Sept. 2021.

Resource Utopia and Dystopia
Excavating Class in Afrofuturist Cli-Fi Film

MARTÍN PREMOLI AND B. JAMIESON STANLEY

The end of oil . . . fuels at once both Utopia and dystopia: it is the crisis that breaks the world into ruin but also the opportunity out of which the possibility of another world might emerge.
—Gerry Canavan, "Retrofutures and Petrofutures: Oil, Scarcity, Limit" (345)

Utopian and dystopian narratives have acquired new urgency as responses to environmental exploitation and climate change. The threat of ecological collapse lends itself to the dystopian, witnessed in texts as different as Octavia Butler's novel *Parable of the Sower* (1993), Roland Emmerich's disaster film *The Day after Tomorrow* (2004), and Roy Scranton's polemic *Learning to Die in the Anthropocene* (2015). But ecological collapse has also illuminated the need for imagining just and sustainable utopian alternatives. As Gerry Canavan argues, utopias emerge from the ruins of crisis, enabling us to reimagine and remake society. How does climate fiction fit into this utopia/dystopia dichotomy? And what might climate fiction tell us about future class conflict, as imagined in dialogue with energy economies? We will address these questions through Afrofuturist cli-fi film.

"Climate fiction" or "cli-fi," coined by journalist Dan Bloom, connotes fictional prose narrative about climate collapse. Yet scholars such as Michael Svoboda apply the term to film, and Rebecca Evans contends that "cli-fi is not in fact a coherent genre but rather a literary preoccupation with climate futures that draws from a wide range of popular genres" (95). Extending this generic expansiveness, we define climate fiction broadly to include film, and to include texts not just about obvious manifestations of an altered climate—such as amplified droughts or storms—but also about energy economies. An analysis of energy economies matters to a conversation about climate fiction and class, we contend, because the current fossil fuel economy (petrocapitalism) has both caused climate change and determined contemporary class relations, and because climate change will provoke different energy economies in the future. We highlight how two Afrofuturist films each imagine an energy economy other than petrocapitalism: a "clean" economy based on the fictional fuel vibranium offers a concurrent alternative to petroleum in Ryan Coogler's *Black Panther*, whereas in Wanuri Kahiu's *Pumzi* a kinetic energy economy emerges after petrocapitalism's collapse.

Relocating the cli-fi conversation to Afrofuturist films about energy extraction and to the speculative Global South raises important perspectives on the transnational operations of class, race, and genre in the era of climate change, recentering how fossil-fueled industrialization in the Global North—the primary driver of climate change—has relied on colonialist patterns of extracting energy, minerals, and human labor. To draw out these patterns and situate our work within critical conversations about climate justice, we begin with a brief overview of Black Anthropocene discourse. We then connect this critical framework to contemporary debates about the geographies of Afrofuturism: while Afrofuturism originated as a term for African American sci-fi, thinking transnationally about Afrofuturism highlights the global dynamics of energy and labor extraction that have produced an uneven climate crisis. Next, we examine the energy economies depicted in the two films, paying attention to scarcity/abundance, labor, class identities, physical spaces, and dystopianism/utopianism. *Pumzi* portrays a future East Africa dependent on kinetic energy, in which scarcity motivates a strict class hierarchy. In our initial reading of this film as a "resource dystopia," *Pumzi* offers a critique of current environmental and labor practices, but not much hope for change. In contrast, *Black Panther* depicts a classless country, Wakanda, powered by an abundant and clean resource known as vibranium. Crafting a "resource utopia" by erasing the classed and racial valences of mining, *Black Panther* may offer more hope than *Pumzi* but provides an insufficient critique of petrocapitalism, positing vibranium as a more perfect petroleum. These films manifest extreme (and opposing) visions of future class relations, enabling us to critique the exploitative dynamics of petrocapitalism and keep the need for a just energy transition central to how we imagine responding to climate change.

THE BLACK ANTHROPOCENE: AFROFUTURISM, EXTRACTION, AND CLIMATE JUSTICE

Octavia Butler's 1993 novel *Parable of the Sower* situates climate change as a key concern for Afrofuturism and, conversely, Afrofuturism as a crucial resource for conceptualizing climate justice. *Parable* depicts residents fleeing a California marred by climate-enhanced drought and rampant inequality. The protagonist, a young Black woman named Lauren, leads a multiracial coalition of climate refugees. Combining an Afrocentric vision of humankind's destiny in space with a critique of privatization, *Parable* presages what scholars are now calling the "Black Anthropocene": a perspective that situates climate change as a product of anti-Black violence, racial capitalism, and fossil fuel extraction.

In *A Billion Black Anthropocenes or None*, Kathryn Yusoff argues that geology, as both discipline and extractive practice, has underwritten liberalism's establishment through colonialism and enslavement. As Yusoff notes, the Anthropocene concept occludes the roles of anti-Blackness and colonial violence in facilitating energy extraction and industrialization, which have caused climate change. Christina Sharpe's work enables us to recognize the ongoing nature of anti-Blackness, reminding us that Black subjects live in the wake of ongoing colonial violence. Adding to these insights, both T. J. Demos and Ta-Nehisi Coates note that whereas neoliberal Anthropocene thinkers would manage climate change through techno-utopian fixes (such as geoengineering) and elide questions of race and class, a Black Anthropocene perspective considers environmental problems "inseparable from social terms of racial capitalism" (Demos) and recognizes the relationship between white supremacy and environmental destruction (Coates 70). Climate change, class inequality, neocolonialism, and anti-Blackness need to be addressed together, turning to root causes such as fossil fuel extraction rather than symptoms being treated through antidemocratic modes of "managing" the climate.

A Black Anthropocene framework thus brings attention to who profits and who suffers from the energy economies that have caused climate change. In our view, this necessitates thinking transnationally, because the extraction of fossil fuels and its resulting harms often occur far from the fuel's consumption. A tank filled up at a Shell station in Nebraska may rely on oil drilling devastating the Niger Delta, for example. In this piece, we think transnationally about Afrofuturism as a multifoliate mode of climate fiction that can question petrocapitalism by imagining different energy economies, whether utopian or dystopian in flavor. Recentering continental Africa as a crucial context both for histories of extraction and for such cli-fi imaginaries, this analysis requires that we attend to the contested geographies of Afrofuturism itself.

In the 1993 article that coins the term, Mark Dery defines Afrofuturism as "speculative fiction that . . . addresses African-American concerns in the context of twentieth-century technoculture—and, more generally, African-American signification that appropriates images of technology and a prosthetically enhanced future" (736). Broadening beyond fiction, film has been an important Afrofuturist medium for expressing what John Akomfrah calls a "digitopic desire": a yearning for utopian possibilities that might be activated by future technologies (qtd. in Keeling 121). The revolution of digital technologies broadened the accessibility and representational possibilities of film (in part by making editing less capital-intensive); nonetheless, Kara Keeling urges film and media scholars not to equate technology with utopian possibility but to instead examine the complex relation between changing technologies, changing representations of race, and ongoing material oppression (144). Similarly, we suggest that an analysis of climate fiction should address how visions of climate futures may hinge upon imagined possibilities for "clean" energy technologies.

While influential chroniclers of Afrofuturism such as Dery and Ytasha Womack have emphasized African American creators, others ask how recentering the African continent might shift expectations. Nigerian American sci-fi giant Nnedi Okorafor suggests in a series of tweets from 2017 that Afrofuturism should refer primarily to writers from the continent: "If we are going to use the word Afrofuturism, African writers from within Africa should be the majority when listing central examples of it. If you are writing an article on Afrofuturism and this isn't the case, that sh*t is inauthentic. . . . As the Black Panther film comes closer to blowing all our minds, I'd like ppl to remember these words."[1] Okorafor anticipates Black Panther's blockbuster success and problematizes this exceptional status going to an American film that reimagines continental Africa. Later the same day, Okorafor posts that she doesn't "care for the word" Afrofuturist, because it's "an American rooted thing."[2] In 2018, Okorafor declares that upon reflection, she "should be called an Africanfuturist, NOT an Afrofuturist."[3] Okorafor's comments suggest the need for an expanded discussion that acknowledges connections and differences across futurist productions from different cultures within Africa and its diasporas.

Wanuri Kahiu, creator of *Pumzi*, assays such an expanded narrative in a 2012 TEDx Nairobi talk. Explaining the origins of Afrofuturism as a term "specifically about African Americans," Kahiu asks what it might mean to "find a place for Afrofuturism in Africa" ("Afrofuturism and the African" 1:45). She emphasizes that "there have always been people in all parts of Africa who have either looked to space, or . . . who are seers," and sees Afrofuturism in long-standing African invocations of myths and the spirit world, such as the Kikuyu myth of Gikuyu and Mumbi, the magical realism of Ben Okri, and Dogon accounts of the planet Sirius B (Kahiu, "Africa & Science Fiction" 3:53; Kahiu, "Afrofuturism and the African"). Kahiu thus rhymes with African American concepts while recentering practitioners from cultural locations across the African continent. Similarly advocating a "planetary" Afrofuturism, Sofia Samatar theorizes "flashpoints" that connect African, Afropolitan, and African American sci-fi without equating them: bricolage or remixology, in which discarded materials and ideas are reclaimed; temporal "entanglement," in which the past becomes an "instrument for survival in the future;" posthuman, alien, and robotic elements; and "passionate attachment to physical African spaces" (187). Samatar and Kahiu alike characterize Afrofuturism as concerned with specific African places or traditions and with how past and future interpenetrate. Together, they provide a schematic that can describe a geographically and culturally expansive Afrofuturism, helping us apprehend its relevance to the global but uneven problem of climate change.

Using the term "Afrofuturism" with an eye to its multiple and contested geographies, we consider how two very differently located and financed film productions—one a Kenyan indie, the other an American blockbuster—each reimagine continental Africa. As white scholars employed by American universities and studying the Global South, we experience racial and class privilege stemming from the global network of extraction that has caused climate change; we are interested in how a transnational take on Afrofuturism can highlight extractive economies in order to invigorate conversations about the class politics and geopolitics of cli-fi. Petrocapitalism is a global phenomenon, meaning that an analysis of climate change and class needs to think transnationally. Afrofuturism can enable this transnational thinking, we suggest, by tracing how extractive energy economies were made possible by the growth of racial capitalism through colonialism, enslavement, and class differentiation, both across and within nations. We argue that by intermingling dystopian and utopian modes, Afrofuturist cli-fi can help all of us revisit our collective past of industrialization fueled by the exploitation of nonhuman nature and particular humans, which must be redressed in order to envision livable climate futures.

RESOURCE DYSTOPIA IN *PUMZI*

The 2009 Kenyan film *Pumzi* pictures what we call a "resource dystopia": an unjust society structured around the scarcity of water and energy after climate collapse. *Pumzi* takes place "35 years after World War III—the 'Water War'" at the Maitu Community, a totalitarian society in East Africa with a strict class hierarchy (0:14). This settlement exists inside a hermetic facility that resembles a space station, perched in a drought-stricken and radioactive desert. The day-to-day operations of the community revolve around rationing water and producing energy. Water reserves are attended by armed guards, one of whom scans a barcode on the protagonist Asha's arm before she can collect her ration. Asha carries water clipped to her belt, and purifies her urine and sweat to refill her plastic bottle. The Virtual Natural History Museum, where Asha works, archives the water crisis and the disappearance of biodiversity: "There Goes the Last Tree," one historical newspaper clipping announces, while another headline describes a "Whole Day Journey in Search of Water" (0:39). These histories are questioned, however, through Asha's dream of plunging into an underground lake, where she sees the roots of a living tree.

Beyond water, the other scarce resource is energy: fossil fuels have been replaced by energy generated by human bodies. A stratified class system surrounds energy production, as we see when Asha strolls by manual laborers on treadmills and rowing machines displayed in the community's main hallway. Flashing signs and a recorded announcement encourage citizens to "do your part" by producing "kinetic energy: zero percent pollution, one hundred percent self-sustainable" (1:53). Although this language implies volunteerism, the laborers' resentful glances at Asha suggest otherwise. A "sustainable" energy economy is achieved through the exertion of lower-class people, calling to mind today's global dynamics of exploited labor and energy extraction. Within *Pumzi*'s world the social hierarchy is built not around race or gender (at least not on terms we'd expect) but class. Nearly all members of this society present as Black; all of the speaking actors present as female-bodied, while male-presenting actors appear as both laborers and guards. Class divisions are defined by roles within the kinetic energy economy.

Although the film does not show how these class positions were assigned, we learn that class status can be changed as a punishment. Asha's routine is disrupted when she receives a package labeled with her name and a set of latitudinal and longitudinal coordinates. Inside is a soil sample with "abnormally high water content" and "no radioactivity" (5:06–5:14). Intrigued, Asha plants the museum's preserved Maitu tree seed in the moist soil. When she reports her findings, her supervisors demote her. Guards drag Asha out of the museum, empty her water bottle, and set her on a rowing machine (10:13). Asha's costume is changed to match the other laborers; her sparkling turquoise eyeshadow is removed. Writing in a different context, Mukti Lakhi Mangharam suggests that like gender, class identity is performative, "achieved through the constant stylization of the body" (97). Asha's body is abruptly restyled to perform a different class identity, and she will now generate power with her kinetic energy.

While a Marxist formulation of labor in energy economies might track how individual laborers are employed to mine energy from the environment, *Pumzi* collapses the distance between laborer and energy source, questioning "who" or "what" is being mined. Whereas fossil fuel economies rely on exploited human labor to extract an energy source, in *Pumzi* exploited human labor *is* the energy source (kinetic energy). With this streamlining, the film demands that viewers confront the centrality of labor exploitation to our present resource dystopia, while anticipating futures of scarcity and intensified exploitation in an altered climate.

RESOURCE UTOPIA IN *BLACK PANTHER*

At first glance, *Black Panther* might not seem like a climate fiction. The film does not foreground weather systems, nor take place in a future characterized by an altered climate (as is the case with *Pumzi*). But because fossil-fueled modernity has caused climate change, we argue that scrutinizing energy extraction is fundamental to climate fiction—and *Black Panther* depicts quite an intriguing energy economy. Whereas *Pumzi* portrays a class-stratified society organized around scarcity, *Black Panther* evacuates class by depicting abundance: the film's "futuristic vision relies on the illusion of infinite resources," as Cajetan Iheka notes (2). This utopian fantasy of an infinite and perfect resource, we argue, problematically enables *Black Panther* to picture technology and clean energy extraction eliminating physical labor, sacrifice zones, and the working class.

Black Panther is an American film based on an American comic strip, but it takes place in a fictional African country, Wakanda, whose depiction utilizes cultural elements from across the continent. Wakandans speak isiXhosa (a South African language), and two written scripts are pictured, one drawing on Nsibidi (an ancient Nigerian pictographic system), and the other a fictive language inspired by "Chinese, Arabic, and Dogon and Murci" elements (Desowitz). Characters from South Africa and the United States render Wakanda a zone of transnational encounter and resource conflict. *Black Panther* thus needs to be understood in relation to Pan-Africanism, postcoloniality, the contested geographies of Afrofuturism, the global stratification of labor, and the politics of resource extraction. We will attempt such a positioning as we consider class dynamics in *Black Panther* under the rubric of resource utopianism.

Nnedi Okorafor's recent contributions to Marvel's comic book series have written complexities of class, gender, and African cultures into the *Black Panther* universe. Okorafor's comic *Shuri: The Search for Black Panther* centers Princess Shuri (rather than her brother, T'Challa) and portrays a Wakanda with characters from many ethnic and class backgrounds. A group of women from diverse classes and ages meets secretly when Wakanda is in trouble; the comic mentions a "Vibranium Extraction Academy," whereas in the film, human labor related to extracting vibranium is invisible (chapter 1). The Wakandan queen, Ramonda, is Zulu; Shuri hears the stories of Wakanda from a griot, or West African storyteller; Wakanda's great baobab tree "is named Grootboom the second, after the original Grootboom in Namibia" (chapter 2). Tensions among African nations appear when King T'Challa meets with a coalition of leaders called the Egungun, as in Yoruba tradition (chapter 4). By flagging the provenances of various cultural elements, Okorafor envisions Wakanda as Pan-African, without generalizing about Africa. Her comics build towards a transnational sci-fi movement with nuanced narratives of the African continent and of gender and class relations.

Okorafor's nuance with regard to class, however, is arguably missing from the *Black Panther* film. The film opens with Wakanda's origin story: "millions of years ago," a meteorite struck central Africa, saturating its geology with vibranium (00:00:15). Vibranium extraction allows Wakanda to create "technology more advanced than any other nation," even while the rest of the world "descended into chaos" (00:01:15–20). Access to vibranium also enables Wakandans to "hide" from the outside world—a point to which we will return. Wakanda is portrayed as an urban techno-utopia, resembling and surpassing the sleek tech-spaces of the Western futurist imagination. An establishing shot of Wakanda's cityscape shows towering, metallic architectural wonders, each conjuring the possibility of an idealized African metropolis. Rather than frame urban spaces as separate from the "natural" world, the city of Wakanda exemplifies ideal environmental intermixing: sparkling rivers cut through skyscrapers and large swaths of greenery suffuse the built environment. The manufactured dualisms that structure the Western imagination and have led to environmental destruction (such as nature/culture) have no place within Wakanda's borders.

Such a harmonious vision translates to the film's social ecology as well. Though Wakanda has a monarchy, the film undercuts any class-based division or rigidity. In one scene, King T'Challa and his love interest, Nakia, stroll through a street market, interacting pleasantly with hawkers and vendors. In an earlier aerial shot, the camera pans over a group of marginal agriculturalists who turn out to be part of Wakanda's "cover," a guise of a poverty-stricken country behind which Wakanda's high-tech city is concealed. Wakanda's organizational dynamics starkly contrast the divisive, claustrophobic, and alienating architectures we encounter in *Pumzi*. Wakanda is an urban utopia, unimpeded by the grid of rigid divisions and inflexible identities often tied to the architectures of cities.

Black Panther organizes this exceptionalism around resource-richness: Wakanda sits atop deposits of vibranium so bountiful that class divisions are unnecessary. Vibranium is characterized as a fossil fuel, yet with none of fossil fuels' negative impacts. As described by the villain Ulysses Klaue, vibranium is both "the most valuable metal known to man" and "not just a metal. They sew it into their clothes. It powers their city, their tech, their weapons" (56:20–30). Energy source, precious metal, and also miracle drug, vibranium even provides superhero powers to Wakanda's king, who drinks from the vibranium-laced "heart-shaped herb."

In real-life sub-Saharan Africa, however, resource abundance has not generated egalitarian societies. Instead, mineral extraction has often motivated colonization and has tended to funnel wealth into walled-off enclaves and then siphon it out of the country. As James Ferguson puts it, "capital does not 'flow' from New York to Angola's oil fields, or from London to

Ghana's gold mines; it hops, neatly skipping over most of what lies in between" (38). Little prosperity accrues near extraction sites, which are run by multinationals headquartered abroad and "often literally walled off with bricks, razor wire, and security guards" (Ferguson 36). But Wakanda's vibranium mine bespeaks openness, in everything from its architecture to its usage patterns. Rather than the cramped space we'd expect in a mine, the vibranium mine is airy and expansive. The high-tech lab where Shuri develops new technologies is located inside the mine. This lab even doubles as a medical unit, where Shuri assists injured CIA agent Ross, explaining that "there is vibranium all around us. That's how I healed you" (1:10:09–1:11:38). The omnipresence of vibranium is a healing force, meaning that vibranium mining lacks the toxic impacts of extracting coal, oil, or natural gas. And while real-world fossil fuels exist in limited supply, the Wakandans "have a mountain full of [vibranium]. They've been mining it for thousands of years and they still haven't scratched the surface" (57:05). The film's fantasy is a clean and infinite resource, allowing Wakanda to figure as a utopia in which energy extraction benefits society and human health without harming the environment.

The vibranium mine contrasts realist and documentary representations of mining in ways that illuminate *Black Panther*'s idealism around class. Mines are often associated with working-class identities: in the United States, for example, the coal miner is a classic figure of the rural working class.[4] This figure is often but not always white, as Yaa Gyasi's novel *Homegoing* (2016) reminds us by foregrounding the post–Civil War labor of incarcerated Black men in coal mines. In South Africa, the mine is a quintessential space of exploited Black migrant labor. Miners were central to union activism against apartheid, and mining has remained a focal point for postapartheid struggles. In 2012, police used assault rifles to suppress striking workers at the Marikana platinum mine, killing thirty-four, as captured in Rehad Desai's documentary *Miners Shot Down* (Uhuru Productions, 2014). The Marikana massacre is South Africa's deadliest use of force against its citizens since Soweto in 1976. Mining, then, spectacularly illustrates the stratification that consigns the (often Black) working class in various national contexts to crushing labor, poor wages, health hazards, and direct violence. But *Black Panther* rewrites the class associations of the mine. Instead of blue-collar workers extracting raw material, we see Shuri's lab-coat labor.

Mines also point to how class is imbricated with environmental shift. Mining arranges working-class experience around natural resource extraction, illustrating how "class identities are mutually constituted not only by our labor, but also by the natural world" (Robertson and Westerman 4). Extracting mineral resources creates precarity for both working-class bodies and "nature." To recognize this requires us to push back against petroculture's attempt to invisibilize both labor and environmental degradation, in part by narrating petroleum as a magical substance that performs work for free. Not unlike plantation slavery or indenture, petrocapitalism offers "the illusion of wealth without work," as "the true costs of oil are externalized to faraway places and to the future" (Wenzel 126, 45). What makes Wakanda a "resource utopia" is that vibranium avoids such costs altogether, externalizing work to a clean raw material and to vaguely defined "technology." Not only does energy appear like magic from the natural environment, but there is a new level of invisibility attached to labor: there are no miners in the mine. *Black Panther*'s egalitarianism thus hinges on eliminating the need for a working class. In this utopia, energy extraction no longer requires physical labor, nor leads to climate-altering emissions.

What are the implications of such an imaginary? Certainly we want to envision futures without labor exploitation, and energy economies that do not imperil the planet. But when attached to the idea of a perfect energy source, this may be a dangerous fantasy. After all, didn't oil seem perfect? The illusion of work without costs has enabled oil to "hijack the imagination" (Wenzel 45). Unbridled resource utopianism is misleading, to say the least. Can this be ameliorated by a combination of utopian and dystopian energies? We will explore this question by turning to the final moments of *Black Panther* and *Pumzi*.

THE DIALECTIC OF UTOPIA/DYSTOPIA

We have shown how *Black Panther* offers a utopian energy economy, while *Pumzi* captures a resource dystopia. Yet the endings of the two films complicate this bifurcation by intermingling utopian and dystopian notes. At *Pumzi*'s climax, Asha breaks out of the Maitu Community and treks across the desert, seeking the coordinates written on the mysterious soil sample's box. She uses her last strength to replant the Maitu seedling, watering it with what remains in her bottle and the sweat from her breasts and back. Asha then shields the plant from the harsh sun with her body and clothing. The film's final shot zooms out toward a bird's eye view as Asha collapses and the tree blossoms upwards through her body. As the camera spirals away, we hear faint sounds of birds, insects, and frogs, and a rumble of thunder followed by rain. We glimpse a green forest on the edge of the desert.

Utopian in the sense of opening new possibilities, this ending allows many readings. Perhaps a healthy forest was hidden all along. Perhaps the forest is a mirage. Or the forest might emerge in the future, seeded by Asha's act of planting and her decomposing organic matter. Alternatively, the forest could be present but radioactive: a reminder that life will continue without us, albeit in unfamiliar forms. By enabling these splintering readings, *Pumzi* suggests hope for ecosystem recovery and an escape from resource totalitarianism, yet comingles this utopian note with dystopian horizons. The film moves from a purer resource dystopia—in which hope existed only in dreams—to one that suggests the duality of hope and desperation in the face of climate injustice.

The ending of *Black Panther* similarly introduces a dialectic between utopia and dystopia. T'Challa travels to Oakland, California, to construct an international social-service project, focused on educating Black kids in poverty. T'Challa promises to end Wakanda's isolationism and share its resources. Through this decision, T'Challa implies that a utopia surrounded by dystopia is no utopia at all. On the surface, his plan seems generous and forward-thinking and could even suggest a global energy transition to vibranium as a potential response to climate change. (It also nods to the original Black Panther political party, founded in Oakland.) Yet this closing scene raises concerns for many critics, because it resonates with shallow humanitarianism and neoliberal approaches to aid. Russell Rickford critiques the "condescending uplift mentality" of T'Challa's gesture ("I Have a Problem"). And Christopher Lebron describes it as "the preferred solution of mega-rich neoliberals: educational programming" ("'Black Panther'"). For these critics, T'Challa's approach is at best a patronizing intervention and at worst an imperialist practice. As such, this closing scene invites dystopian possibilities into the film's construction of resource utopia.

Rather than frame this as a collapse of *Black Panther*'s utopian imaginary, however, it is possible to view this ending as a dialectical step toward utopia. The film concludes without further fleshing out T'Challa's plan; it neither activates nor avoids the problems mentioned above. Instead, the film encourages skeptical viewers to rigorously question and imagine what a global, anti-racist, and anti-imperial response to climate change might look like. What sort of education is best suited to empower the dispossessed and racially disenfranchised? How might local initiatives articulate with a global consciousness that is essential for combatting war, climatic disruptions, domination, and exploitation in Africa, America, and beyond? How might educational programs be coupled with radical political moves, such as charging the United States with crimes against humanity, as some nations attempted to do in the early moments of the Movement for Black Lives (Lebron)? Though *Black Panther* refrains from answering such questions, it moves us closer to a utopianism that engages with, rather than shies away from, the fraught consequences of imagining utopia in a world marred by histories of resource violence, dispossession, and dehumanization.

CONCLUSION

We began this essay with Gerry Canavan's remarks on the affordances of dystopia and utopia. For Canavan, dystopian modes should be considered alongside their utopian counterparts: the troubles of our world merit discussion, but we must also undertake the critical work of imagining livable futures. Such interest in thinking beyond dystopia resonates with recent critiques of Euro-American cultural fixation on apocalypse: as numerous scholars have noted, narratives that locate apocalypse in the future may efface the histories and ongoing experiences of genocide and racism that Black and Indigenous communities face.[5] While we agree with these critiques of mainstream apocalypticism, we have argued that resource utopianism also carries complex baggage: it overlooks the material realities and labor politics that accompany processes of resource extraction. As Imre Szeman has argued, utopian fictions have a history of imagining resolution through scientific innovations that are "in perfect synchrony with the operations of the capitalist economy: problem solved, without the need for radical ruptures or alterations in political and social life" ("System Failure" 813). Utopian and dystopian narratives, then, have both been guilty of eliding the patterns of inequality and violence that give rise to an uneven climate crisis; dystopia and utopia both entangle with Indigenous and Black dispossession and the pillaging of resources.

Intersecting this conversation about utopia/dystopia with a consideration of cli-fi and class, this essay has offered a comparative analysis of two Afrofuturist films with a focus on extraction—a social and material concern that impacts our ability to imagine "the shape of futures to come" as climate change advances (Szeman, "Afterword" 389). Our reading of *Black*

Panther examines how its much-discussed vision of a high-tech and powerful Africa hinges upon another feature of the film, which has often escaped critical commentary: vibranium. As a seemingly perfect fuel, vibranium allows the film to occlude the exploited labor and class hierarchies that surround real-world petroleum extraction and consumption. *Pumzi*, meanwhile, takes a more critical stance on the capacities of a society built on resource extraction. In this film the missing resource is a primary signifier, determining the labor relations of the society depicted. Comparing these texts through the lens of extraction, therefore, has allowed us to consider where exploitative race and class relations are made visible, versus where they are occluded, across utopian and dystopian forms.

By reading these Afrofuturist films as climate fictions, we have underscored how energy extraction drives racialized and globalized class relations, and noted the importance of redressing energy-related exploitation as we respond to climate change. Ultimately, our hope has been to emphasize the importance of both utopian *and* dystopian thinking, particularly as they relate to the processes and promises of resource extraction. This comparative approach emphasizes the need to think outside an either/or dichotomy (either we embrace resource extraction or we fully condemn it) when it comes to envisioning our relationship with energy. While there is no perfect fuel, it is possible to imagine and cultivate more sustainable and just relations with the resources that do exist on Earth. Afrofuturist cli-fi film's dialectic between utopian and dystopian modes offers a fuller picture of the violences and potentialities that have attended petrocapitalism, all while emphasizing the need to radically reimagine planetary futures.

NOTES

1. Nnedi Okorafor (@Nnedi), Twitter, October 18, 2017, 5:05 a.m., https://twitter.com/Nnedi/status/920576681747865600; 5:09 a.m., https://twitter.com/Nnedi/status/920577568847421440. The initial tweet in the thread is no longer available.

2. October 18, 2017, 5:12 a.m., https://twitter.com/Nnedi/status/920578362996871168.

3. November 4, 2018, 12:08 p.m., https://twitter.com/Nnedi/status/1059130186883448833.

4. See Robertson and Westerman, in which mining is discussed as a signal working-class occupation.

5. See, for example, Zamora, Whyte, and Ford III.

WORKS CITED

Butler, Octavia. *Parable of the Sower.* Grand Central Publishing, 2012.
Canavan, Garry. "Retrofutures and Petrofutures: Oil, Scarcity, Limit." *Oil Culture,* edited by Ross Barrett and Daniel Worden, University of Minnesota Press, 2014, pp. 331–49.
Coates, Ta-Nehisi. *Between the World and Me.* Spiegel & Grau, 2015.
Coogler, Ryan, director. *Black Panther.* Walt Disney Studios Motion Pictures, 2018.
Demos, T. J. "To Save a World: Geoengineering, Conflictual Futurisms, and the Unthinkable." *e-flux journal,* no. 94, 2018, n.p. https://www.e-flux.com/journal/94/221148/to-save-a-world-geoengineering-conflictual-futurisms-and-the-unthinkable/.
Dery, Mark. "Black to the Future: Interviews with Samuel R. Delany, Greg Tate, and Tricia Rose." *South Atlantic Quarterly,* vol. 92, no. 4, 1993, pp. 735–78.
Desowitz, Bill. "'Black Panther': How Wakanda Got a Written Language as Part of Its Afrofuturism." *IndieWire,* 22 Feb. 2018. https://www.indiewire.com/2018/02/black-panther-wakanda-written-language-ryan-coogler-afrofuturism-1201931252/. Accessed 21 July 2020.
Evans, Rebecca. "Fantastic Futures? Cli-fi, Climate Justice, and Queer Futurity." *Resilience: A Journal of the Environmental Humanities,* vol. 4, nos. 2–3, 2017, pp. 94–110.
Ferguson, James. *Global Shadows: Africa in the Neoliberal World Order.* Duke University Press, 2006.
Ford, James Edward, III. "When Disaster Strikes: On the Apocalyptic Tone of Hip Hop." *ASAP/Journal,* vol. 3 no. 3, 2018, pp. 595–622. DOI: 10.1353/asa.2018.0041.
Iheka, Cajetan. *African Ecomedia: Network Forms, Planetary Politics.* Duke UP, 2021.
Kahiu, Wanuri. "Africa & Science Fiction: Wanuri Kahiu's 'Pumzi.'" Interview by Oulimata Gueye. Filmed and edited by Masha Kosobokova, *YouTube,* 16 Dec. 2013. https://www.youtube.com/watch?v=SWMtgD9O6PU/.
———. "Afrofuturism in Popular Culture: Wanuri Kahiu at TEDxNairobi." Afrofuturism and the African. *TEDx,* July 2012, Nairobi. https://www.youtube.com/watch?v=PvxOLVaV2YY. Accessed 18 Mar. 2023.
———, director. *Pumzi.* Focus Features, 2009.
Keeling, Kara. *Queer Times, Black Futures.* New York UP, 2019.
Lebron, Christopher. "'Black Panther' Is Not the Movie We Deserve." *Boston Review,* 17 Feb. 2018. http://bostonreview.net/race/christopher-lebron-black-panther. Accessed 1 July 2021.
Mangharam, Mukti Lakhi. "Revealing Fictions: Neo-liberalism, Domestic Servants, and Thirty Umrigar's *The Space Between Us.*" *Ariel: A Review of International English Literature,* vol. 49, no. 1, 2018, pp. 79–106.
Okorafor, Nnedi. *Shuri: The Search for Black Panther.* Illustrated by Leonardo Romero and Jordie Bellaire. Marvel Worldwide, 2019.
Rickford, Russell. "I Have a Problem with 'Black Panther.'" *Africa Is a Country,* 22 Feb. 2018. https://africasacountry.com/2018/02/i-have-a-problem-with-black-panther. Accessed 1 July 2021.

Robertson, Christina, and Jennifer Westerman. "Introduction: Toward a Working Class Ecology." *Working on Earth: Class and Environmental Justice,* edited by Robertson and Westerman, U of Nevada Press, 2015, pp. 1–9.

Samatar, Sofia. "Toward a Planetary History of Afrofuturism." *Research in African Literatures,* vol. 48, no. 4, 2017, pp. 175–91. https://muse.jhu.edu/article/690428/.

Sharpe, Christina. *In the Wake: On Blackness and Being.* Duke University Press, 2016.

Svoboda, Michael. "Cli-Fi on the Screen(s): Patterns in the Representations of Climate Change in Fictional Films." *Wiley Interdisciplinary Reviews: Climate Change,* vol. 7, no. 1, 2016, pp. 43–64.

Szeman, Imre. "Afterword." *Fueling Culture: 101 Words for Energy and Environment,* edited by Imre Szeman, Jennifer Wenzel, and Patricia Yaeger, Fordham UP, 2017, pp. 389–94.

———. "System Failure: Oil, Futurity, and the Anticipation of Disaster." *South Atlantic Quarterly,* vol. 106, no. 4, 2007, pp. 805–23.

Wenzel, Jennifer. *The Disposition of Nature: Environmental Crisis and World Literature.* Fordham UP, 2020.

Whyte, Kyle Powys. "Our Ancestors' Dystopia Now: Indigenous Conservation and the Anthropocene." *The Routledge Companion to the Environmental Humanities,* edited by Ursula K. Heise, Jon Christensen, and Michelle Niemann, Routledge, 2017, pp. 206–15.

Womack, Ytasha. *Afrofuturism: The World of Black Sci-Fi and Fantasy Culture.* Lawrence Hills Books, 2013.

Yusoff, Kathryn. *A Billion Black Anthropocenes or None.* University of Minnesota Press, 2019.

Zamora, Lois Parkinson. "The Myth of Apocalypse and the American Literary Imagination." *The Apocalyptic Vision in America: Interdisciplinary Essays on Myth and Culture,* edited by Zamora, Bowling Green U Popular P, 1982, pp. 97–138.

Dreaming a Decolonized Climate
Indigenous Technologies and Relations of Class and Kinship in Cherie Dimaline's The Marrow Thieves

JESSICA CORY

Climate crises rage across the world. Yet the dominant rhetorical strains in Western society focus on individual lifestyle choices and technological solutions, ignoring the outsize carbon footprints of the large corporations and military interests whose lobbyists shape our neoliberal systems of governance. This shortsighted emphasis on technology and individualism rather than governmental or corporate accountability clearly represents a capitalist response to a capitalism-induced (and arguably, colonialism-induced) crisis. Not only will such a blinkered approach further perpetuate the racist, classist, and heteropatriarchal systems of oppression and extraction that Christian Parenti terms "the catastrophic convergence," it is also unlikely to limit emissions to safe levels without causing severe atmospheric or geological upset (7). To build a just and sustainable world, we must look beyond the parameters set by corporate persons.

Against this impoverished vision of climate futurity, Indigenous thought, with its capacious ability to imagine otherwise, offers a radical corrective. Considering the problem of climate and technology from an Indigenous perspective yields several important and interrelated questions. Who decides what counts as technology, and who controls it? Who or what, including nonhuman kin, might be harmed by technology, and in what ways might it increase or exacerbate ongoing inequalities and oppressions? What does the use of technology ignore? And how might Indigenous lifeways and technologies suggest a path towards climate mitigation without themselves becoming subject to yet another instance of violent, colonial extraction?

Indigenous intellectuals discuss these questions and theorize climate change in both scholarly and creative works (and texts that move across or between these categories). Potawatomi biologist Robin Wall Kimmerer writes extensively about Traditional Ecological Knowledge (TEK), knowledge that is experienced through connection to, and reciprocity with, place. Such reciprocity, as I get to shortly, engages with class by inherently being anticapitalist, as it cannot exist in greed or exploitation. Unfortunately, as Kimmerer discusses in her well-known book *Braiding Sweetgrass,* TEK is often not accepted by mainstream university science, largely because of science's racist and classist history in westernized countries. To expand upon TEK's usefulness as a technology, Kyle Powys Whyte, also Potawatomi, in much of his work explains how tribal sovereignty allows various peoples to utilize TEK in thinking about and creating Indigenous futures. Whyte notes that one way such futurity can be imagined is through Indigenous climate fiction ("Indigenous Science"). As Whyte explains, Indigenous peoples have already experienced apocalypses and thus have unique perspectives to share when it comes to writing about climate change and the Anthropocene (a concept that he and many other Indigenous intellectuals critique). There are many excellent examples of Indigenous cli-fi, such as Louise Erdrich's *Future Home of the Living God,* Alexis Wright's *The Swan Book,* and Melissa Tantaquidgeon Zobel's *Oracles,* each offering insight into matters of emplacement, land sovereignty, evolution (and devolution), adoption (a nod to the Indian Child Welfare Act), pregnancy, and other issues that have been affected by colonial law. While it may seem obvious, because many everyday readers (and arguably, literature scholars) may have limited experience with Indigenous literature, it is important to distinguish between cli-fi written by Indigenous authors (which is considered Indigenous literature) and cli-fi that simply includes Indigenous characters, often in an appropriative fashion. As Briggetta Pierrot and Nicole Seymour report, many works of climate fiction "explicitly invoke Indigenous peoples only to absent and sometimes even appropriate their experiences and traditions" (95) and focus on the fall of Western civilization (i.e. whiteness) rather than on the global ecological imbalance that disproportionately affects Indigenous peoples and communities of color, in yet another example of class consciousness (or lack thereof) in the cli-fi genre.

The Marrow Thieves, Métis author Cherie Dimaline's 2017 award-winning novel, theorizes classism (frequently based on race) and technology in ways that highlight Indigenous survivance and placemaking in postapocalyptic Canada. Dimaline particularly shows how such survivance gives way to hope for Indigenous peoples amid yet another apocalypse, a hope that counters the frequent solastalgia present in much contemporary environmental discussion. While the Canadian landscape is ravaged by climate change in the novel, it is also ravaged by Recruiters. These Recruiters, European settlers,[1] target Indigenous peoples because the Recruiters have lost the ability to dream, a gift that Indigenous peoples retain. One might say that the Recruiters are experiencing or embody solastalgia, a term used to describe a type of sadness or grief associated with the changing environment and one's human connection to that environment. These Recruiters believe that the bone marrow of Indigenous persons somehow houses their dreaming faculty. Driven by envy and despair, they set about capturing anyone with Indigenous blood and extracting their marrow via futuristic technology. As Dimaline demonstrates, however, their knowledge and machinery are no match for Indigenous epistemologies and ontologies.

RACE, CLASS, AND WHOSE IDEAS "COUNT" AS TECHNOLOGY

The Recruiters' process of marrow extraction in the novel is obviously a continuation of the genocide beget by settler colonialism. Yet it also allegorizes the classed (often via racism), extractive nature of technology-driven climate responses, designed for and by elite interests, that ignore Indigenous perspectives and ways of knowing. Early in the text, Miigwaans, a middle-aged two-spirit queer (2SQ) Anishnaabe[2] man and one of the novel's main characters, outlines the stakes of Dimaline's intervention in conversations about climate change and technology, by his understanding of biology via TEK: "Dreams get caught in the webs woven in your bones," he explains. "That's where they live, in that marrow there . . . You are born with them. Your DNA weaves them into the marrow like spinners . . . That's where they [the Recruiters] pluck them from" (18–19). Miigwaans's description of dreaming and DNA demonstrates an Indigenous epistemology, a solidly technological understanding that, alongside the mechanical technologies of the Recruiters, leads the reader to consider why some ways of being and knowing are seen as "technological" while others are not.

Such barriers to viewing TEK as "not technology" are inherently classist, as Kimmerer explains in much of her work. Western white supremacy has long influenced Western science and often assumes that its scientific methods and educational systems are the best way to understand one another and our connections to land and other-than-human kin. As Kimmerer discusses in "The Fortress, the River, and the Garden," such a superiority complex purposefully omits TEK in traditional science-based education. Kimmerer notes that her "non-Native science students . . . are well schooled in the scientific paradigm, so much so that they are unaware of the existence of alternative worldviews. . . . They are very often surprised to learn of the very existence of the indigenous [sic] worldview—and stunned to find that it has been purposefully omitted from their education" (72). Correcting such purposeful omissions is part of what makes the work of Kimmerer, Dimaline, Tantaquidgeon Zobel, Wright, and other Indigenous writers so important for sharing the power and importance of Indigenous ways of being and knowing with an even broader audience.

PREVIOUS APOCALYPSES, COLONIZATION, AND THE ANTHROPOCENE

To better understand Indigenous epistemologies and ontologies, and therefore TEK and how it works within the novel, we need to understand the differences between settler and Indigenous temporalities and reactions to climate chaos.[3] Many Indigenous studies scholars discuss Indigenous survival of prior apocalypses in order to reframe the current climate crisis from an Indigenous perspective. Whyte, for example, consistently emphasizes that Indigenous concepts of temporality differ from those of settler populations and that settlers view current Anthropocene conditions as apocalyptic because they have not been inhabiting Indigenous lands for thousands of years. Due to this truncated time horizon, he suggests, settlers lack the broader perspective of Indigenous peoples, who have experienced previous episodes of climatic change and passed down knowledge of how to adapt to them and thrive. In a recent article, Whyte holds that such knowledge is a "form of technology" that has allowed and continues to allow Indigenous communities to react to and plan for changes in the Earth's climate ("Indigenous Climate Change"). Here, he also argues that capitalistic, colonizer technologies are extraction-based and rely on coal and carbon, while those technologies employed and pioneered by Indigenous peoples are often more place-based and allow their communities to find solutions that benefit their lands and waters as well as their human populations.[4]

THE DANGERS OF EXTRACTION AND THE ROLE OF AFFECT

Indigenous solutions to climate change that move away from extractivist technologies make sense not only from a logistical perspective but also from a decolonial one. As Leanne Betasamosake Simpson explains in her chapter "Nishnaabeg Anticapitalism," extraction goes beyond exploiting what colonialism has defined as "natural resources," for it also steals "children from parents. Children from families. Children from the land. Children from our political system and our systems of governance.... In this kind of thinking, every part of our culture that is seemingly useful to the extractivist mindset gets extracted. The canoe, the kayak, any technology we had that was useful was extracted and assimilated into the culture of the settlers without regard for the people and the knowledge that created it" (75).

Importantly for the aims of this volume, Nishnaabeg Anticapitalism also reduces the classism that continues to harm both Indigenous and non-Indigenous peoples. Because this ideology is based in relationship and reciprocity and not exploitation and extraction, it creates the possibility for relationships that can over time build sustainable, supportive communities that meet the needs of all involved, rather than societies in which many struggle just to stay alive despite such a society having some of the greatest capital wealth and technological advances. I want to draw particular attention here to the ways that Simpson's insight—"any technology we had that was useful was extracted and assimilated"—echoes and corresponds with the events of Dimaline's novel. What both Indigenous feminist writers note here is that technologies (including TEK) need to be based in relationship, not in how much money they will generate or how they can be used to exploit or extract from communities and the planet.

Dimaline's reframing of technology and her emphasis on TEK in *The Marrow Thieves* encourages a reconceptualization of the climate chaos that drives the Recruiters to hunt the marrow in the first place. Indeed, as the climate scholar Mike Hulme suggests, "When solutions to previously framed problems are no longer forthcoming or lead to dangerous adventurism, we should be willing to restructure the problem" (122). Along similar lines, Whyte points out that many contemporary "solutions" to climate change, such as geoengineering, pose severe threats to Indigenous peoples and their lifeways. If Indigenous epistemologies, like those shared by Kimmerer, and Dimaline's character Miigwaans, can provide a preliminary map for how to reframe (and perhaps mitigate) climate change in keeping with Whyte's thought, two significant barriers nonetheless arise. First, how might Indigenous technologies be invoked without simply recapitulating histories of extraction and exploitation? And how might these ways of being and knowing be (re)envisioned as alternate, radical technologies capable of generating new ways of imagining and responding to climate change?

Central to the novel's treatment of climate change, class, and technology is the affect of hope, as the lack of hope creates the Recruiter class, whose desperation drives them to continue the genocide of their ancestors. In much the same way, aggressive proposals to alter the climate through the use of scattershot geoengineering technologies reflect misplaced optimism and threaten vulnerable peoples. For readers of Dimaline's text, nonetheless, it may be difficult to appreciate the importance of something as apparently frivolous as hope in a world where climate chaos has left "most of the rivers cut into pieces and lakes left as grey sludge puckers on the landscape" (21). But as she explains in a 2017 interview, "Hope is the backbone of our survival, and it's the core of our strength" (Henley). Part of Dimaline's explanation for Indigenous hope is that "we have already survived an apocalypse'" ("Is This The One?"), a notion prevalent in the scholarship of many Indigenous intellectuals, including Whyte, who writes, "Indigenous peoples . . . approach climate change having already been through transformations of their societies induced by colonial violence" ("Indigenous Science" 224). This harrowing, ongoing experience of long apocalypse, Dimaline and Whyte suggest, provides Indigenous peoples with a body of advantageous knowledge that effectively functions as, and should be considered, a form of technology, a system of tools for navigating and thriving within the world as we find it. *The Marrow Thieves* implicitly locates the capacity to hope in TEK and similar technologies of survival, and around them the novel constructs a metaphoric nexus centered on bone marrow and dreaming.

Meanwhile, the settlers in *The Marrow Thieves*, new to catastrophe, fearful for the end of the world, and forlorn of hope, "lost their minds, killing themselves and others and, even worse for the new order, refusing to work at all. . . . [T]hose who could afford it turned to sleep counselors, took pills to go to bed and pills to wake up, and did things like group hypnosis" (Dimaline 88). With such passages, the novel frames white settlers as suffering from the same maladies that all too often plague Indigenous peoples, and especially Indigenous youth, in the contemporary world—an issue that Dimaline laments in several interviews. In this fictional reversal, she suggests that continued colonization by European settlers "rebounds back to the colonizer," as Audra Mitchell has argued regarding the work of Aimé Césaire and Frantz Fanon. This process of colonial "rebounding" manifests in the text as a literal loss of the ability to dream, from which the other maladies spring. The settlers, rather than confronting the past and seeking hopeful reparation, instead begin another round of technologically mediated violence, seeking the marrow, which, they desperately believe, may yet prove capable of saving them from the horrors they have inflicted on themselves.

Recruiters operate the extraction centers to mine the Indigenous populations of marrow, killing them in the process; curiously, however, readers never actually see the Recruiters use the marrow to aid in dreaming. This important omission may suggest that the marrow is being used not to incite dreams or to endure the climate crisis, but for some other, even more insidious purpose that passes undefined within the text. A lacuna of this sort opens space within the text for readers to imagine the present through what we know of the past. Crucially, then, readers do witness the construction of extraction centers, which the novel refers to as "Schools." School #47E, for example, is described as "a fallacy of glass and steel against the dusty expanse of the north shore clearing, like a middle finger thrown up into the sky, built in record time" (173). These facilities clearly reference the residential schools in which many Indigenous children were shorn of their cultures and even killed, and encourage reflection on the ways in which these extraction centers serve to continue (as well as metaphorize) such genocide.

The novel makes clear that the extraction centers are built *after* the climate crisis has already deepened into a general cataclysm, thus no forethought or planning took place (or, if it did, it was ineffective). Essentially, they were constructed as a last-ditch effort by the settlers and Recruiters to save themselves. Therefore, not only are places like School #47E constructed as a means to extract marrow, but the extraction centers themselves instantiate a perverse, murderous rendition of settler hope, as they provide the Recruiters and settlers a beacon to look toward that signifies something is being done to mitigate their solastalgia. Treating the solastalgia, of course, does not fix the climate crisis, but treating the effects that only the Recruiters and settlers experience tracks with their selfish motivations. After all, if the climate crisis was mitigated, it would benefit everyone, and those with power would not want those they consider to be lesser humans to benefit in any way. Constructing large buildings in a time when economic and construction resources are likely scarce due to the climate crisis also speaks to the settler-Recruiters' socioeconomic status. Their concrete imposition on the land, too, displays their understanding of and connection with their local environs, a disconnection that they extend to Indigenous bodies, which they believe are beneath them.

The absence of humane feeling and environmental connection in the Recruiters manifests even more strongly in the brutality of the extraction process itself. In the scene in which Minerva, the elder of Miigwaans's kinship group, has her marrow forcibly extracted, Recruiters #1 and #3 appear as frankly monstrous. One is described as "sadistic," while the other thinks, "The chase was the crux. After that, who cared how the savages screamed or cried" (172). The historically resonant ways that the Recruiters mistreat Minerva, the Anishnaabe elder they have abducted, reflects settler European views of race and class in regard to Indigenous peoples. The language used to describe marrow extraction—"processing," for example—further deepens the Recruiters' dehumanization of Minerva and, by extension, all Indigenous people, much in the way that a poultry farmer might refer to "harvesting" a chicken. Because the Recruiters do not consider Indigenous bodies to be people, or if they do, people of a lower class, they are unable to view TEK and other epistemologies as technology, and refuse to consider any possibility of working together to mitigate the climate crisis. Instead, they view Indigenous bodies as objects for extraction. Like many imperial and military technologies, the marrow processing technology used by the Recruiters was created with the express knowledge and purpose of committing genocide against a lower class they consider subhuman at best.

RACE, CLASS IDENTIFICATION, AND DNA TECHNOLOGIES

Broadly speaking, *The Marrow Thieves* comprehends class through the racialization of Indigenous and white communities, largely erasing the Black presence in Canada. Unfortunately, this erasure mirrors present-day Canadian understandings of racial categories and race relations.[5] The only Black characters in *The Marrow Thieves* appear near the end: "two black women . . . stirring beans and talking about a shared memory back from the city" (223). Frenchie, the novel's sixteen-year-old protagonist, realizes that the Black women "were Guyanese," for, as he explains, "After the weather got violent and the islands were battered, the West Indian population here had swollen." Perhaps these women joined with the Indigenous peoples' camp due to shared racial oppression or, perhaps, due to their perception of themselves as "indigenous" to Guyana, creating a sort of pan-Indigenous community.[6]

The novel does not clarify whether the Guyanese women retain the ability to dream or whether the Recruiters are targeting them for their marrow. Nonetheless, the presence of the women within the Indigenous camp strongly suggests that they are seeking a haven from the Recruiters, who apparently target anyone they perceive as nonwhite. Given the tendency of contemporary realities to find their way into dystopian fictions, this should not be particularly surprising.[7] From the outset of the colonial project, surveillance efforts, augmented by technologies of violence, have targeted Black and Indigenous bodies alike. Indeed, Dimaline reveals that, in composing *The Marrow Thieves*, she sought to represent the continuance of these modern-day and historical oppressions, and that her novel foments a response against them. Regarding the genocide in the novel, she explains that she wanted her readers to think, "Well, this can't happen. We need to make sure it doesn't happen" (Henley).

The genocide depicted in *The Marrow Thieves* evinces a similar conception of race, as the European settlers who have lost the ability to dream turn their destructive technologies on Indigenous peoples, whom they hunt like wild game. This futuristic genocide obviously mirrors the classed, colonial histories and ongoing oppressions meted out upon the bodies of Indigenous peoples. The novel's race-based taxonomical systems also hearken to the pseudo-scientific legacy of Black and Indigenous racialization in what we now call North America; in this way, *The Marrow Thieves* speaks to how notions of race and class evolve over time, often due to unethical, and frequently unconscionable, applications of technology.[8] Along these lines, Kim TallBear's research focuses on DNA and notions of blood quantum as methods of defining Indigenous peoples (and specifically, Native Americans) as a racial category. The *Marrow Thieves*, with its emphasis on DNA, marrow, and blood as loci of colonial extraction, thus finds stirring analogs in contemporary Indigenous scholarship and raises important questions about the histories and applications of technological processes as well as the classism that can result from the reliance on blood quantum and DNA.

DNA technologies play a central role in *The Marrow Thieves*, with their often totalizing potential for (mis)identification and (mis)application. Dimaline's text criticizes notions of DNA-derived racial purity through Miigwaans's recounting of the early days of Recruitment: "They asked for volunteers first," he says. "Put out ads asking for people with 'Indigenous bloodlines and good general health' to check in with clinics for medical trials" (89). This European focus on "bloodlines" and marrow speaks to the perpetuation of race via blood quantum by European practitioners of the same sorts of "science" that spawned eugenics and other categories used to dehumanize nonwhite human beings. Such classed and racialized technological practices have consigned nonwhites to socioeconomic marginalization, with serious environmental implications such as limited access to traditional homelands, limited property ownership, and increased exposure to toxic hazards and climate-change risks, risks that likely could be avoided or mitigated through Indigenous land sovereignty and TEK.[9]

KINSHIP AND CEREMONY AS TECHNOLOGY

As Dimaline demonstrates throughout *The Marrow Thieves,* and as Whyte, Kimmerer, and other Indigenous intellectuals note, connection to each other and the land is only possible through respect and reciprocity, neither of which can exist fully if intertwined with classism, extraction, or exploitation, making such connections anticapitalist. Despite (or perhaps in spite of) the horrors inflicted upon them in *The Marrow Thieves,* Dimaline's Indigenous characters marshal a strong collective response, using kinship networks and ceremonial actions not only to overcome the Recruiters but to survive this latest apocalypse. The technologies, as these are indeed networks that connect the Indigenous characters to one another, to their ancestors, and across time and space, allow for reciprocal, respectful connection to flourish, resulting in Indigenous resurgence.

Combining kinship and ceremony, Miigwaans carries the "glass vial" labeled "66542G, 41-year-old male, Euro-Anishnaabe" on his person throughout the novel (215). The vial is only half-full, and Frenchie imagines that Miigwaans must have "IDed [it] as Isaac." We learn that Miigwaans and Isaac, his partner, had been captured by the Recruiters and taken to an extraction center, though Miigwaans was able to escape. Later, he returned to the facility, armed with a rifle. He could not save Isaac, but he was able to overtake a truck driven by a center employee. In the man's truck were crates full of boxes containing "rows of glass tubes" filled with DNA—essentially the only remaining evidence of Miigwaans's relatives—labeled with a series of numbers, biological sex, age, and colonizer determination of their race or racial makeup. Rather than leaving the samples with the employee,

Miigwaans "loaded the crate in the back and just drove away with them all" (Dimaline 144). He explains, "I couldn't live with the people being served up like a club sandwich to the dreamless. So I tried to take them home" (Dimaline 145). In this powerful scene, Miigwaans clearly identifies these relatives as kin, regardless of their DNA, location, or other identifying factors, and he knows that because they are kin, he has a responsibility to them, a responsibility to provide them dignity and peace.

While Miigwaans may not be able to save their physical bodies, he knows that these "remains" are still his kin and they deserve repatriation. He may not be able to bury all of them in their precise homelands, but he can still honor their bodies and spirits through a ceremony that connects all participants to one another and to the land: "I drove to the lake," he reflects, "one of the last ones I knew still held fish. Got as close as I could from the road and then trekked in, back and forth, one box at a time. Then I camped there for four days. I sang each of them home when I poured them out. It rained, a real good one, too. So I know they made it back" (145). Crucially, Miigwaans seeks out a lake that "still held fish," as human-fish relationships are key to particular Indigenous epistemologies (especially to certain Arctic groups, as Zoe Todd notes in her essay "Fish Pluralities"). The fact that Miigwaans can find such a lake in a world ravaged by climate change further underscores his knowledge of, and connection to, local lands and waters, as made possible through his embrace of TEK and other essential Indigenous technologies of inhabitation and placemaking.

Miigwaans, however, is not the only character to engage in ceremony throughout the novel. We also see Minerva's lifetime of connections and learning, made manifest when she burns School #47E to the ground:

> she called on her blood memory, her teachings, her ancestors. That's when she brought the whole thing down.
>
> She sang. She sang with the volume and itch and a heartbreaking wail that echoed through her relatives' bones, rattling them in the ground under the school itself. Wave after wave, changing her heartbeat to drum, morphing her singular voice to many, pulling every dream from her own marrow and into her song. And there were words: words in the language that the conductor couldn't process, words the Cardinals couldn't bear, words the wires couldn't transfer.
>
> As it turns out, every dream Minerva had ever dreamed was in the language. It was her gift, her secret, her plan. She'd collected the dreams like

bright beads on the string of nights that wound around her each day, every day until this one. (172–73)

While Minerva's act does not halt the climate crisis, it does prevent a particular aspect of the convergence from worsening, and it certainly saves Indigenous lives. Though School #47E is a single site and this fire, of course, did not cause the demise of all the Recruiters, the ruination of the building and its occupants does transform Indigenous futurities in significant ways within the text. Minerva's dreams, each one "dreamed . . . in the language," allow for the preservation of her kin and strengthen those kinship ties across generations, a sharp contrast from the settler goals for dreaming, which appear to be relief of solastalgia and a continuation of their everyday systems of oppression and extraction. Instead of continuing "settler business as usual," Minerva's dreams and resultant actions instruct other captured Indigenous peoples on how to recreate the damage, essentially allowing them to take down the whole system of extraction centers and those who run them, primarily through using the technologies of Indigenous languages and ways of knowing, such as TEK.

Understanding these and other Indigenous methods of knowing and being as technologies that may contribute solutions not only to the climate crisis but also to Parenti's "catastrophic convergence" of racialized, classed, and gendered oppression accomplishes two goals. First, viewing Indigenous epistemologies and ontologies as technologies directly confronts the colonial definitions of technology and who should or does have access to it; and secondly, such a framing centers Indigenous ways of knowing and being, upsetting the current Canadian power dynamic, which privileges white, upper-class individuals and their knowledge systems. Ultimately, considering Indigenous perspectives as scientific allows for the possibility of Indigenous resurgence and helps Native and non-Native peoples alike to survive, thrive, and potentially prevent further climate impacts from damaging the most economically vulnerable.[10]

These relationships with land and with one another shine further light on the matter of how Indigenous lifeways and technologies might supply strategies of climate mitigation without being themselves extracted in yet another instance of classed, colonial violence. Ultimately, TEK holds that land, in Schilling's words, cannot be owned and must be "shaped by something other than economic profit" (12). Capitalism, however, as an economic system driven by profit and exploitation, will only exploit TEK for its own ends and will continue colonial violence. If we are to realize TEK's potential to help humanity and our nonhuman relations survive and even potentially mitigate climate change, we will have to let go of capitalism and instead learn to make kin, as Donna J. Haraway has suggested.[11] Obviously, this will require radical shifts in actions and perceptions. Non-Native people, including myself, will have to trust Indigenous communities and allow them to lead. They will make the key decisions regarding their lands—which is to say, all lands. Are these changes possible? Doubtlessly. Will we enact them, and if we do, will they prove sufficient? That remains unseen.

The Marrow Thieves provides ample examples of why society requires such change, and the power of Indigenous leadership and technologies in enacting and surviving it. The ability of Indigenous leadership to maintain and remember critical knowledge for communities to thrive in the present is a key technology for those working to create self-determined Indigenous futures, especially futures lived in a particular place. In regards to climate change, the goal of Indigenous ways of knowing go beyond planning and adapting; they allow for what Megan Bang and coauthors refer to as "viable futures of survivance" (38–39). Bang and her colleagues utilize the stories of those peoples native to the Chicago/Shikaakwa to learn about and connect with the place as Indigenous land. They explain that incorporating these lessons into Indigenous self-conceptions "means working to move our practice beyond historicized us/them dichotomies and willfully contradicting common narratives of assimilated and landless urban Indians toward longer views of our communities and our homelands not enclosed by colonial timeframes" (Bang et al. 39). More concretely, viewing the land in this way, and teaching others how to view the land in this way, upsets the dynamics of settler colonialism, challenges settler sovereignty, and unleashes possibilities for Indigenous futurity that are not bound to "colonial conceptions of land" or class distinctions (Bang et al. 43). Part of how these epistemologies accomplish the reframing that they create is through experiencing land and its inhabitants as kinship relations, relations based on respect, reciprocity, and responsibility, not on class or extractivism.

Just as Bang and her colleagues (re)story Chicago/Shikaakwa, Dimaline in *The Marrow Thieves* (re)stories Canada. Their texts marshal the technology of TEK to restore the position of "land as the first teacher" and to elevate Indigenous ways of knowing and being (Bang et al. 49). These writers and many others engage in Indigenous survivance and futurity, despite the seeming omnipresence of colonization and ongoing climate crisis.

By learning from and listening to the land in a respectful, reciprocal relationship, the practitioners of Indigenous technologies—fictional and real, living and beyond life—pass these crucial ontological frameworks to future generations, allowing for the hope not only of Indigenous resurgence but also the survival of life on Earth, our home.

NOTES

1. I chose "settlers" here rather than "descendants of European settlers" because the processes of colonization and land theft remain ongoing, and instances of past violence have not been adequately remediated.

2. Dimaline employs this spelling throughout the novel, and my usage follows hers.

3. There has also been much discussion of how colonialism is directly responsible for the current Anthropocene. Simon L. Lewis and Mark A. Maslin, in their article "Defining the Anthropocene," suggest that European colonization resulted in a significant "golden spike," meaning that colonization and its long-term effects may be responsible for our current Anthropocene, in what they have named the Orbis hypothesis. Zoe Todd and Heather Davis have also argued that positioning our current epoch as beginning at colonization "allows us to understand the current state of ecological crisis as inherently invested in a specific ideology defined by proto-capitalist logics based on extraction and accumulation through dispossession—logics that continue to shape the world we live in and that have produced our current era" (764). Audra Mitchell's "Decolonising the Anthropocene" is a good introduction to this topic as well.

4. Whyte observes that while Native Nations are finding their own solutions that work with their local environments, part of this innovation is out of necessity, as he notes in "Indigenous Science (Fiction) for the Anthropocene," "in my work on climate justice, I have documented literatures that show how even the green solutions to climate change commit and risk environmental injustice against Indigenous peoples, no different from the fossil fuel industries to which these solutions pose as alternatives" (237–38).

5. For more information on Black erasure in Canada, see Dionne Brand's *A Map to the Door of No Return* or the work of Katherine McKittrick, particularly chapter four, "Nothing's Shocking: Black Canada," in her book *Demonic Grounds: Black Women and the Cartographies of Struggle*.

6. It does seem pertinent that Dimaline created these Black women as Guyanese, as Black indigenization in Guyana has a peculiar history that involves the displacement of Indigenous peoples in the Caribbean, which is the focus of Shona Jackson's book, *Creole Indigeneity: Between Myth and Nation in the Caribbean*.

7. Mark Rifkin analyzes this aspect of dystopian worlding in Native and Black novels in his monograph *Fictions of Land and Flesh*.

8. Kim TallBear's *Native American DNA: Tribal Belonging and the False Promise of Genetic Science* explores how such racialization began and has evolved; she focuses

particularly on what is now the US, though her research can certainly be applied transnationally. In this nuanced account, she acknowledges that some tribes, as sovereign nations, do employ DNA testing for a variety of purposes, which further complicates issues of bioethics.

9. Dorceta E. Taylor's *Toxic Communities: Environmental Racism, Industrial Pollution, and Residential Mobility* and Rob Nixon's *Slow Violence and the Environmentalism of the Poor* both broadly discuss the intersections of race, class, and environmental hazards. There are also location-specific texts that examine these intersections, such as Dana E. Powell's *Landscapes of Power: Politics of Energy in the Navajo Nation* and *Wastelanding: Legacies of Uranium Mining in Navajo Country* by Traci Brynne Voyles.

10. To learn more about Indigenous resurgence, Leanne Betasamosake Simpson's *As We Have Always Done: Indigenous Freedom through Radical Resistance* is particularly helpful.

11. I reference Haraway here because her critique of capitalism and championing of kinship are quite well known. However, it should be noted that because she concludes *Staying with the Trouble* by advancing depopulation theories, which have disproportionately impacted Indigenous communities (and other communities of color), I generally avoid using her work in the analysis of Indigenous texts.

WORKS CITED

Bang, Megan, Lawrence Curley, Adam Kessel, Ananda Marin, Eli S. Suzukovich III, and George Strack. "Muskrat Theories, Tobacco in the Streets, and Living Chicago as Indigenous Land." *Environmental Education Research*, vol. 20, no. 1, 2014, pp. 37–55. https://doi.org/10.1080/13504622.2013.865113.

Brand, Dionne. *A Map to the Door of No Return*. Penguin Random House / Vintage Canada, 2011.

Davis, Heather, and Zoe Todd. "On the Importance of a Date, or Decolonizing the Anthropocene." *ACME: An International Journal for Critical Geographies*, vol. 16, no. 4, 2017, pp. 761–80.

Dimaline, Cherie. *The Marrow Thieves*. Dancing Cat Books, 2017.

Erdrich, Louise. *Future Home of the Living God*. Harper Perennial, 2018.

Henley, James. "The Message YA Novelist Cherie Dimaline Has for Young Indigenous Readers." *CBC*, 7 July 2017,

Hulme, Mike. *Can Science Fix Climate Change: A Case against Climate Engineering*. Wiley, 2014.

"Is This the One? The Marrow Thieves in the Fight for the Book Canada Reads." *Rakuten Kobo*, 8 Mar. 2018. https://www.kobo.com/blog/themarrowthieves.

Jackson, Shona N. *Creole Indigeneity: Between Myth and Nation in the Caribbean*. U of Minnesota P, 2012.

Kimmerer, Robin Wall. *Braiding Sweetgrass: Indigenous Wisdom, Scientific Knowledge and the Teachings of Plants*. Milkweed Editions, 2013.

———. "The Fortress, the River, and the Garden: A New Metaphor for Cultivating Mutualistic Relationship between Scientific and Traditional Ecological Knowledge." *Contemporary Studies in Environmental and Indigenous Pedagogies: A Curricula of Stories and Place*, edited by Andrejs Kulnieks, Dan Roronhiakewen Longboat, and Kelly Young, Sense Publishers, 2013, 49–76.

Lewis, Simon L., and Mark A. Maslin. "Defining the Anthropocene." *Nature*, vol. 519, 2015, pp. 171–80. https://www.nature.com/articles/nature14258.

McKittrick, Katherine. "Nothing's Shocking: Black Canada." *Demonic Grounds: Black Women and the Cartographies of Struggle*, by McKittrick, 91–119. U of Minnesota P, 2006.

Mitchell, Audra. "Decolonising the Anthropocene," *Worldly*, 17 Mar. 2015. https://worldlyir.wordpress.com/2015/03/17/decolonising-the-anthropocene/.

Nixon, Rob. *Slow Violence and the Environmentalism of the Poor*. Harvard UP, 2013.

Parenti, Christian. *Tropic of Chaos: Climate Change and the New Geography of Violence*. Nation Books, 2011.

Pierrot, Briggetta, and Nicole Seymour. "Contemporary Cli-Fi and Indigenous Futurisms." *Departures in Critical Qualitative Research*, vol. 9, no. 4, 2020, pp. 92–113.

Powell, Dana E. *Landscapes of Power: Politics of Energy in the Navajo Nation*. Duke UP, 2018.

Rifkin, Mark. *Fictions of Land and Flesh: Blackness, Indigeneity, Speculation*. Duke UP, 2019.

Schilling, Dan. "Introduction: The Soul of Sustainability." *Traditional Ecological Knowledge: Learning from Indigenous Practices for Environmental Sustainability*, edited by Melissa K. Nelson and Dan Schilling, Cambridge UP, 2018, 3–14.

Simpson, Leanne Betasamosake. *As We Have Always Done: Indigenous Freedom through Radical Resistance*. U of Minnesota P, 2017.

TallBear, Kim. *Native American DNA: Tribal Belonging and the False Promise of Genetic Science*. U of Minnesota P, 2013.

Taylor, Dorceta E. *Toxic Communities: Environmental Racism, Industrial Pollution, and Residential Mobility*. New York UP, 2014.

Todd, Zoe. "Fish Pluralities: Human-Animal Relations and Sites of Engagement in Paulatuuq, Arctic Canada." *Études/Inuit/Studies*, vol. 38, nos. 1–2, 2014, pp. 217–38. https://www.jstor.org/stable/24368324.

Voyles, Traci Brynne. *Wastelanding: Legacies of Uranium Mining in Navajo Country*. U of Minnesota P, 2015.

Whyte, Kyle P. "Indigenous Climate Change Studies: Indigenizing Futures, Decolonizing the Anthropocene." *English Language Notes*, vol. 55, nos. 1–2, 2017, pp. 153–62. https://doi.org/10.1215/00138282-55.1-2.153.

———. "Indigenous Science (Fiction) for the Anthropocene: Ancestral Dystopias and Fantasies of Climate Change Crisis." *Environment and Planning E: Nature and Space*, vol. 1, nos. 1–2, 2018, pp. 224–42. https://journals.sagepub.com/doi/10.1177/2514848618777621.

Wright, Alexis. *The Swan Book*. Giramondo Publishing, 2013.

Zobel, Melissa Tantaquidgeon. *Oracles*. U of New Mexico P, 2017.

PART II

Class Differentiation and Climate Risk

PART II

Class Differentiation and Character Risk

Climate-Change Fiction and Poverty Studies

Kingsolver's Flight Behavior, Diaz's "Monstro," and Bacigalupi's "The Tamarisk Hunter"

DEBRA J. ROSENTHAL

If we log the mountain, then the trees are gone. But the debt isn't. Does it make sense to turn everything upside down just to make one payment? Like there won't be another one next month, and the month after that?
—Barbara Kingsolver, *Flight Behavior*

For its nuanced attention to a terrible ecological consequence of our carbon economy, Barbara Kingsolver's best-selling and critically acclaimed novel *Flight Behavior* (2013) has been hailed as a major work in the growing genre of cli-fi (climate-change fiction).[1] However, I see *Flight Behavior* as also making a significant contribution to the interdisciplinary field of poverty studies. The passage above compellingly encapsulates the novel's overlapping themes of environmental degradation and socioeconomic struggle. *Flight Behavior* tells the story of Dellarobia Turnbow, a frustrated, low-income, stay-at-home young mom in rural Tennessee who makes the startling discovery of millions of monarch butterflies roosting in her husband's family's forest. An entomologist travels to Feathertown to study the anomaly and realizes that the butterflies' aberrant behavior is due to calamitous global climate change. Much of the conflict in *Flight Behavior* revolves around whether the Turnbow family should escape their perpetual financial hardship by destroying the natural world around them through a clear-cutting of their hundreds of acres of mountaintop trees. In the passage from the novel cited above, Dellarobia debates the strategy of temporarily getting out of debt by logging their only resource, which will ultimately result in the family being bereft of both trees and money. In *Flight Behavior,* Kingsolver provides readers with an incisive analysis of issues facing low-income workers, such as the economics of farm life, sheepshearing, balloon payments on equipment, wage inequality, women's employment, the finances of childcare, and problems paying rent.[2] Such plot developments illustrate economic issues that directly relate to anthropogenic climate change in the real world; for example, farming in general produces large amounts of methane and carbon dioxide from both animals and farm equipment, and the deforestation eliminates carbon sinks that would absorb the greenhouse gases produced by the farming.[3] Since wealth inequality and climate change are both socially constructed forces of economics and politics, an "ecopoverty" critical lens—of reading one in terms of the other—can reveal the exploitation of the poor and connect it to the exploitation of the earth.[4]

Before I discuss *Flight Behavior* through an "ecopoverty" perspective, I want to recognize that sometimes the fields of environmental studies and poverty studies might seem at odds: a biocentric approach so important to an environmental aesthetic needs to foreground nonhuman nature—for example, Kingsolver's monarch butterflies and the changing weather patterns in Tennessee. Oppositely, a reading of *Flight Behavior* through a poverty studies lens would be committed to focusing on the Turnbows' lived experiences and identities.[5] What's at stake when literary works could appear on a syllabus for a course on environmental studies as well as on a syllabus for a course on poverty or wealth inequality? What questions arise at the often contradictory intersection of poverty studies and climate change fiction? My analysis of *Flight Behavior* will be complemented by readings of two other works that could similarly be placed at the imbrication of the two genres: Junot Diaz's "Monstro" and Paolo Bacigalupi's "The Tamarisk Hunter." Because they appear in high-profile publications, Diaz's and Bacigalupi's stories stand as important examples of the overlap of ecopoverty themes: Diaz addresses the Dominican Republic upper class's ability to avoid a disease caused by climate warming that devastates the impoverished, while Bacigalupi's story imagines how an anthropogenic drought in the American Southwest restructures society to disadvantage the working poor.

Before I turn to a literary discussion, I want to frame my ecopoverty analysis with a brief discussion about climatological and economic reports that similarly find the conjunction of planetary atmospheric change and poverty studies to be relevant. I then want to provide an overview of why the conjunction of cli-fi and poverty in literary representation, as opposed to scientific or economic representation, presents some conflicts and then how the two genres complement each other. If we recognize that both intergovernmental climate scientists and economists agree that it is imperative to look at the intersecting concerns of climate change and financial disparities, then literary scholars might benefit from a similar investigation of the overlap in genre. I will demonstrate that the genres of cli-fi and poverty studies are at once resistant to each other and simultaneously politically akin, and thus that studying literary works at the intersection of the two genres can heighten political advocacy to ameliorate planetary warming.

Before the publication of *Flight Behavior*, "Monstro," and "The Tamarisk Hunter," major scientific reports on climate change disseminated crucial information about the changing atmosphere's effects on the world's poor.[6] Affirming that "climate change is a serious risk to poverty reduction that threatens to undo decades of development efforts," the Organization for Economic Co-operation and Development clearly understands the intricately linked concerns of socioeconomic struggle and anthropogenic global warming (*Poverty and Climate Change* v). Economists similarly investigate the relationship between global warming and income inequality: to take one of many examples, in an article in *Applied Economic Perspectives and Policy*, economic researchers Thomas Hertel and Stephanie Rosch ask, "What are the likely *impacts* of rising temperatures and changing rainfall patterns on agriculture and poverty?" (Hertel and Rosch 357). Their report emphasizes not only agriculture but goods and services needed by the poor that can be negatively affected by changing weather. I find that their economic analysis of agriculture, climate, and poverty elucidates the literary representations of such issues and thus reinforces the importance for humanities scholars of considering the effects of planetary warming on the world's low-income earners.

While this conjunction of cli-fi and poverty makes complete sense in the scientific and economic communities, the literary representation of the overlap of the two fields can sometimes run into challenges. For example, the genres of cli-fi and poverty studies might seem to conflict with each other regarding their temporal settings, or where in time such works take place. Since we have not yet experienced a complete climate collapse, nor any of the three "pictures" that Margaret Atwood lays out in her thought experiment ("It's Not Climate Change"), the genre of cli-fi is often speculative and set in the future. Its premises are predicated on informed guess and not on actual lived experience. Thus, the genre of poverty studies stands in great contrast to cli-fi in terms of temporal setting, because the long history of the literary representation of poverty in American life has depended on depicting the actual lived experiences of people facing great material deprivation. From antebellum poverty discourse, to the Great Migration, to Progressive Era reforms, to the Depression, to Appalachian studies, to reservation literature, to urban studies, to Matthew Desmond's Pulitzer-Prize-winning *Evicted* (2016) and more, it has been critically important for writers to accurately and sensitively depict people's real-life challenges as they live on the margins of society. Poverty studies is not considered a speculative genre; writers derive their stories from ample real-life evidence, often personally experienced, of the struggles of low-income survival.

While cli-fi and poverty studies might seem at odds in terms of their representations of speculative conditions of life versus actual existence, they share the similar challenge of trying to be relevant and urgent to readers. Works of fiction that fall into the categories of cli-fi or poverty studies often overlap in their goal of being politically meaningful and efficacious to readers. It is important for literary scholars to consider whether and how fiction attuned to both the environment and to economic inequality can intervene in political discourse and possibly motivate readers to move towards reversing or ameliorating planetary damage and its devastating socioeconomic effects on the world's poor. Hayden Gabriel and Greg Garrard note that many readers might think that there could only be two types of writing about earth's climate: "either mimetic (writing novels that represent climate change) or exhortatory (writing non-fiction that communicates climate science with passion and urgency)" (Gabriel and Garrard, "Reading and Writing" 117). However, they remind us that literature's capaciousness can actually generate a multitude of responses to the scale of climate change and that perhaps fiction is uniquely situated to speed up what scientists lament as the "knowledge-action gap" that causes cognitive dissonance and prevents people from acting when they acquire frightening knowledge (Garrard 297).

The genres of cli-fi and poverty studies share the same challenge of moving readers to a position of deep concern or action. Rob Nixon discusses cli-fi's inherent challenge in motivating readers in terms of what he calls slow violence, which refers to the climatological effects of greenhouse gas emissions that do not tend to attract as much attention as large explosions or such catastrophes as hurricanes or earthquakes. The slow, gradual pace of climate change (although rapidly accelerating in recent years) challenges the human imagination. If we cannot "see" the violence, we are less motivated to act with urgency. Big blockbuster movies and novels that promise excitement, action, and violence tend to draw the major crowds. Nixon is right to point out that quieter movies and novels that attempt to track the slower movement of planetary warming over time might be harder pressed to attract a wide audience. Cli-fi writers hope that the literary imagination can help us understand the scale and urgency of what Knadler terms "necropolitical neglect" that "inflict[s] a gradual collateral damage disproportionately on the lives of the poor and people of color" (Knadler 22) and be moved to political awareness and action.

On the one hand, the rather too-slow pace of planetary warming may be too boring and not exciting enough to attract readers to a novel. Yet on the other hand, the representation of a too-violent environmental disaster may produce cognitive dissonance. Timothy Clark refers to this disjuncture as "scale framing" in that "the time scales at issue may challenge forms of narrative geared to an easily identifiable section of lived human time" (143). For example, the Tyndall Centre for Climate Change Research published a report called "Is This Climate Porn? How Does Climate Change Communication Affect Our Perceptions and Behavior?" The study looked at whether popular representation of global warming spurred readers or viewers towards action; in other words, do images of a dire future motivate audiences? Thomas D. Lowe, the author of the Tyndall Centre's report, labels "climate porn" the fast-action violence that Rob Nixon claims attracts the biggest following. The study hopes that a compelling story can "enable the audience to examine a difficult social and environmental problem from an informed yet quasi-fictional perspective" (Lowe 3). To the contrary, however, the study instead presents initial findings that stories, fiction, and movies that convey the very real dangers of environmental degradation and socioeconomic inequality can actually thwart their intended political awareness and action. The "slow violence" that Nixon fears might not attract attention actually proves to be *not* as ineffective as riveting sugar-high violence that numbs or jades the audience and paralyzes them into inaction. Although his study is based on a small sampling of undergraduate students, Lowe suggests that "whilst 'shock' may make compulsive news, it may distance individuals from the reality of the risk, thus reducing the likelihood that they will act to mitigate the risk" (Lowe 6). Thus, while cli-fi is timely and pertinent, the representation in popular culture of the devastation wrought by the carbon economy can either be too boring and thus dismissed or else too intense and thus alienating. This argument pertains to the endings of *Flight Behavior*, "Monstro," and "The Tamarisk Hunter": they might either motivate the readers to want to change their environmental and political behavior, or the works may cause readers to feel helpless in the face of such environmental ruin.

A similar pedagogical conundrum about the efficacy of cli-fi to stimulate political agency may also hold with poverty studies. After teaching a course on the literature of poverty, John Marsh doubts that such an educational opportunity actually helps students learn about such a pressing social issue. He argues that to think that teaching about poverty can help ameliorate it "is to fall prey to a pervasive, favorite myth in the United States today, one that holds that problems of social justice, including and especially poverty, can be solved through education. They cannot. And believing that they can does considerably more harm than good" (Marsh 605). My own years of teaching the literature of poverty corroborate some of what Marsh argues: since professors should not impose their own personal beliefs on students, it becomes difficult for me when students insist that the poor suffer due to their lack of effort. My urge towards advocacy somewhat fails when I realize that I should not force my own agenda or beliefs on my students. I also face a conflict in use-value: while I aim for my students to have a deeper understanding of the historical arc of poverty in the US, we end up "using" real people's stories of impoverishment and hardship to reinforce my students' middle-class identity. It is easy for students to feel deeply for an author or character who struggles economically, but then the students close the book with a sigh and feel grateful that they do not have to face such indignities. I also agree with Marsh's harsh realization that "we may try to understand the poor, or poverty, but what matters, finally, is our own critical thinking about them. (Or worse yet, what finally matters is our grade in the course.)" (Marsh 614). I feel the same conflicts with my students, but the doubt is lessened somewhat by the heavy service-learning orientation of my course. Students enhance their classroom learning by working throughout the semester with the same group of homeless, incarcerated, or otherwise impoverished adults. Developing a personal relationship with those facing gross material hardship lessens the distance between the issues we read about and the way people experience those issues in real life.

While the above paragraphs outline how cli-fi and poverty studies share the commonality of possibly facing roadblocks in getting readers to understand the issues' urgency, both genres have another conundrum in common: how anthropogenic climate change affects current ideas about the local versus the global. For example, the generic conventions of place-based realism challenge the discursive representation of climate change and poverty. Historically, American literary regionalism and contemporary environmental literature emphasize the specificity of location or bioregion. Writers who try to evoke a sense of rootedness or place rely on ecological indicators—such as weather, topography, seasons, and local customs—to evoke the particularity of a locale. However, a changing climate threatens to disrupt the very foundational essence of place-based literature. Regionalism's devotion to biome uniqueness and autonomy gets undermined by the leveling factor of planetary collapse (Malewitz 716). Yet, just as scholars consider the dual nature of the pace of cli-fi literature—whether the inherent slow violence remains too uninteresting, or its devastating consequences too numbing—so, too, could scholars see two sides to the regionalist devotion of cli-fi literature. Rather than being antithetical to place-based literature, planetary warming could actually positively reinforce the specific identity of a geographic location since each bioregion will become ecologically devastated in a regionally different way, and thus solidify bioregional distinctiveness and identity. The technological advances and machinery that dot the landscape in order to adapt to changing weather patterns also eventually define the characteristics of the area and thus alter the original identity of "regionalism." Part of the local color of a region might come to be particular pieces of hi-tech industrial equipment, such as wind turbines, flood dams, or water pipes. Ironically, according to Malewitz, various "climate-change infrastructure might become the central marker of regional difference in an era of anthropogenic climate change" (Malewitz 727). "The Tamarisk Hunter" by Bacigalupi illustrates this concern well—the "Straw" water transport system that scars the draught-stricken landscape might come to be its defining regional feature. But, on the other hand, the same large-scale machinery is used to mitigate the effects of climate change around the world, and their ubiquity thus threatens to homogenize landscapes; asserting local identity could come to be seen as a form of resistance to globalization. Asserting a regionalist identity, once considered given and ahistorical, can, under the threat of climate change, ironically come to be seen as "a means of resisting the imperialist dimensions of globalization" (Heise 7).

Climate change also affects received wisdom about regionalism because ecocriticism's presumed deep connection to a sense of a local place occludes the wider effects of globalism and planetary warming. Mehnart points out that ecocritics rely too heavily on an "ethics of proximity," and that "localism" prevents us from seeing larger global processes. In other words, devotion to regionalism may naively miss the larger forces affecting that very region (Mehnart 62). If we apply this idea to poverty studies, we may realize that defining "our" poor by nearby neighborhoods, or the catchment area of a university's social outreach, might occlude the inbound approach of normally faraway economic migrants. For example, Kingsolver's Dellarobia Turnbow in Tennessee slowly becomes aware of the plight of the Delgado family, who can be seen as both economic and climate migrants from Mexico. Reading *Flight Behavior* through an ecopoverty lens permits readers to see previously unacknowledged links between Dellarobia and the Delgado family. Similarly, Junot Diaz's unnamed narrator's wealth allows him to escape from the Dominican Republic to the US and thus avoid the spread of disease from climate warming. And Bacigalupi's Lolo likely will end up an economic climate-change migrant when his water source and income get cut off.

Considering *Flight Behavior* together with "Monstro" and "The Tamarisk Hunter" might rankle some readers, because the former can fall into a different cli-fi subgenre than the latter two. Thus, examining the three together can illuminate two differing strands of cli-fi: "the narrative of catastrophe" and "the narrative of anticipation." According to Sylvia Mayer and Alexa von Mossner, while the narrative of catastrophe "explores the risk of climate change by creating a future fictional world when climate collapse has already occurred, the narrative of anticipation focuses on the present moment when the climate collapse can still be avoided, when it is still a risk scenario that needs to be fully grasped in order to be averted" (13). As a novel of anticipation, *Flight Behavior* focuses on a "strong sense of uncertainty and controversy" that faces those who do not fully understand or who want to deny their human agency in the upcoming disaster (Mayer, "Explorations" 26).

Although Mayer discusses *Flight Behavior* as a risk narrative of anticipation, she does so exclusively in terms of risk due to climate change. Because

Flight Behavior, "Monstro," and "The Tamarisk Hunter" also thematize socioeconomic inequality, I would argue that we can similarly read them as risk narratives of anticipation and of catastrophe in poverty studies. In other words, we can see them as risk narratives of anticipation of economic deprivation, of social marginalization, of financial default, of educational inequality, or of the looming threat of poverty. As I have been outlining, an ecopoverty perspective shifts readers' attention from one focused exclusively on the environment to one on ecosocial justice. Because much of cli-fi literature is speculative, due to its reliance on scientific predictions or estimates of what life might possibly be like due to extensive planetary warming, Mehnart refers to the lack of actual lived experience under climate catastrophe as "time-delayed hazards" (Mehnart 59). In poverty studies, however, we do not have such a need for hypothesized future estimates about quality of life—literature that thematizes socioeconomic struggle powerfully portrays the actual lived reality of people facing conditions of impoverishment. Cli-fi literature is based on what Mehnart calls "second-hand non-experiences," because no one has actually lived through a climate apocalypse. Again, this is the opposite of the work done in poverty studies that seeks to represent the known and current reality of living with restricted material resources.

Having set up the above discussion about the overlap of cli-fi and poverty studies, I'd like to now make some observations about *Flight Behavior* when examined through an ecopoverty lens. The Turnbows face two major obstacles to their plan to gain financial security through deforestation. First, anthropogenic climate change has led to heavy rains that have caused ecologically and financially catastrophic mudslides on the properties of neighbors who clear-cut on their mountains. If the Turnbows do deforest their mountain, they may similarly risk losing their home and farm due to a massive mudflow when the next heavy rains arrive. Second, since the trees on the Turnbow property marked for clear-cutting now unexpectedly serve as an overwintering haven for millions of climate-refugee monarch butterflies, the family's decision to log will have devastating ecological consequences for a species. The novel also derides irresponsible media outlets that foster climate-change denial among low-income, uneducated rural folk, who might then become complicit in the destruction of their own natural resources.

Flight Behavior parallels two stories: one addresses the journey of working-poor protagonist Dellarobia Turnbow from being a dissatisfied stay-at-home low-income mom planning an affair with a telephone repairman, to becoming a more mature and self-aware woman who leaves her husband to pursue an education, a career, and financial stability. The second arc of the novel addresses the migration of millions of Mexican monarch butterflies that aberrantly overwinter in Feathertown, Tennessee, rather than in Michoacan; the novel provides the reader with a thorough understanding of how climate change could tragically cause a species to be wiped out.

While Kingsolver could present a condescending view towards an uneducated teen mom, she instead sympathetically crafts Dellarobia as a smart and sarcastic protagonist trapped in an early marriage to a low-wage farm and construction worker. Kingsolver carefully puts in many class markers so that middle-class readers understand the characters to be lower class. For example, Dellarobia distinguishes her friend Crystal by her big hair and wonders about Crystal naming her sons Jazon and Mical: "what kind of mother misspelled her kids' names on purpose?" (29). When Dellarobia looks at herself through the PhD students' eyes, she sees herself as a redneck (162), and she understands that Billy Ray Hatch's hillbilly ways are mocked by well-to-do outsiders (187). Gavin Jones posits that such literary representations of poverty have "inevitably been as much a cultural as an economic issue" (Jones, "Poverty" 771). Such scenes demonstrate Dellarobia's double consciousness of class—as both the judger and the judged. An ecopoverty reading of the novel offers a vital contribution to reading environmental literature for its critique of the middle-class sport of making fun of the rural white impoverished people who will suffer disproportionately from planetary warming.

Flight Behavior coalesces cli-fi narrative and the literature of poverty when Dellarobia and her financially strapped family must make decisions regarding the nesting of the climate-refuge butterflies on their property. The character Ovid Byron, a lepidopterist, attributes the monarchs' presence to a "bizarre alteration of a previously stable pattern" that points to a "continental ecosystem breaking down," caused by anthropogenic climate change (228). Alterations to the biotic system from climate change affect human economic difficulty as the Turnbows' earnings are limited by the heavy rains caused by a warming planet.

Dellarobia's husband, Cub, agrees with his father's decision to try to get out of debt by selling his family's tract of forest to a lumber company for clear-cutting.[7] The Turnbows desperately need the huge sum of money, but rising temperatures due to climate change have forced monarch butterflies to migrate from Mexico and settle in the very patch of land that the lumber company wants to purchase. Cub cannot afford to worry about conserving nature and cannot see the possible long-term effects of endangering a vulnerable species when his children have needs now. The developers' offer to clear-cut puts in relief the novel's concerns with both environmental and socioeconomic issues and the ways that cli-fi productively challenges parochial regionalist concerns. This tension calls to mind the epigraph that set up this paper. Because of their precarious economic situation, the Turnbows find it difficult to prioritize long-term planetary health when their bills need to be paid immediately. Dellarobia makes it evident that sacrificing the environment might provide financial relief for a short time but might not be a beneficial long-term economic solution.

Dellarobia's father-in-law, Bear, will only change his mind about logging if he stands to gain money. Naydan astutely notes that "in his devotion to capitalist ideals, [Bear] sustains a sort of patriotism, at least according to Dovey's definition of reverence of wealth as patriotic in America" (Naydan 167). However, readers do sympathize with Bear, because he stands to lose a lot as his balloon payment on farming equipment comes due and the heavy rains have prevented him from securing contracts. Selling his forest is an immediate solution to his financial woes. Murphy points out that clear-cutting "becomes an example of how people can be persuaded by the consumerist culture in which they live to make decisions that run counter to their own personal long-term interests, as well as the long-term health of their human communities, their ecoregional communities, and the biosphere" (Murphy 159). According to Goodbody, farmers usually prefer clear-cutting over selective felling because of higher profits (Goodbody 50). The combination of hard-core science about planetary vulnerability, and readers' sensitivity to the Turnbows' lived experience of limited material resources, brings questions of ecosocial justice to the fore. Trexler calls these issues "anthropocene economics for the working poor" (Trexler 228) and recognizes that middle-class consumers unfairly benefit from a high-carbon lifestyle. The Turnbow family exemplifies the lower class that produces a lower-impact carbon footprint and is taught that climate change is a hoax but who then suffer more from the extravagances of the upper-class's proclivity to burn fossil fuels.

The Turnbows' hardscrabble, poverty-line status derives in large part from their lack of opportunity to attend college. Their generational poverty will be inherited by their children, because they do not think it important or likely for their offspring to receive a higher education. Dellarobia remarks, "Kids in Feathertown wouldn't know college-bound from a hole in the ground. They don't need it for life around here. College is kind of irrelevant." Yet at the same time, Dellarobia also realizes that "educated people had powers." Kingsolver's novel makes evident that although education is crucial to understand and combat climate change, the halls of academe can also avoid recognizing that the poor disproportionately bear the impact of environmental degradation and cannot sacrifice immediate survival needs for far-off gain.[8]

Kingsolver brings together cli-fi and poverty studies when the novel offers a critique of how the educated middle class's approach to ameliorating climate change disregards the lived experience of those at or around the poverty line. For example, Dellarobia is approached by Leighton Akins, an environmental activist, who asks her to pledge to reduce her carbon footprint. Dellarobia and her husband, Cub, struggle to feed their family and so find it absurd to pledge to reduce their air travel (when they can't afford to fix the car) or to stop buying bottled water, when they rely on a well. They also cannot comprehend the pledge's insistence that they buy more energy-efficient appliances, when they cannot afford to buy any new appliances at all. Dellarobia recognizes that "an environmentalist stance, as valid as its goals may be, often goes hand in hand with an unacknowledged privileged socioeconomic status, and that the response to environmental problems of poorer people is to a large extent motivated by socioeconomic insecurity and fear" (Mayer, "Explorations" 29).

Are Dellarobia and Leighton on opposite sides of the "green gap"? Leighton wants Dellarobia to pledge to do her part to help with climate mitigation, which tend to be defined by most policymakers as "human intervention to reduce the sources or enhance the sinks of greenhouse gases" ("Summary" 4). Yet her low socioeconomic status means she already does not benefit from a cozy wasteful lifestyle. Ross argues that such a green gap "has already opened up between the eco-oases of affluent carbon-conscious communities and the human and natural sacrifice zones on the other side of the tracks, where populations have to fight to breathe clean air and drink uncontaminated water" (Ross, "Climate Change" 41). While the Turnbow family has clean air and water, they are still on the other side of the green gap and, ironically, live a low-carbon-impact lifestyle that affluent city folk try to emulate. Yet the Turnbows still struggle financially and sometimes miss paying bills—for example, their electricity gets cut off and cannot power the generators Ovid Byron uses to study the butterflies. Ovid pays the Turnbows' bill in order to continue his research. Economic globalization thus proves to be a force twinned by global climate change.

Dellarobia's pursuit of an advanced education as a woman mirrors some challenges faced by such climate refugees as the Delgado family from Michoacan. Climate change will likely impact women worldwide more seriously than it will affect men, because of "social roles, discrimination, and poverty" (Gaard 70). According to Gaard, "women's gender roles restrict women's mobility, impose tasks associated with food production and caregiving, and simultaneously obstruct women from participating in decision making about climate change, greenhouse gas emission, and strategies for adaptation and mitigation" (Gaard 70). The Delgado family as well, if they manage to stay in Tennessee or elsewhere in the US, will likely increase their reliance on fossil fuels, because Latin American immigrants usually increase their carbon footprints when they move north (Ross 39).

But Kingsolver levels some of her most biting criticism at unfocused, overzealous climate activists who do not have accurate information. For example, when students from the local community college show up to protest in an effort to save the monarchs, they go to the wrong house. Kingsolver portrays the British knitting eco-do-gooders Nelda and Myrtle as naïve and bumbling "slactivists." They squat on the Turnbows' land and knit figures of butterflies as their chosen form of resistance. By posting updates about their knitting activities on social media, they attempt to raise awareness about the butterflies' plight due to anthropogenic climate change. Dellarobia doesn't understand how the knitters have the financial means to support their yarning resistance. Through the knitting protesters, Kingsolver raises questions about the most effective type of activism and who has the socioeconomic means to engage in activism.

Flight Behavior thematizes migration and flow not only through the monarch butterflies' flight behavior but through the circulation of low-cost goods that problematize conservation and green attitudes. While Dellarobia values the craftsman expertise of her parents, she also benefits financially by shopping in cheap dollar stores. One of the novel's most extraordinary scenes occurs in chapter 7: Kingsolver dissects the problem of worldwide circulation of cheap items and shows the interdependence of people and goods, just as the butterflies are dependent on their rapidly changing environment. The mass migration of crappy products made by low-wage workers and purchased by other low-wage earners stands in ironic contrast to the natural flow of the butterflies from exploited South to privileged North and back again. This scene in the dollar store twins ecologic and economic injustices by contrasting the circulation of the monarchs to the circulation of cheap crap that threatens to "naturalize" as timeless and ahistorical the bottom-line market profit of disposable plastic trinkets.

While climate amelioration and mitigation stand as extremely urgent, it is possible that Dellarobia and her young son Preston's ability to adapt by the end of the novel undermines the urgency to stop anthropogenic climate change. By leaving her husband, arranging amicable child custody, and pursuing an education, Dellarobia shows that she can adapt to change. She convinces her small son that migrating back and forth between her household and his dad's will actually make him stronger. I strongly disagree with Linda Wagner-Martin's claim that Dellarobia dies at the end of the novel (Wagner-Martin 197). Instead, I understand the ending to indicate that Dellarobia survives and thrives. However, a possible unintended takeaway message from the novel is that climate disaster might not be all bad: we can adjust and adapt, which will make us stronger.

While *Flight Behavior* conjoins cli-fi and poverty studies in what Mayer would call a narrative of anticipation, Junot Diaz's "Monstro" thematizes both issues in a narrative of catastrophe. Published in *The New Yorker* as a piece of high-brow fiction, "Monstro" is a narrative of catastrophe that depicts an already changed Earth. "Monstro" tells the first-person story of a rich, privileged, spoiled (and unnamed) Brown University student—"a flash priv kid" (Diaz 107)—from the Dominican Republic who hangs out with other rich brats as a terrible disease, buoyed by a hot climate, ravages the poor over the border in Haiti. Looking for work, the narrator returns to the sweltering heat of his home in the Dominican Republic, with its "oletime climate change" (Diaz 108). The narrator informs us that "shit, a hundred straight days over 105 degrees F. in our region alone, the planet cooking like a chimi and down to its last five trees—something berserk was bound to happen" (Diaz 107).

The narrator and his friends remain unconcerned about the spread of a global-warming disease since it only affects the socioeconomically marginalized. The changed climate causes the "negrura" disease to spread: "the infection showed up on a small boy in the relocation camps outside Port-au-Prince, in the hottest March in recorded history" (Diaz 1). The new disease is something strange and unprecedented: "A black mold-fungus-blast that came on like a splotch and then slowly just started taking you over, tunneling right through you—though as it turned out it wasn't a mold-fungus-blast at all. It was something else. Something new" (Diaz 107). In this story, the planet is heating up so dramatically that the diseased skin of the infected come to resemble the coral reefs that once existed, as if some sort of somatic substitution took place: "coral reefs might have been adios on the ocean floor, but they were alive and well on the arms and backs and heads of the infected" (Diaz 107).

While "Monstro" clearly can claim a place on a cli-fi syllabus, it could equally appear on a poverty studies syllabus for its critique of wealth inequality in the face of a climate collapse. The narrator makes it clear that a combination of an economic depression and draught conditions forces him to return from college to live with his mother in the Dominican Republic: "I wouldn't have come to the Island that summer if I'd been able to nab a job or a summer internship, but the droughts that year and the General Economic Collapse meant nobody was nabbing shit" (Diaz 108). "Monstro" cleaves a difference between the impoverished victims and the uninfected wealthy. For example, the narrator's best friend, Alex, comes from such a wealthy family that Alex was kidnapped and ransomed as a child. In contrast, the poor are forced to live in relocation camps in Haiti. But authorities do not worry about the spread of the disease, since it only affects low-status Haitians. The narrator comments, "And since it was just poor Haitian types getting fucked up—no real margin in that" (Diaz 107). According to Leyshon, Diaz is fascinated by "outbreak stories." In an interview, Diaz says that "if it's true that writing the future is just another way to write the present, then my present is all about climate change, inequality, capitalism's cruel optimism, femicidal violence, and the survival, against all odds, of the utopian imagination" (Leyshon). In Diaz's hands, the apocalyptic cli-fi plot horrifies readers while emphasizing the rich/poor disparity. Sarah Quesada argues that with the story's zombie ending, "this Caribbean sic-fi journey is, in essence, a futuristic account of an unimaginably prosperous sugar island, turned darkly decadent, whose only hope is found in an allegorical signifier—that is, the legend of the living dead" (291). It is clear in the story that the brunt of the suffering from heat and the spread of disease will be borne by those with the fewest resources.

Likewise, Paolo Bacigalupi's "The Tamarisk Hunter" imagines how different economic classes form due to the "postnatural condition" of high-tech climate-change mitigation (Malewitz). "The Tamarisk Hunter" tells the story of Lolo, who lives in the American Southwest, which has been turned into a desert due to the "Big Daddy Drought." Lolo eeks out a living as a "water tick": the government pays him to dig up water-sucking tamarisk plants for state water-conservation efforts. To Lolo, being a water-tick "is a living; where other people have dried out and blown away, he has remained: a tamarisk hunter, a water tick, a stubborn bit of weed" (Bacigalupi 511). Poorly paid, Lolo gets around by camel in the Colorado River Basin as he rides past one "eviscerated town" after another (513). To secure himself an income in the future, Lolo breaks the law by secretly replanting some tamarisks in a hidden area. He wants to tell his friend Travis about his "insurance plan" of reseeding tamarisks to guarantee himself continued work, but he realizes "the stakes are too high. Water crimes are serious now, so serious Lolo hasn't even told his wife, Annie, for fear of what she'll say" (515).

In "The Tamarisk Hunter," wealthy Californians have secured water rights and constructed a wall to keep others out. This type of futuristic scenario is not too far-fetched: according to du Shutter, "climate change with more frequent and extreme drought and floods and less predictable rainfall is already affecting the capacity of some communities to feed themselves, and is destabilising markets" (33). As one of the "have nots," Lolo lives on the margin of unemployment and poverty. He fears that the federal government will deprive him of his small earnings and bankrupt him due to his "crime" of working against California's exclusive access to water rights: "They'll want him all right. Put him on a Straw work crew and make him work for life, repay his water debt forever" (520). Bacigalupi suggests that planetary warming has been rather rapid, because Lolo recognizes one of the "guardies" as a former childhood friend, from before anthropogenic climate change brought on the drought. Lolo recalls that "they played football together a million years ago, when football fields still had green grass and sprinklers sprayed their water straight into the air" (522). Clearly this nostalgic memory of lush lawns and sprinklers is meant to shock readers into realizing that our everyday lawns could become extinct and nothing more than a fond memory. In the suspenseful ending, Lolo thinks the guardies will arrest him for his water crimes. Instead, Lolo finds out that the Department of the Interior decided to end the water bounty-payout program and that he will be unemployed (524). He realizes he will have no other way of eeking out a living: "What am I supposed to do, then?" (525). The guardies offer him an early buyout of $500 and the small consolation that "it's enough to get you north. That's more than they're offering next year" (525). The story ends with Lolo and Annie, already low on the socioeconomic scale, facing even more dire impoverishment due to the excesses of the carbon economy.

An ecopoverty reading of these three fictions effectively conjoins ecological and economic inequity. Studying the overlap of the genres of climate fiction and poverty studies makes more urgent the necessity to consider the twinned maltreatment of our environment and of the poor. One danger of literarily portraying damaged environments is that human and planetary suffering becomes aestheticized in order to produce a satisfying reading experience. Yet, because economic and scientific reports of catastrophic environmental damage and of the dire and growing income gap between rich and poor are not enough alone to move the public towards ameliorative action, the literary imagination has much to contribute to a discussion of how we can change public policy to move us towards more green and equitable lives.

NOTES

1. Gregers Andersen is correct to assert that the term "cli-fi" should only be used "to describe fictions that specifically employ the scientific paradigm of anthropogenic global warming in their plots" (Andersen 856).

2. Gavin Jones's *American Hungers* directs much-needed attention to writers who have been concerned with poverty in the US, including Herman Melville, Theodore Dreiser, Stephen Crane, Edith Wharton, James Agee, Richard Wright, and Rebecca Harding Davis.

3. These quick fixes will eventually loop back and harm those originally trying to escape trouble, constituting one of Timothy Morton's "strange loops." In a heartbreaking real-life parallel, a school in Newton Falls, Ohio, is planning to raise money by selling timber on the school grounds. A school graduate's reaction exactly mirror's Dellarobia's point: "After the money has been spent, all we will be left with is the eyesore of a fragmented forest that will take a hundred years or more to regenerate. The need for money will still be there" http://www.tribtoday.com/news/local-news/2018/06/falls-schools-plan-timber-harvesting/. Many thanks to Kyle Keeler for pointing out this article and reminding me of Morton's idea.

4. The environmental justice (EJ), ecojustice, and anti–environmental racism movements have brought much-needed attention to structural disparities that make it more likely that impoverished, disenfranchised communities will suffer from a toxic landscape. The EJ movement shares much in common with green cultural studies, ecopoetics, and environmental literary criticism. The EJ movement can be defined as "the right of all people to share equally in the benefits bestowed by a healthy environment. We define the environment, in turn, as the places in which we live, work, play, and worship" (Adamson, Evans, and Stein 4). An ecocritical or green reading,

which I am doing of cli-fi literature, certainly can be considered one aspect of the EJ movement. In general, however, EJ "primarily names a social movement, plural and engaged in the urgency of local campaign work" (Clark, *Cambridge Introduction* 88). While we literary critics certainly aspire for our textual analyses to be effective in the world, I realize that my readings of the conjunction of cli-fi literature and poverty literature are not the same as on-the-ground activism as done by EJ activists.

5. Poverty literature certainly depicts the landscape or built environment of those facing socioeconomic hardship, and cli-fi fiction definitely has a decidedly human interest as well.

6. For example, see the *Fifth Assessment Report* published by the Intergovernmental Panel on Climate Change.

7. Dellarobia's parents also both lost their livelihood when mass production of cheap crap supplanted the appreciation for handmade furniture and hand-tailored clothes. Chapter 7 of *Flight Behavior* is particularly stunning for the way Dellarobia and Cub discuss their relationship, money, and environmental concerns in the dollar store.

8. John Marsh argues to the contrary. He maintains that a guiding myth of American culture is that "problems of social justice including and especially poverty, can be solved through education. They cannot. And believing that they can does considerable more harm than good" (Marsh 605).

WORKS CITED

Adamson, Joni, Mei Mei Evans, and Rachel Stein, editors. *The Environmental Justice Reader: Politics, Poetics, and Pedagogy.* U of Arizona P, 2002.

Andersen, Gregers. "Cli-fi and the Uncanny." *ISLE*, vol. 23, no. 4, 2016, pp. 855–66.

Atwood, Margaret. "It's Not Climate Change—It's Everything Change." *Medium*, 28 July 2015. https://medium.com/matter/it-s-not-climate-change-it-s-everything-change-8fd9aa671804.

Bacigalupi, Paolo. "The Tamarisk Hunter." *Loosed upon the World: The Saga Anthology of Climate Fiction*, edited by John Joseph Adams, Saga Press, 2015, pp. 511–25.

Clark, Timothy. *The Cambridge Introduction to Literature and the Environment.* U of Cambridge P, 2011.

———. "Some Climate Change Ironies: Deconstruction, Environmental Politics, and the Closure of Criticism." *The Oxford Literary Review*, vol. 32, no. 1 (2010), pp.131–49.

de Schutter, Olivier. "Eco-farming Addresses Hunger, Poverty and Climate Change." *Pacific Ecologist*, no. 21, 2012, pp. 33–37.

Diaz, Junot. "Monstro." *New Yorker*, 4 and 11 June 2012.

Gaard, Greta. "Ecofeminism." *Keywords for Environmental Studies*, edited by Joni Adamson, William A. Gleason, and David N. Pellow, New York UP, 2016, pp. 61–63.

Gabriel, Hayden, and Greg Garrard. "Reading and Writing Climate Change." *Teaching Ecocriticism and Green Cultural Studies*, edited by Garrard, Palgrave Macmillan, 2012.

Garrard, Greg. "Conciliation and Consilience: Climate Change in Barbara Kingsolver's *Flight Behavior.*" In *Handbook of Ecocriticism and Cultural Ecology*, edited by Hubert Zapf, Berlin, Walter de Gruyter, 2016, pp. 117–29.

Goodbody, Axel. "Risk, Denial and Narrative Form in Climate Change Fiction: Barbara Kingsolver's *Flight Behavior* and Ilija Trojanow's *Melting Ice.*" Mayer and von Mossner.

Heise, Ursula. *Sense of Place and Sense of Planet: The Environmental Imagination of the Global.* Oxford UP, 2008, pp. 39–58.

Hertel, Thomas W., and Stephanie D. Rosch. "Climate Change, Agriculture, and Poverty." *Applied Economic Perspectives and Policy*, vol. 32, no. 3, 2010, pp. 355–85.

Jones, Gavin. *American Hungers: The Problem of Poverty in US Literature, 1840–1945.* Princeton UP, 2008.

———. "Poverty and the Limits of Literary Criticism." *American Literary History*, vol. 15, no. 4, 2003, pp. 765–92.

Kingsolver, Barbara. *Flight Behavior.* Harper, 2012.

Knadler, Stephen. "Narrative Slow Violence: Post-reconstructions Necropolitics and Speculating beyond Liberal Antirace Fiction." *J19: The Journal of Nineteenth-Century Americanists*, vol. 5, no. 1, 2017, pp. 21–50.

Leyshon, Cressiday. "This Week in Fiction: Junot Diaz." *The New Yorker*, 27 May 2012.

Lowe, Thomas D. "Is This Climate Porn? How Does Climate Change Communication Affect Our Perceptions and Behavior?" Tyndall Centre for Climate Change Research, December 2006.

Malewitz, Raymond. "Climate-Change Infrastructure and the Volatilizing of American Regionalism." *Modern Fiction Studies*, vol. 61, no. 4, 2015, pp. 715–30.

Marsh, John. "The Literature of Poverty, The Poverty of Literature Classes." *College English*, vol. 73, no. 6, 2011, pp. 604–27.

Mayer, Sylvia. "Explorations of the Controversially Real: Risk, the Climate Change Novel, and the Narrative of Anticipation." Mayer and von Mossner, pp. 21–37.

Mayer, Sylvia, and Alexa Weik von Mossner, editors. *The Anticipation of Catastrophe: Environmental Risk in North American Literature and Culture.* Universitatsverlag Winter, 2014.

Mayer, Sylvia, and Alexa Weik von Mossner. "Introduction: The Anticipation of Catastrophe: Environmental Risk in North American Literature and Culture." Mayer and von Mossner, pp. 1–15.

Mehnart, Antonia. "Things We Didn't See Coming—Riskscapes in Climate Change Fiction." Mayer and von Mossner, pp. 51–65.

Morton, Timothy. "The Oedipal Logic of Ecological Awareness." *Environmental Humanities*, no. 1 (2012) 7–21.

Murphy, Patrick D. "Pessimism, Optimism, Human Inertia, and Anthropogenic Climate Change." *Interdisciplinary Studies in Literature and the Environment*, vol. 21, no. 1, 2014, pp. 149–63.

Naydan, Liliana M. *Rhetorics of Religion in American Fiction: Fundamentalism and Fanaticism in the Age of Terror.* Bucknell UP, 2016.

Nixon, Rob. *Slow Violence and the Environmentalism of the Poor.* Harvard UP, 2013.

Poverty and Climate Change. Organization for Economic Co-operation and Development. http://www.oecd.org/env/cc/2502872.pdf.

Quesada, Sarah. "A Planetary Warning? The Multilayered Caribbean Zombie in 'Monstro.'" *Junot Diaz and the Decolonial Imagination,* edited by Monica Hanna, Jennifer Harford Vargas, and Jose David Saldivar, Duke UP, 2016.

Ross, Andrew. "Climate Change." *Keywords for Environmental Studies,* edited by Joni Adamson, William A. Gleason, and David N. Pellow, New York UP, 2016, pp. 37–40.

"Summary for Policy Makers." Intergovernmental Panel on Climate Change (IPCC), 2014. http://www.ipcc.ch/pdf/assessment-report/ar5/wg3/ipcc_wg3_ar5_summary-for-policymakers.pdf.

Trexler, Adam. *Anthropocene Fictions: The Novel in a Time of Climate Change.* Harvard UP, 2015.

Wagner-Martin, Linda. *Barbara Kingsolver's World: Nature, Art, and the Twenty-First Century.* Bloomsbury, 2014.

Learning to Survive
Place-Based Education in Strange as This Weather Has Been *and* Parable of the Sower

JENNIFER HORWITZ

In the past several decades, educators at all levels of the US education system have become increasingly concerned with the negative impacts that education has on the environment. In particular, environmental educators have warned that the promise of upward mobility entrenched in the dominant school system too often mandates a disassociation from place. In his critique of higher education in particular, Wendell Berry writes that universities have functioned "to uproot the best brains and talents, to direct them away from home into exploitative careers in one or another of the professions, and so to make them predators of communities and homelands, their own as well as other people's" (51–52). Since an intimate relationship or connection to place can be pivotal in developing a land ethic, or a moral responsibility to the earth, it is with grave consequence that US formal education discounts and directly opposes students' attachments to local places.[1]

In response to the environmentally disastrous dominant education system, place-based education has grown in popularity as an important corrective.[2] Although there are many names for this kind of education, and each has its own emphasis—including land education, community-based education, and experiential learning—common to all is the call to have students engage with their immediate material surroundings in order to "provide people with the experience and knowledge needed to care for our environments" (Gruenewald, "Foucauldian Analysis" 73). One of the first to coin the term "place-based education," Laurie Lane-Zucker captures the core of this educational movement when he writes, "Place-based education might be characterized as the pedagogy of community, the reintegration of the individual into her homeground and the restoration of the essential links between a person and her place" (Sobel ii). If place-based education offers the learning needed to restore students' relationships to their local environments—and the earth more generally—the pedagogical framework, dominated by an ideology of rooting oneself in place, begs the question: what does a grounded, earth-based education look like when staying and learning in place is deadly?

Where people live and go to school is intimately connected with structures of class privilege, since poverty and housing discrimination often force disenfranchised people to live near toxic waste sites.[3] In this essay, I examine Ann Pancake's *Strange as This Weather Has Been* (2007) and Octavia Butler's *Parable of the Sower* (1993), two climate fiction (cli-fi) novels that represent the experiences of victims of environmental injustice, to argue that the experiences of people living in toxic or uninhabitable places must inform place-based educational theory. Otherwise, the pedagogy risks becoming meaningless, or worse, harmful, to students in frontline communities. By bringing literary perspectives to bear on place-based education, this article has diverse experiences with place speak back to the ecologically essential yet largely exclusive pedagogical theory with the aim of making place-based education not only more inclusive but also more effective.

A dominant and persistent strand of American environmentalism assumes that the experience of place is neutral and thus universal. For example, the writing of transcendentalists, which is foundational to American environmentalism, approaches experiences in nature as inherently good and replicable for anyone. Famously, Thoreau leaves for the Walden Woods in order to live "deliberately." Although he roots himself in and is attuned to that place, at the same time, he believes that his experience at Walden can be translated into universal American ideals; indeed, place often becomes a conduit for him to meditate on and promote values like individualism and self-reliance. In believing that what holds true for him at Walden holds true for other people in other places, Thoreau erases differences in relationship to place. Importantly, environmental humanists have challenged these romantic and universalized Euro-American conceptualizations of place. In his formative essay, "The Trouble with Wilderness," William Cronon shows how ideas of the sublime have made certain places—and the experiences of the white elite in those places—more worthy of protection than others. Mei Mei Evans similarly demonstrates that ideas of what is "natural" and "wild" are not only culturally constructed but also function to foreclose those locations to women, people of color, and other marginalized groups. By acknowledging the social situations that shape people's experiences with the environment, ecocritics have diversified discourses of place, and it is critical that place-based educational conversations do the same.

My analyses align with the work of educators who intend to counter a universalized, Western education with one that is alert to the particularities of place, which includes the experiences of people in those places. In fact, foundational place-based educational theorists like David Sobel and David Orr first began to define and develop a pedagogy of place as distinct from environmental education specifically because the latter, housed in the natural sciences, was "too narrow," and they recognized the need for "a broader and more inclusive fashion" of learning about natural and built environments that encompassed landscapes and ecosystems, people and neighborhoods (Sobel 8). Instead of studying either a biotic community or a human one, educators and students, through a focus on "place," can center the entanglements between the human and the more-than-human world.

As made evident, place-based education is dependent upon the local: the particular human and biotic community in which students are embedded is where essential ecological learning happens. But famously, Ursula Heise has critiqued place-based US environmentalism for its failure to grapple adequately with theories of globalization, which posit "that the increasing connectedness of societies around the globe entails the emergence of new forms of culture that are no longer anchored in place" (10). Instead of eliding the increasing connectedness of the planet, however, place is often the site in which those connections can be made most immediate and material to students. In her "ethnography of global connection," Anna Tsing shows that the local necessarily leads to the global, and vice versa, since the work of the universal "is enacted in the sticky materiality of practical encounters" (1). In other words, global systems, networks, and problems manifest in local iterations that are apparent only when we encounter and attend to the specificity of place. As the global is best understood in and through the particular, students today need educational experiences that champion the close and careful study of place.

While place-based education is a pedagogical framework full of potential for the planet, particularly in our time of global climate change, certain bedrock assumptions continue to limit it. The educational theory is dominated by the language of "staying put" and "digging in," of teaching students to value "reintegration" into their homeplace. This is most salient in Orr's distinction between "resident" and "inhabitant," which is a distinction that has been repeated by many scholars when discussing a pedagogy informed by place: "A resident is a temporary occupant, putting down few roots and investing little, knowing little, and perhaps caring little for the immediate locale beyond its ability to gratify.... The inhabitant, in contrast, 'dwells' ... in an intimate, organic, and mutually nurturing relationship with a place. Good inhabitance is an art requiring detailed knowledge of a place, the capacity for observation, and a sense of care and rootedness" (*Ecological Literacy* 130). When inhabitance is an "art," it becomes a matter of individual ability and effort. In Orr's terms, someone is a resident or inhabitant based entirely on their own volition. If the person cares enough about the place, they will learn to become long-term inhabitants; if not, they will be occupants merely passing through.[4] Interestingly, Orr acknowledges the class associations with residency, saying, "Residence requires cash and a map. A resident can reside almost anywhere that provides an income" (130). He fails, however, to consider that choosing to stay put can also be a privilege. Environmental justice leaders like Robert Bullard have shown that ecological hazards disproportionately impact impoverished communities and communities of color; and yet, this attention to how class and race interact with the environment falls away in Orr's generalized discussion on "good inhabitance." While Orr's terminology, particularly the need to inhabit or dwell in a place, is useful in combatting a dominant cultural trend of increasing alienation from the earth, it risks ignoring and thereby perpetuating the systemic inequities that have led to the climate crisis.

Strange as This Weather Has Been and *Parable of the Sower* advance this educational theory by representing protagonists who must navigate what it means to be an inhabitant in hazardous places. Pancake's Lace grows up in a poor, white coal town in West Virginia, where mountaintop-removal mining leaves behind sludge in the water and slurry impoundments that may flood at any moment, while Butler's Lauren grows up in a Black, middle-class family living in the California of the near future, where the effects of climate change have led to increased violence and chaos. Together, these cli-fi novels show how the fossil fuel industry and climate change exacerbate social disparities, and, subsequently, how learning to integrate into one's local environment is not always an invariable and uncomplicated good. By highlighting class differences in relationships to place, *Strange as*

This Weather Has Been and *Parable of the Sower* offer more expansive imaginings of place-based pedagogies in practice: they envision an environmental education that is not only more attentive to class-based experiences in places but also more responsive to increasingly unstable ones.

LEARNING THE FUTURE OF A PLACE

The common narrative about the US education system as the means through which individuals can achieve social mobility and middle-class aspirations is condensed in the first several pages of *Strange as This Weather Has Been*, when Lace moves through her schooling with the hope of getting as far away as she can from her poor hometown. Growing up in an Appalachian community, Lace internalizes from a young age, as many poor and working-class children do, the message that "your place is more backwards than anywhere in America and anybody worth much will get out soon as they can" (3).[5] Indeed, she comes to think of her home as "just a holding pen" and arrives at West Virginia University with the promise that she will "never look back" (3–4).

If *Strange as This Weather Has Been* opens with Lace "getting out," the rest of the novel can be seen as her unlearning this lesson. Lace initially returns home not because she wants to but because she has to: after falling for the good-looking, baby-faced Jimmy Make and getting pregnant, Lace drops out of college and finds herself in the very position that she had been determined to escape. Rather than discount the material hardships of living in a place with little financial opportunity or security, Pancake's novel manages to acknowledge those hardships while reassessing a capitalist value system: when Lace's mother brings her into the woods to forage for food the family needs, Lace rediscovers the gifts of a place that people inside and outside of it have deemed worthless. "When I first got started," Lace explains, "it was just the plants I'd expected Mom to reteach me, things I could sell, but she knew she couldn't teach that without the other, and when I look back now, I see how much else I relearned" (139). Through this time with the land, Lace learns a connection to the place around her and realizes the truth in her mother's mantra, "You can live off these hills . . . everything was put in them for a reason" (94). Despite her family's poverty, the earth and her regained knowledge of it sustain Lace and her growing baby. Her traditional schooling, in other words, gets replaced with the core didactics of place-based education: once Lace no longer intends to leave her home and instead learns to become an inhabitant, she develops a seemingly life-giving, harmonious relationship to place.

However, *Strange as This Weather Has Been* illustrates the need for a place-based education that teaches students more than an attachment to the land, by featuring a place marred by the dual abuses of the poor and the earth. Mountaintop-removal mining, a process of blasting off the tops of mountains to reach the seams of coal, which has been in the background of the novel, moves to the foreground of Lace's concerns years later when she catches one of her sons knee-deep in the creek by their house with two dead fish in his hands. Realizing the poisons in the runoff will affect more than fish, Lace joins community members who use the local Dairy Queen she works at as a classroom space to learn about the dangers of coal mining: "They'd taught themselves chemistry, geology, hydrology, biology, politics, law. It was amazing what all they'd taught themselves, Loretta with nothing but a high school diploma and Charlie without even that, but when I mentioned it once to Charlie, he just grunted, 'You'd be surprised how quick you learn about something that's on the verge of killing you'" (268). Through shared investigation, Lace and the others study and mobilize against the imminent hazards of mountaintop removal, from chemical leaks to cancer-causing dust, flyrock to flash flooding. A key aspect of Lace learning to reinhabit her hometown, then, is learning to identify and disrupt the injustices that threaten it.

In attempting to make room within place-based education for the need for social change, David Gruenewald theorizes a place-based education combined with critical pedagogy, taking what he suggests is "the best of both worlds": the conservationist focus of the former with the critical consciousness, or *conscientization,* of the latter ("Best of Both Worlds"). Gruenewald's work is an important example of theorizing place-based education in a way that does not erase class difference—and while students can simultaneously learn to conserve *and* transform a place, as Gruenewald argues, this activist component most often falls away in conversations about place. For example, Scott Russell Sanders, who advocates for the "discipline of staying put" (xv) and the "salvation in sitting still" (101), makes this argument against the impulse to leave for somewhere better: "There are no privileged locations. If you stay put, your place may become a holy center, not because it gives you special access to the divine, but because in your stillness you hear what might be heard anywhere" (115). The value of investing in place indeed remains relevant everywhere, but sentiments about the holiness of each patch of land fail to acknowledge that staying put is easier and more beneficial for someone in an economically advantaged place. To say that there are no privileged locations ignores the many disparities that exist among them and the need to do something about it, to ignore that humans are perpetrators of environmental damage as well as agents of environmental healing. For Sanders, as for many place-based educators and writers, an emphasis on a connection to place eclipses action for it.

In contrast, Lace does not lose sight of either element of care for her impoverished and exploited place. Informed by the teachings of her mother, from whom she learns to reinhabit her home, and of the neighbors, from whom she learns to recognize the ways that home is uninhabitable, Lace models how these two lessons might work together in her powerful statement at the end of the novel: "What I do know, after almost two years of not even getting anybody to listen, much less take action, is this: the best way to fight them is to refuse to leave. Stay in their way—that's the only language they can hear. We are from here, it says. This is our place, it says. Listen here, it says. We exist" (314). For Lace, place-based learning culminates in committed social action to stay and protect her home. This decision has serious consequences for people who live in contaminated environments, most of whom already have limited access to resources, and in the moments before making such a choice, Lace considers the impact it will have on her children's health: "I can't lose my kids. I can't leave my place. One more time, the terrible choices. . . . Stay here without my kids. Leave the place with them. Or keep my kids here with me and risk losing them altogether" (313). Unfortunately, the need to put bodies on the line, especially in frontline communities, in order to protect the environment is not new. In a talk on "environmental martyrdom," Rob Nixon points out that across the world, and particularly in the Global South, environmentalists have faced imprisonment and targeted assassination for their resolve to protect their homes and the earth. In fact, on average over the past decade, an environmental activist has been killed every two days (McGrath). As Nixon and others remind us, the victims of environmental injustice are often the most vital players in the struggle against those injustices.

The consequences of Lace's self-sacrifice are slower and less exceptional than in the examples of environmental martyrs Nixon provides, but they are equally grave. Because the novel closes with Lace's heroic decision to stay, the aftermath of this decision is best revealed through the life of the woman on whom Lace is based. When Pancake first met Judy Bonds while in West Virginia helping her sister make a documentary on mountaintop removal, she did not know that Judy would inspire the central character in her first novel. At the time, Judy had been fired from her job at Pizza Hut for speaking out against coal and was just beginning her work for a new grassroots organization, but she would go on to become known as "the godmother of the anti-mountaintop removal movement" (Pancake, "Creative Responses" 411). In 2011, four years after the publication of *Strange as This Weather Has Been,* Judy died of brain cancer at the age of fifty-eight. As Pancake explains, "Water tests of the creek outside [Judy's] house—the creek where her grandson held the dead fish—show that it contains polyacrylamide, a cancer-causing agent used for coal processing" (411). Lace foresaw that inhabiting this place would prove deadly, just as the toxins that seep from the water into Judy's body and brain confirm. The fictional and real stories here help us to see that place-based education demands a greater, and often the greatest, sacrifice from individuals in the most vulnerable positions.[6]

Since individuals and places have different life spans, acting on behalf of one will always be at odds with the welfare of the other in a region where poor people and the earth are considered disposable by all who profit from extractive industries. When the timeframe of an individual is rejected, however, then characters learn to see that the welfare of people and places are one and the same; as one person puts it, "What we're doing to this land is not only murder. It is suicide" (179). Though Lace's actions are self-sacrificial, she is motivated by a more collective definition of survival. Because she may very well die before mountaintop removal is banned from her home—and Judy, the woman on whom Lace is based, does—the success of this environmental justice work depends on individuals learning to act together across time. In fact, learning to care for a place in *Strange as This Weather Has Been* requires knowledge that accrues throughout and beyond the life span of an individual, and no less than three generations of women participate in this educative process. When Bant, Lace's daughter, whom she was carrying as she learned to forage, discovers in the final pages of the novel that the first blasts have been made into the next and closest mountain, memories return to her of being in that place with her mother and grandmother and, finally, of her grandmother's words, "You can live off these mountains. Put you in a little garden, and you can live off these here" (355). Repeated by Lace and Bant throughout, this critical lesson traverses the reading time of the novel, emulating communal knowledge shared across time. In the end, equally imperative as Lace deciding to stay to protect her place is her daughter echoing that same decision when her father offers to take her away. For Lace and her family, the "good inhabitance" that Orr describes as an art is, instead, a fatal fight for the future of a place that they love more than themselves.

LEARNING A FUTURE PLACE

While *Strange as This Weather Has Been* portrays place-based education as promoting class-based environmental justice action when students learn to extend roots beyond themselves, *Parable of the Sower* offers an adaptation of this pedagogy when the model of refusing to leave, or staying in place, is unavailable. Mobility can be a class privilege, as reflected in the "getting out" narrative, but so too can it be a matter of survival. Like Lace, Lauren faces the decision to stay in or leave the community she has known her whole life. Despite her boyfriend trying to convince Lauren "to get out of this dead-end neighborhood," she makes the selfless decision to stay in her Robledo neighborhood to help provide for her family (140). She even gives a commanding sermon that ends with a sentiment akin to Lace's: "*We persist*. This is our place, no matter what" (135). Her tale diverges from Lace's, however, when a group of "pyro addicts" decide to inhabit her home and burn and pillage her neighborhood, forcing her to escape. Another character captures this same experience when describing his own circumstances: "I didn't decide to leave. I escaped" (264). Lauren's forced displacement in 2027 shows that any place-based educational theory will become antiquated if it does not pay attention to the experiences of students who must learn an affiliation and responsibility to place while on the move.

This especially rings true because more and more people are being, and will be, uprooted by climate change. Though climate change, much like other environmental dangers, is not an equal-opportunity threat, *Parable of the Sower* foretells a time, and not so far into the future, when its impacts are not siloed to poor communities and communities of color. Lauren herself predicts this at the beginning of the novel when describing how the impact of an uncommonly early and powerful hurricane left for dead many of the "street poor who have nowhere to go," which brings her to the realization that "one way or another, we'll all be poor some day" (15). While not negating the fact that climate change differently impacts people, Lauren acknowledges that those affected will only grow in number—and exponentially. In fact, she herself becomes a "street poor" about halfway through the novel. And while Lace faces insecure and unsafe living conditions because she is born into a poor community, Lauren faces them despite her middle-class status. Her father teaches at a university, and the racially mixed gated neighborhood she lives in signals a degree of social and economic capital. In illustrating the demolition of this more privileged community, *Parable of the Sower* forces its readers to confront a world where the majority of individuals are unable to control their own physical or social mobility.

By shifting the timeframe, Butler's dystopia makes visible the futility of "getting out" of a world altered by climate change; consequently, an education system built on the guarantee that individuals can get ahead in the world topples. Lauren's stepmother, for example, looks to the fact that both she and her husband have PhDs as reason to believe that they will be able to get out of the neighborhood crumbling around them. But when she calls about reserving a spot in Olivar, a company-owned town where residents are given protection in exchange for becoming indentured servants, she discovers that their educational backgrounds are not enough to ensure livable wages even there (120). Shortly after these top degrees are reduced to pennies, unable to provide the Olamina family with a way out of calamity, the novel expunges all trace of our current education system, which endorses individual success at the expense of all else—including, in the case of Olivar, one's freedom. When Lauren's father, who has continued leaving the walls of the neighborhood to teach at the nearby college, fails to return from one such trip, the final tie to a traditional educational institution is severed. In so doing, *Parable of the Sower* makes room for "what the time needs" (325); a changed earth, the novel insists, requires an education that responds to this new reality.

Significantly, Lauren is positioned as a teacher, particularly after the death of her father, the professor. During her time in Robledo, she takes charge of teaching the young people in the neighborhood to read, and after her forced displacement from her home, she continues teaching literacy skills to the diverse set of companions she collects while walking north. Earlier, when considering how she might make money outside her gated community, she comes up with this plan: "I wonder if there are people outside who will pay me to teach them reading and writing. . . . I might even be able to teach some Earthseed verses along with the reading and writing. Given any chance at all, teaching is what I would choose to do" (124). This is exactly what Lauren does, albeit for free, and through lessons from *Earthseed: The Books of the Living*, which theorize ways to survive and shape immense change, Lauren not only teaches people to read but also to think and act anew in a time of climate crisis. One of the central objectives of Earthseed is revealed in the moment Lauren discovers the name for her teachings: "Well, today, I found the name, found it while I was weeding the back garden and thinking about the way plants seed themselves, windborne, animalborne, waterborne, far from their parent plants. . . . Even they don't have to just sit in one place and wait to be wiped out" (78). Infused in the Earthseed verses is this insistence on movement and enduring to take root once more, like the seeds featured in the titular parable that closes *Parable of the Sower*. When a place is unsurvivable—whether it be Robledo or the even more dreadful and oppressive places the other poor, multiethnic characters in the novel hail from—instead of "just sit[ting] in one place and waiting to be wiped out," Lauren teaches the drive and ability to become rooted in a future place.

Earthseed pedagogy, then, stands as a place-based education in a place where the present is unsustainable. In Robledo, this means learning skills that will enable people to live outside the gated neighborhood. Lauren starts by studying books on medical emergencies, gunmanship, and basic living skills and tries to convince her friend Joanne to do the same: "I'm trying to learn whatever I can that might help me survive out there" (58). Lauren makes a case for learning to confront the reality of a particular place, even when that reality is that they will need to leave. In contrast to Lauren, her father refuses to entertain the possibility of leaving and instead digs deeper into a community and, more broadly, a world order, that is fast unraveling. When he hears about the conversation with Joanne, he reprimands Lauren for the "scare talk," to which she responds: "It wasn't scare talk. We do need to learn what we can while there's time" (64). While her father denies that humans have changed the climate of the earth and "wait[s] for the old days to come back" (57), Lauren looks ahead to how she might survive and rebuild after her home is destroyed.

Even as Lauren's Earthseed pedagogy anticipates life elsewhere, it is specifically not rootless; unlike a traditional education that has students hungering for elsewhere, resulting in people with allegiances nowhere, as soon as Lauren hits the road, she searches for a secure place to inhabit. Despite being unable to spend more than a few days in any one location, Lauren leads her fellow travelers always toward "a home base" (276), which becomes an actual family home when they meet Bankole, whose sister is living on his land in northern California. Unlike Lace's initial plotting to "get out" of her small mountain town, Lauren's movement away from her homeplace is simultaneously an exit *and* a movement toward a future one. Mitchell Thomashow, one of the few place-based educators to contend with the experience of migration, coined the term "place-based transience" to reconcile how people might move through places while still caring for them: "It is in the comings and goings of people, landscape, flora, and fauna that this place is connected to a broader and deeper ecological experience. One's transience merely puts place in perspective—it enriches the process of passing through" (182). Thomashow intends to consider how learning from place might work under transitory circumstances, and yet the only way he can imagine this is by making "the process of passing through" enriching. As with Orr, Sanders, and other prominent environmental educators, Thomashow's conceptualization of a pedagogy of place is based exclusively on a pleasurable relationship to the land. But just as Lauren's experience in Robledo is tumultuous, so too is her experience in the many places in which she stops during her travels along the California coast. As she faces life-threatening fire storms, predatory gangs, and a constant shortage of food and water, Lauren does not live well in these places, with each one worse than the other: she survives.

Importantly, this does not negate her ability to pass on or enact place-based knowledge, and at the end of Lauren's long journey is Acorn. When Lauren and her band finally arrive at Bankole's property, they expect a thriving household but find only bones and ashes. After much debate on whether they should stay or leave, a return to the question that dominated the first half of the novel, Lauren asks each person if they will commit themselves to this place. Person by person, they agree to stay at Acorn until Harry, the last to decide, hesitates: "I want something of my own . . . Land, a home, maybe a store or a small farm. Something that's mine. This land is Bankole's" (322). Harry correctly knows that this place is not his, but neither will it be Bankole's; though Bankole owns the land, Butler has shown how little property rights matter to the forces that reign on this climate-changed earth. Instead, Harry's—and everyone's—best and only hope is a place collectively shared, cared for, and protected, since individuals simply do not survive in the US of the future. Thus, Acorn functions not only as a community that rewrites the capitalist structure of private property but also as a place where success depends on bringing together people from a range of class and racial backgrounds. Lauren points out that Bankole's sister and her husband could not have kept a good watch by themselves, but "if we work together, we can defend ourselves" (321). In addition to a human community, Lauren knows that they need a robust biotic community in order to survive, and she suggests that their first step be to plant a winter garden. After Harry sheds his last, lingering devotion to individualism, as well as the impulse to look for somewhere better, and agrees to participate in Acorn, the group goes about enacting a collective vision of survival in which they live in relation to, and dependent upon, each other and the earth.

In the end, though Lauren cannot save Robledo and her human and more-than-human neighbors who shared her home, she remains committed to transformation and conservation in the hopes of building a new place-based community that will endure. This is apparent in her investment in the future life of Acorn—she prioritizes the protection of the community's children, "the ones we have now and the ones we will have" (321)—as well as her investment in Acorn's past lives. She suggests a ceremony for all the group's relatives who have died, and in choosing to plant acorns as part of this tribute and in calling the commune Acorn, Lauren memorializes her previous home. When families in the old neighborhood had wanted to cut down their oak trees to plant "something useful," her father had convinced them not to, having learned from a book on Indigenous peoples of California that acorns could be used to make bread, knowledge which proved vital when flour from more water-intensive crops like wheat became scarce (64). Carrying this knowledge with her, Lauren ensures that the inhabitants of Acorn will reap the many benefits of the acorns she brought with her from Robledo, showcasing place-based learning that continues beyond a single place. In using knowledge from one place to sustain another, Lauren teaches that roots, including those that are transported and replanted, are invaluable when inhabiting our unpredictable and increasingly terrifying earth.

EARTHSEED PEDAGOGY FOR TODAY

As we continue to deny our reliance on the earth, climate change and its heightened effects force swelling numbers of people to migrate. As just one example, experts cite climate change as a major factor in the Syrian war, with sustained droughts causing 1.5 million people to move between 2006 and 2011 to the country's cities, which were then unable to support such a population influx with basic resources like clean water (Taylor). Even wealthier countries like the US have been unable to escape the effects of climate change when wildfires in California and unprecedented hurricanes in different parts of the nation have left many without homes. Because a two-degree warming will significantly raise sea levels, and most of the population in the US, as well as the rest of the world, lives on coastlines, we will face a future in which forced migration will be a part of many people's lived experience.

As a genre that brings to light our current world order built on class stratification and the fossil fuel industry, and future iterations of such a world, cli-fi offers the vital imaginative—and educative—space for teachers to consider and explore how pedagogies, including place-based ones, might anticipate and account for an increasingly unstable planet. In the two novels I have discussed here, Lace and Lauren demonstrate that place-based education today and into the future is less about learning never to leave a place and more about learning how to act on behalf of economically devastated and exploited places. While the ability to sink roots somewhere, especially for those in frontline communities, often remains outside one's control due to socioeconomics, and will increasingly become so because of climate change, these two cli-fi novels develop and impart diverse imaginings of good inhabitation—as "Earthseed," a term that includes a grounded ("earth") as well as a portable ("seed") way of coexisting with place, encapsulates. If we, as educators, continue to ignore, marginalize, or deny differences in people's relationships to place, then we will continue to fall short in achieving educational change that promotes collective action for survival, which requires the efforts of everyone. As Lauren reminds us in a key Earthseed verse, "Learn or die" (279), the stakes of learning have never been higher as we discuss and imagine the type of education needed for the planet today.

NOTES

1. For more on the erasure of place in US formal education, see a range of scholars including Joni Adamson, bell hooks, and Vine Deloria Jr. and Daniel Wildcat.

2. Environmental educators like David Sobel and David Gruenewald have been foundational to the place-based education movement on the elementary and secondary school levels, while John Elder, David Orr, and Mitchell Thomashow have helped to cultivate a discussion about place in higher education. In addition, millennia before any educational movement, Indigenous peoples have learned from and located knowledge in place, which the writing of Gregory Cajete, as just one example, underscores.

3. See Richard Hofrichter's *Toxic Struggles* and Dorceta Taylor's *Toxic Communities*, which establish the connection between low-income class status and exposure to toxicity as well as document the growing efforts of the environmental justice movement to spotlight this injustice.

4. Wallace Stegner expresses the same sentiment as Orr in his distinction between "boomers" and "stickers." A growing culture of sustainability in the American West, he writes, "is the product not of the boomers but of the stickers, not of those who pillage and run but of those who settle, and love the life they have made and the place they have made it in" (xxvii).

5. Haas and Nachtigal's *Place Value* illustrates how students in rural communities are taught to believe that their place is valueless and that "the good life" is necessarily located elsewhere, while Corbett's *Learning to Leave* offers a case study of such a phenomenon.

6. The novel also does not condemn people who choose to leave, as seen especially in its treatment of Avery, a character who lived through the horrific Buffalo Creek disaster as a child and who flees his home as a young adult.

WORKS CITED

Adamson, Joni. *American Indian Literature, Environmental Justice, and Ecocriticism: The Middle Place*. U of Arizona P, 2001.

Berry, Wendell. *Home Economics: Fourteen Essays*. Counterpoint, 2009.

Bullard, Robert D., editor. *Confronting Environmental Racism: Voices from the Grassroots*. South End Press, 1999.

Butler, Octavia E. *Parable of the Sower*. Updated ed., Grand Central Publishing, 2000.

Cajete, Gregory. *Look to the Mountain: An Ecology of Indigenous Education*. Kivaki Press, 1994.

Corbett, Michael. *Learning to Leave: The Irony of Schooling in a Coastal Community*. Fernwood Publishing, 2007.

Cronon, William. "The Trouble with Wilderness; or, Getting Back to the Wrong Nature." *Uncommon Ground: Rethinking the Human Place in Nature*, edited by Cronon, W. W. Norton, 1995, pp. 69–90.

Deloria, Vine, Jr., and Daniel R. Wildcat. *Power and Place: Indian Education in America*. Underlining ed., Fulcrum Publishing, 2001.

Elder, John, editor. *Stories in the Land: A Place-Based Environmental Education Anthology*. Orion Society, 1998.

Evans, Mei Mei. "'Nature' And Environmental Justice." *The Environmental Justice Reader: Politics, Poetics, and Pedagogy*, edited by Joni Adamson, Evans, and Rachel Stein, U of Arizona P, 2002.

Gruenewald, David A. "The Best of Both Worlds: A Critical Pedagogy of Place." *Educational Researcher*, vol. 32, no. 4, 2003, pp. 3–12. *JSTOR*, doi:10.2307/3700002.

———. "A Foucauldian Analysis of Environmental Education: Toward the Socioecological Challenge of the Earth Charter." *Curriculum Inquiry*, vol. 34, no. 1, Taylor & Francis, 2004, pp. 71–107.

Haas, Toni, and Paul M. Nachtigal. *Place Value: An Educators' Guide to Good Literature on Rural Lifeways, Environments, and Purposes of Education.* Eric Clearinghouse on Rural, 1998.

Heise, Ursula K. *Sense of Place and Sense of Planet: The Environmental Imagination of the Global.* Illustrated ed., Oxford UP, 2008.

Hofrichter, Richard. *Toxic Struggles: The Theory and Practice of Environmental Justice.* U of Utah P, 2002.

hooks, bell. *Belonging: A Culture of Place.* Routledge, 2008.

McGrath, Matt. "Over 1,700 Environment Activists Killed in Decade—Report." *BBC News,* 29 Sept. 2022. www.bbc.com.

Nixon, Rob. "Environmental Martyrdom and the Defenders of the Forest." Global Spaces, Local Landscapes, and Imagined Worlds. Northeast Modern Language Association (NeMLA) 49th Annual Convention, 13 Apr. 2018, Omni William Penn Hotel, Pittsburgh, PA. Keynote address.

Orr, David W. *Ecological Literacy: Education and the Transition to a Postmodern World.* State U of New York P, 1991.

Pancake, Ann. "Creative Responses to Worlds Unraveling: The Artist in the 21st Century." *The Georgia Review,* vol. 67, no. 3, 2013, pp. 404–14.

———. *Strange as This Weather Has Been: A Novel.* Shoemaker & Hoard, 2007.

Sanders, Scott Russell. *Staying Put: Making a Home in a Restless World.* Beacon Press, 1994.

Sobel, David. *Place-Based Education: Connecting Classrooms and Communities.* 2nd ed., Orion Society, 2004.

Stegner, Wallace. *Where the Bluebird Sings to the Lemonade Springs: Living and Writing in the West.* Reprint ed., Modern Library, 2002.

Taylor, Dorceta. *Toxic Communities: Environmental Racism, Industrial Pollution, and Residential Mobility.* NYU Press, 2014.

Taylor, Matthew. "Climate Change 'Will Create World's Biggest Refugee Crisis.'" *The Guardian,* 2 Nov. 2017. www.theguardian.com.

Thomashow, Mitchell. *Bringing the Biosphere Home: Learning to Perceive Global Environmental Change.* Reprint ed., MIT Press, 2003.

Thoreau, Henry David. *Walden: Or, Life in the Woods.* CreateSpace Independent Publishing Platform, 2017.

Tsing, Anna Lowenhaupt. *Friction: An Ethnography of Global Connection.* Illustrated ed., Princeton UP, 2005.

Settler Apocalypses
Race, Class, and the Erasure of Indigenous Resilience in Alaskan Cli-Fi

JENNIFER SCHELL

According to the authors of the Alaska chapter of the federal government's *Fourth National Climate Assessment*, "Alaska is on the front lines of climate change and is among the fastest warming regions on Earth. It is warming faster than any other state, and it faces a myriad of issues associated with a changing climate" (Markon et al. 1190). The list includes thawing permafrost, melting glaciers, and vanishing sea ice, as well as wildland fires, ocean acidification, biodiversity loss, and infrastructure damage. Perhaps not surprisingly, a number of nonfiction writers have sought to document the cultural and economic issues caused by these environmental problems. For example, in a chapter in *Early Warming*, Nancy Lord addresses the ironies of "last chance" tourism in the Iñupiaq village of Kaktovik, where residents welcome wealthy tourists, who expend enormous amounts of money and fuel to travel to the Arctic to see wild polar bears before they go extinct.[1] Throughout the chapter, she also highlights some of the other difficulties confronting the inhabitants of this North Slope community, most of which involve the prospect of oil development in the Arctic National Wildlife Refuge (ANWR). At every turn, Lord stresses that opinions on these matters vary dramatically depending on the individual and their relationship to the coercive operations of resource extraction, settler colonialism, and corporate capitalism in Alaska.

As a whole, *Early Warming* elaborates the cultural and economic complexities of life in a part of the United States where anthropogenic climate change affects every organism, often in unpredictable and dangerous ways. Insofar as its interest in this subject is concerned, this nonfiction book is not an anomaly. Other examples include Charles Wohlforth's *The Whale and the Supercomputer*, Elizabeth Kolbert's *Field Notes from a Catastrophe*, Gretel Ehrlich's *In the Empire of Ice*, Seth Kantner's *Swallowed by the Great Land*, and Dahr Jamail's *The End of Ice*. Though stylistically and tonally different, these texts also describe the dramatic changes occurring in circumpolar Alaska and their profound impact on the region's human and nonhuman inhabitants. Like *Early Warming*, most of them discuss colonialism and capitalism and confront their complicated legacies in Alaska.

For some reason, Alaskan climate novels tend not to engage with these complexities, especially insofar as their representations of Alaska Natives are concerned.[2] Some, such as Susannah Waters's *Cold Comfort* and Don Rearden's *The Raven's Gift*, possess admirable intentions but elect to elaborate what April Anson calls "settler apocalypse narratives" (63). As such, they tell deterministic stories of social, economic, and environmental collapse that perpetuate problematic colonialist tropes, such as the "vanishing Indian" and "white savior." Taken together, these novels position Alaska Natives not as resilient, resourceful people but as powerless victims of settler colonialism, corporate capitalism, and climate change. In so doing, they provide further support for Briggetta Pierrot and Nicole Seymour's claim that "intentionally or not, some mainstream cli-fi functions in large part to justify settler colonialism" (107).

As a naturalistic novel with an apocalyptic bent, *Cold Comfort* describes the fate of a fourteen-year-old Iñupiaq girl named Tammy, who obsesses over climate change as a means of coping with her impoverished living situation and her sexually abusive father. Resentful and rebellious—not to mention self-destructive—she forms an intimate relationship with her eighteen-year-old cousin and participates in an ecoterrorist plot to sabotage drilling machinery in ANWR. Caught in the cold, she freezes to death on the tundra shortly after her companions cause an accidental explosion. In its various chapters, *Cold Comfort* highlights issues of race and class in an attempt to position climate change as a problem of environmental justice. As it does so, it simplifies the situation, positioning all Iñupiat—rural and urban—as "vanishing Indians," helpless casualties of deterministic economic and environmental forces.

An example of apocalyptic fiction, *The Raven's Gift* describes the experiences of a young couple, John and Anna Morgan, employed as teachers in Nunacuak, a tiny Yup'ik village on the banks of the Kuskokwim River.[3] Shortly after their arrival, the couple witnesses the effects of the unequal distribution of wealth in Alaska as a mysterious illness sweeps through the impoverished community and decimates its population. Throughout, *The Raven's Gift* contextualizes contemporary social and environmental problems—poverty, epidemic disease, and climate change—by engaging in nuanced discussions of Alaskan history. While these portions of the novel are rich and complex, others advance reductive tropes. In the chapters that describe postplague Alaska, John assumes the role of "white savior," taking charge of a small band of otherwise helpless Yup'ik survivors, most of whom are children. Much like *Cold Comfort*, then, *The Raven's Gift* also reinforces settler colonial ideals by participating in a project of Indigenous erasure.

ENVIRONMENTAL APOCALYPSE AND ALASKAN HISTORY

Over the last twenty years, contemporary authors have produced a hefty amount of climate fiction, much of it apocalyptic or postapocalyptic. Although these modes of writing were once embraced by environmentalists for their perceived ability to catalyze change, they have recently come under scrutiny for their complicity with settler colonialism and the forms of capitalism affiliated with it. According to Kyle Whyte (Potawatomi), "Indigenous people do not always share quite the same science fiction imaginaries of dystopian or apocalyptic futures when they confront the possibility of a climate crisis." As he explains, this is because "the hardships many non-Indigenous people dread . . . are ones that Indigenous peoples have endured already due to different forms of colonialism: ecosystem collapse, species loss, economic crash, drastic relocation, and cultural disintegration" (226). In his view, anthropogenic climate change represents not a single catastrophe but the latest in a long series of social and environmental crises created by colonialism and capitalism working together to exploit the world's human and nonhuman resources.

Building on this idea, April Anson describes what she calls "settler apocalypse" narratives, "stories that tell of the end of the whole world but are, in reality, specific to white settlers" (63). Importantly, these narratives possess an ironic element, for they often "reinforce the exclusionary violence and ecological devastation they so often seek to diagnose and disrupt" (61). While Anson applies the term to ecofascist texts, Pierrot and Seymour expand the archive to include examples of contemporary climate fiction and film that perpetuate the "vanishing Indian" trope into the twenty-first century. As they demonstrate, this trope has performed a similar function across time. In the past, it served as a justification for the appropriation of land and resources for nationalist and capitalist purposes. In the present, it works to "maintain the colonial status quo even as [it] imagine[s] a drastically altered world that has *resulted from it*" (107). Given their investment in tropes that enact Indigenous erasure and perpetuate settler colonialism, *Cold Comfort* and *The Raven's Gift* belong on the list of "settler apocalypse" stories enumerated by Anson, Pierrot, and Seymour. They are important to mark as different from others of their kind, though, because they feature Indigenous characters and communities, ostensibly in a well-intentioned effort to draw attention to the impact of climate change on them. As such, they possess an overwhelming amount of irony.

Before discussing the intricacies of *Cold Comfort* and *The Raven's Gift*, I want to highlight some of the aspects of Alaskan history that they obscure, especially those that support Whyte's and Anson's claims about Indigenous and settler apocalypses. Efforts to colonize Alaska and exploit its human and nonhuman resources did not begin in earnest until 1742 when the survivors of Vitus Bering's Second Kamchatka Expedition straggled into Avacha Bay with several bales of sea otter pelts that they gathered in the Aleutians. Impressed by the quality of these furs, Russian traders—with the support of government officials in St. Petersburg—launched an oppressive, destructive colonial enterprise that lasted for the next hundred years. Interested in profit as opposed to settlement, they enslaved Unangax̂ hunters and forced them to slaughter sea otters and fur seals in record numbers (Jones 42). In addition to commandeering their labor, the Russians engaged in what Amitav Ghosh calls "conflict through inaction," a devastating form of biopolitical warfare that involved spreading alcohol and epidemic diseases among the Unangax̂, many of whom died for lack of resistance and medical care (Ghosh 171; Fortuine 103).

Throughout the nineteenth century, American entrepreneurs and their employees flooded into Alaska, establishing whaling stations, sealing camps, gold mines, salmon canneries, and lumber mills. As they did so, they perpetuated the North Pacific's reputation as a place filled with what Jason Moore calls "cheap nature," human and nonhuman resources available below cost for appropriation by imperialist power structures (89). Note that much like their Russian predecessors, most Americans preferred not to settle in Alaska; instead, they pillaged its resources, concluded their business, and relocated to warmer climates. Environmentally speaking, they launched a series of collapses as they massacred fur seals, bowhead whales, and musk ox, pushing these animals to the brink of extinction and beyond.[4] According to Harold Napoleon (Yup'ik)—whose writing inspired the pandemic portions of *The Raven's Gift*—the Americans also spread measles and influenza among Alaska Natives, killing an estimated 60 percent of the population by 1900. Alcohol, a popular item of trade among American workers and Indigenous people, only exacerbated this epidemiological disaster (21).

As the twentieth century progressed, bureaucrats, missionaries, and teachers—many of whom worked for boarding schools—arrived in Alaska. Importantly, they helped to inaugurate the transition of Alaska from resource to settler colony. Embracing the goal of assimilation endorsed by the Bureau of Indian Affairs, these individuals engaged in systematic regimens of cultural genocide against Alaska Natives. Boarding school teachers—just like those mentioned in *Cold Comfort*—punished students for speaking Indigenous languages, and missionaries forbade proselytes from participating in traditional activities such as the potlatch and Kivġiq (Messenger Feast).[5] Some individuals subjected their charges to physical and sexual abuse. All told, these various assimilationist projects inflicted trauma that lasted for generations as survivors and their descendants grappled with a host of problems caused by cultural dislocation, including suicide, substance abuse, and violent crime (Sharp and Hirshberg iii).

Over time, Alaska achieved statehood, settlement continued, and American oil companies set out to locate the vast reserves of petroleum rumored to lie buried beneath the Arctic tundra. In 1968, they discovered a massive deposit, initially estimated at ten billion barrels of oil, on state-owned land near Prudhoe Bay. With development stymied by the fact that Alaska lacked the infrastructure to bring Arctic oil to market safely and easily, the companies decided to build an overland pipeline, stretching from the North Slope to Prince William Sound. Although they sought to follow the pattern of resource development established by Russian fur traders and their American successors, they found their plans disrupted by several unresolved Indigenous land rights issues.

After learning that oil companies planned to build the pipeline on their ancestral lands, Alaska Natives mobilized, forming the Alaska Federation of Natives (AFN) to protect their interests. Lawsuits were filed and permits were rescinded. To expedite what promised to be a protracted series of negotiations, the state created the Land Claims Task Force, which included representatives from Alaska Native communities as well as various government officials. Their efforts resulted in the passage of the Alaska Native

Claims Settlement Act (ANCSA), a controversial, assimilationist piece of legislation designed to extinguish any outstanding land claims and introduce Alaska Natives to neoliberalism and corporate capitalism.[6] ANCSA stipulated that the federal government create a network of for-profit regional and village corporations and transfer the settlement assets—$962.5 million and forty-four million acres of land—to them for management. Significantly, the regional corporations also received the subsurface mineral rights to their property (Dunaway 141; Tuck 241). Thus, all Alaska Natives became corporate shareholders, receiving dividends based on the profitability of their business ventures, including mining and drilling projects on settlement land.

Just six years after ANCSA was signed into law, oil companies finished the Trans-Alaska Pipeline System (TAPS) and began production at Prudhoe Bay. Over the course of the next ten years, the field yielded ever-increasing amounts of oil, ultimately reaching a peak of 1.5 million barrels per day in 1988. Nowhere have the economic benefits and social inequities that attended this development been more evident than in the North Slope Borough, a municipality incorporated in 1972 by its Iñupiaq inhabitants. Since it includes Prudhoe Bay as part of its tax base, the Borough has been able to accumulate wealth and invest in civic improvements, providing residents with modern housing, running water, and flush toilets (Brewster 16–17). Despite its prosperity, it has not been able to alleviate the elevated cost of living in its villages—$11.00 for a gallon of milk in Utqiaġvik—caused by high transportation costs for goods and services. Many, if not most, of the Alaska Native villages located outside the Borough possess equally high costs of living and lack basic infrastructure and amenities. Their residents tend to live at or below the poverty line.

All told, the settlement process in Alaska created complicated economic and environmental realities for the state's Indigenous people. Climate change has only compounded the complexities, as recent debates about drilling in ANWR demonstrate. Established in 1980, the Refuge consists of eighteen million acres of northern tundra and boreal forest, encompassing the breeding ground of the Porcupine caribou herd and the ancestral homeland of the Gwich'in Athabascan people, who refer to it as "Iizhik Gwat'san Gwandaii Goodlit" or "The Sacred Place Where Life Begins" (Dunaway 33). Notably, ANWR also includes Iñupiaq territory and the village of Kaktovik. Although most of the Refuge is designated as wilderness—and, therefore, is protected from development in perpetuity—its coastal plain is not. Since

1980, many federal lawmakers from Alaska and elsewhere have introduced legislation to exploit this loophole and open ANWR to oil development.

Among Alaska Natives, opinions on this issue vary. Most Gwich'in oppose drilling in the Refuge, for fear that it will endanger the caribou that are so important to their food security and cultural traditions (Dunaway 8). As such, they tend to support the efforts of the Gwich'in Steering Committee, a transnational Indigenous advocacy group, whose members work with conservation organizations to lobby legislators, promote environmental justice, and protest oil drilling. The matter is more complicated for the Iñupiat of Kaktovik. Some residents—especially those allied with the Arctic Slope Regional Corporation (ASRC), which possesses subsurface rights to a portion of the coastal plain—support oil development for its potential to bring economic prosperity to their community (Dunaway 142–45). Others argue that drilling poses threats to the numerous nonhuman organisms that live in the Arctic, including the bowhead whales that are essential to Iñupiaq culture. They also emphasize that the fossil fuel industry—and the oil it produces—contributes to climate change and exacerbates its impacts. As this evidence indicates, Alaska Native people are not monolithic in their opinions about fossil fuel development; rather, they possess a range of opinions, depending on their employment status and economic stature, as well as their subsistence traditions, spiritual beliefs, and environmental commitments.

When taken together, these historical details demonstrate that anthropogenic climate change represents just one of many social and environmental disruptions that Alaska Natives have experienced since the onset of colonization. As such, they testify to the accuracy of Whyte's and Anson's claims about Indigenous and settler attitudes toward climate apocalypse. At this point, it is crucial to emphasize that none of these crises destroyed Alaska Native people or their cultures. This is because they developed what Gerald Vizenor (Anishinaabe) calls strategies of survivance that represent "renunciations of dominance, tragedy and victimry." By maintaining an "active sense of presence" in their communities, Alaska Natives preserved—and, in some cases, revived—their cultural traditions for future generations, often merging modern and traditional lifeways (Vizenor viii). Thus, Gwich'in and Iñupiaq hunters use rifles and bomb darts instead of arrows and harpoons, but they still hunt caribou and whales, just as their ancestors did thousands of years ago. At the same time, Alaska Native people also learned to contend with government bureaucracies, educational institutions, conservation groups, and scientific organizations to advocate for the development of environmental resources, protection of sacred land, continuation of subsistence rights, and enactment of climate justice.

SUSANNAH WATERS'S *COLD COMFORT* AND THE "VANISHING INDIAN" TROPE

One of the first Alaskan cli-fi novels, *Cold Comfort*, has attracted attention from a number of literary critics, including Adam Trexler and Karsten Levihn-Kutzler. Although they discuss the book's treatment of capitalism and tendency toward determinism, neither mentions its investment in "vanishing Indian tropes" and settler colonialism (Trexler 193–94; Levihn-Kutzler 12–14). Taking into account all of these aspects of the novel, I emphasize that *Cold Comfort* ignores much of the cultural and economic history described above, preferring instead to position all Iñupiat—no matter where they live or how much money they earn—as members of an impoverished underclass that is doomed to extinction. According to the calculus of the novel, the future belongs to settler-colonial Alaskans, prosperous members of the middle class, who are well prepared to survive a future marked by the ravages of climate change.

As Fairbanksans, Tammy and her family members—especially her father, Bill—serve as stereotypical representatives of urban Iñupiat. An abusive alcoholic and climate-change denier, Bill works as a cook for an oil company on the North Slope. His schedule, two weeks in Prudhoe Bay and one week in Fairbanks, gives him plenty of spare time to hunt, fish, and drink. Obsessed with his eldest daughter, he sexually assaults her at almost every opportunity. While it does not provide much historical detail, the novel attributes Bill's abusiveness and destructiveness to the cultural dislocation he suffered as a victim of assimilationist residential schools. According to the novel, Bill attended "an Indian Bureau school in Oklahoma, where he got beat up by the teachers . . . every time he forgot to speak English" and where he learned nothing about Iñupiaq culture (Waters 27).

As the novel makes clear, no amount of wealth can ameliorate the issues that Tammy's family experiences. Although Bill is "making more money than he's ever made," everyone is still profoundly unhappy (Waters 16). To make matters worse, their house is slowly sinking into the thawing permafrost underneath it, just "like the *Titanic*, tipped up and heading under" (11). In a futile attempt to address this catastrophe, Bill requests an evaluation from the Fairbanks Permafrost Technology Foundation, whose technician declares the building an uninhabitable "liability" (141). Instead of following the suggested course of action—selling their home to the Foundation and buying it back once it is fixed—Bill decides to excavate the foundation and reinforce it himself. This project ultimately ends in failure when the structure collapses into the mire and kills him.

Although they live in the rural community of Shishmaref, as opposed to Fairbanks, Tammy's first cousin George and his family members—especially his father, Cliff—experience their fair share of difficulties. According to the novel, most of these issues stem from their inability to merge modern and traditional lifeways. As George explains, "My dad, all he's ever wanted to do was live on the island, hunt, fish, get enough food to feed us all, enough furs to trade to buy the other things we need—oil, fuel—just enough to share out with everyone else and get by. . . . But that kind of life's impossible now" (Waters 99). For George, these cultural and economic issues are worsened by climate change. After a whaling accident kills a community member, he blames environmental factors, telling his father, "Akpayuk made a bad decision. He couldn't judge the weather because nobody can any more. He couldn't read the signs because the signs have all changed" (161). Shortly thereafter, he launches into an extended discussion of public health issues, focusing on the "modern disease[s]" that plague Iñupiaq communities: "You know what the major cause of death is today for Inupiats? Cancer. You know what we're getting arrested for? Number one: assaulting one another. Number two: driving drunk. Number three: sexual abuse of our own kids" (161). Note that George belongs in the third category—though he never admits it and the novel never addresses it—for he commits statutory rape and incest with Tammy. When Cliff protests that "there are problems, sure. But it's possible to find a balance," George issues a definitive, uncompromising statement on the matter: "The things we need, to continue living the way we always have, are being destroyed" (161–62).

If *Cold Comfort* presents the situation of the Iñupiat—both rural and urban—as precarious, then it characterizes the position of white, middle-class Alaskans as secure. At the midpoint, the novel introduces Dave Dervish, Tammy's former science teacher. A recent arrival in Alaska, he lives in a well-appointed log cabin with his wife, Helen, who is pregnant with their first child. When Dave invites Tammy and George to a dinner party at his home, Tammy experiences an epiphany regarding the fate of humanity: "These are the people . . . who will somehow adapt themselves, whatever happens; these are the people who will survive what's coming if anyone does. They will manage to invent something at the last minute, at two seconds to midnight, something that will preserve their calm, flat spaces and they will endure in these spaces" (Waters 180). As she sees the situation, white Americans—those who possess wealth and resources—will survive the coming climate apocalypse, not more vulnerable populations of people handicapped by racial and economic oppression.

Instead of contradicting this viewpoint, *Cold Comfort* reinforces it by concluding with the deaths of all of its major Iñupiaq characters. As noted above, Bill perishes when his house collapses into thawing permafrost, and George and Tammy die of exposure at Prudhoe Bay after an unexpected explosion derails their sabotage mission. What is important to emphasize here is that, symbolically speaking, this ending characterizes all Iñupiat as doomed to extinction because their lifeways—rural or urban, traditional or nontraditional, wealthy or poor—are incompatible with the modern world. These are not resilient, resourceful people who have endured across time by employing survivance strategies and traditional knowledge; rather, they are textbook examples of "vanishing Indians." In the end, then, *Cold Comfort* serves as an ironic justification of the colonialist and industrialist practices that it attempts to condemn.

DON REARDEN'S *THE RAVEN'S GIFT* AND THE "WHITE SAVIOR" TROPE

Although *The Raven's Gift* has not attracted as much critical scrutiny as *Cold Comfort*, TiaAnna Tidwell (Nunamiut) has described it as a "settler colonial fantasy of belonging" that depends upon the effacement of Indigeneity (37). Insofar as this insight is concerned, this scholarship jibes with mine. Tidwell, however, is more interested in the gendered dimensions of this erasure than the environmental, while it is these that I wish to highlight and examine. For the most part, *The Raven's Gift* contains fairly realistic representations of the environmental justice issues confronting the residents of the Yup'ik villages in southwestern Alaska. As it demonstrates, almost all of the problems that they experience—poverty, food insecurity, mining projects, climate change—can be attributed to the long, uneven history of capitalist resource-development in Alaska. Though these portions of *The Raven's Gift* are rich, complicated, and insightful, the ending of the book is more problematic. Instead of showcasing the resiliency of the Yup'ik during the pandemic, it casts them as helpless victims of circumstance. Incapable of saving themselves when they run out of resources, some turn to cannibalism while others wait for help to arrive from outside the community.

As an example of apocalyptic cli-fi, *The Raven's Gift* represents something of an anomaly, because anthropogenic climate change is not the primary cause of the epidemiological catastrophe that occurs in the novel. This is especially odd, given that experts have long warned about the advent of new infectious diseases caused by global warming (Markon et al. 1200–4). Importantly, though, *The Raven's Gift* positions climate change as one of many social and environmental problems—caused by settler colonialism and industrial development—that make the Yup'ik more vulnerable to the mysterious disease that infiltrates their community. In its prepandemic sections, it weaves together descriptions of the effects of climate change *and* poverty. In so doing, it highlights a host of issues that contribute to the precarity of the Yup'ik, including education, assimilation, erosion, suicide, weather, nutrition, and infrastructure.

One of the most complex discussions of these issues takes place in a prepandemic conversation between John and his friend Carl. Perplexed by the lack of basic amenities in Nunacuak, John asks, "Do you think we'll ever get running water in the houses?" After responding in the negative, Carl elaborates, blaming the problem on the lack of fossil-fuel resources in southwestern Alaska. As he explains, "If we had oil wells here, or if there were more *kass'aqs* [white people], maybe then" (Rearden 153). Somewhat ironically, he attributes the social and economic issues in the village to the lack—not the presence—of settler colonialism and industrial development along the Kuskokwim.

Shortly thereafter, Carl notes that southwestern Alaska possesses some mineral wealth—especially gold and copper—but he observes that it is unlikely to ameliorate the situation of the villagers. According to Carl, "Some company is putting a gold mine up the Kuskokwim. Maybe if they take a couple billion dollars of gold out they will think about helping us get running water, but I doubt it." Surprised by this news, John asks for more information, and Carl tells him that he opposes the Donlin Mine because it "could really cause some problems for our fishing on the Kuskokwim" (Rearden 153). As he emphasizes, though, many of his friends and relatives support the project for its employment opportunities: "People round here need work so bad, though. I don't see anyone stopping that mine. Climate change is killing all our salmon. Commercial fishing is all but dead here on the Kuskokwim" (154).

To underscore the hopelessness of the situation, Carl contrasts responses to the proposed Donlin Mine with attitudes toward the proposed Pebble Mine, another potentially destructive extraction project located in southwestern Alaska. As he speculates, "Those Natives there over the ridge, I think some people will help try to fight the mine," but only because it threatens "the headwaters of the world's last great wild salmon run." In his estimation, the Yup'ik who live along the Kuskokwim are unlikely to receive such support, because "who cares much about what happens around here, to us? They never did. Never will. We're the invisible people" (Rearden 154).[7] What is important to note here is that Carl manages to highlight and juxtapose many of the factors that in his opinion contribute to the impoverished situation of the Yup'ik, including climate change, resource development, environmental politics, and settler colonialism.

As *The Raven's Gift* shifts from its prepandemic to postpandemic timeline, it remains preoccupied with complex social and environmental issues, explicitly linking the new epidemic to those experienced during the colonial era. Thus, in a conversation with a surviving elder, John learns that "Yup'ik people been seeing bad sicknesses since when *kass'aqs* come here. Not the ducks. Not the birds that did this to the people. I've seen these kind of diseases before. When I was little *piipiq*. Smallpox, measles, influenza—so bad mostly everyone all on the river and tundra villages dies" (Rearden 41). Note that in its descriptions of Yup'ik responses to epidemic disease, the novel chooses to focus on helplessness as opposed to community strength and adaptive resiliency.

Competing for scarce resources, most of the Yup'ik survivors in *The Raven's Gift* resort to lawless acts of violence, including horrific displays of murder and cannibalism. Importantly, these latter acts have no historical precedent. During a visit to the region in 1877, anthropologist Edward Nelson—whose book *The Eskimo about Bering Strait* provided background for the novel—investigated the issue and declared that he found "no positive evidence that cannibalism had been practiced by the natives" during times of famine and disease (270). In the context of the book, the characterization of the Yup'ik as cannibals serves to heighten the dramatic tension surrounding the pandemic and the apocalypse it causes. Not insignificantly, it also perpetuates enduring stereotypes about Indigenous people as "savages," who choose to resort to barbarism in the face of food insecurity and socioeconomic collapse.

A few characters refuse to commit murder or cannibalism. Incapable of helping themselves—perhaps because of age, gender, or disability—Maggie, Rayna, and Alex decide to wait for help to arrive from outside the community. Eventually, John discovers Maggie and Rayna hiding in abandoned houses and leads them to an isolated encampment where Alex and a small group of young people are avoiding the chaos. As one of the only adult survivors, he assumes a leadership role among the children. Here, it is important to note that John is not a typical "white savior" figure, for his racial and ethnic ancestry is ambiguous. Apparently, his grandfather met his grandmother when he was stationed in the Aleutian Islands during World War II, and she may or may not have been Alaska Native. Another complication occurs at the end of the novel when Rayna performs a mystical ceremony involving a woven grass mat and a herd of caribou and adopts John into the Yup'ik community.

Throughout most of the novel, though, John sees himself as a white man. Just before he arrives in Nunacuak, he characterizes himself as "one of three white men living in a Yup'ik village in the middle of nowhere" (56). For the most part, the community residents also regard John in this way. During prepandemic times, Alex refers to his teacher as "some *kass'aq* like you," and during postpandemic times, Rayna asks Maggie to "tell us a story, in *kass'atun*, so John will understand" (162). In the end, then, John represents something akin to a "white savior" figure, who rescues the Yup'ik from both the pandemic and themselves. According to *The Raven's Gift*, these people survived all manner of threats to their existence across time, but they cannot survive this disease without the help of outsiders.

All this is to say that, much like *Cold Comfort*, *The Raven's Gift* takes the form of a settler apocalypse narrative that rehearses tired tropes that perpetuate settler colonialism and the various forms of capitalist development affiliated with it. Ignoring important historical precedents, these novels just cannot imagine what Grace L. Dillon (Anishinaabe) calls a "vibrant Indigenous presence," a future in which Alaska's Indigenous people survive and thrive independent from their colonizers (4). These failings are important to mark, for they simply do not jibe with reality. They are also prohibitive to forging the multiracial environmental coalitions that activist Naomi Klein believes could help shield "all of us from a future of climate chaos" (380). As she posits, Euro-American settlers who wish to form these coalitions "will have to become the treaty and land-sharing partners that [their] ancestors failed to be" (387). They will also have to eliminate colonialist tropes from their climate fiction.

NOTES

1. The Iñupiat are an Inuit people who reside in the northernmost coastal regions of Alaska. Iñupiaq is the singular and adjectival form of Iñupiat. It also refers to the language spoken by these people (Sakakibara 4).

2. Alaska Native is an inclusive term used to refer to the Indigenous peoples living in what is currently the state of Alaska.

3. The Yup'ik live in southwestern Alaska on the shores of the Bering Sea.

4. Bowhead whales and fur seals survived, but musk ox were eradicated from Alaska by 1900. They were reintroduced in the 1930s as part of a US government agricultural project. For more on these environmental issues, see Bathsheba Demuth's *Floating Coast: An Environmental History of the Bering Strait* (15–70), Briton Cooper Busch's *The War against the Seals: A History of the North American Seal Fishery* (95–122), and Peter C. Lent's *Muskoxen and Their Hunters: A History* (154–56).

5. For the Haida, Tlingit, and Tsimshian, potlatches are communal feasts and gift exchanges, commemorating births, deaths, or other important events. They were banned in the United States until 1934 (Carter). For the Yup'ik and Iñupiat, Kivġiq is a midwinter festival held between distant or rival villages to celebrate successful whaling ventures. Outlawed by missionaries in the early twentieth century, it was revived by the Iñupiat in 1988 (Sakakibara 174–82).

6. Opinions on ANCSA vary. Donald Craig Mitchell calls it "the most generous and innovative aboriginal claims settlement in U.S. history" (10). However, Eve Tuck (Unangax̂) condemns it as an "ideological invasion on Alaska Native life and land" (249), and Thomas R. Berger criticizes it for creating problems of inequity in Alaska's Indigenous communities (26–47).

7. Carl refers to actually existing projects. Opposition to Pebble Mine has been fierce for the reasons Carl describes. Opposition to Donlin Mine has been markedly less so.

WORKS CITED

Anson, April. "'Master Metaphor': Environmental Apocalypse and the Settler States of Emergency." *Resilience: A Journal of the Environmental Humanities*, vol. 8, no. 1, 2020, pp. 60–81.

Berger, Thomas R. *Village Journey: The Report of the Alaska Native Review Commission*. Farrar, Straus, and Giroux, 1985.

Brewster, Karen, editor. *The Whales, They Give Themselves: Conversations with Harry Brower, Sr.* U of Alaska P, 2004.

Busch, Briton Cooper. *The War against the Seals: A History of the North American Seal Fishery.* McGill-Queen's UP, 1985.

Carter, Blythe. "Tlingit Potlatches." *Haines Sheldon Museum*, 2013. www.sheldonmuseum.org/vignette/tlingit-potlatches/. Accessed 29 July 2021.

Demuth, Bathsheba. *Floating Coast: An Environmental History of the Bering Strait.* W. W. Norton, 2019.

Dillon, Grace L. "Introduction: Indigenous Futurisms, *Bimaashi Biidaas Mose*, Flying, and *Walking towards You*." *Extrapolation*, vol. 57, nos. 1–2, 2016, pp. 1–6.

Dunaway, Finis. *Defending the Arctic Refuge: A Photographer, an Indigenous Nation, and a Fight for Environmental Justice.* U of North Carolina P, 2021.

Fortuine, Robert. *Chills and Fever: Health and Disease in the Early History of Alaska.* U of Alaska P, 1989.

Ghosh, Amitav. *The Nutmeg's Curse: Parables for a Planet in Crisis.* U of Chicago P, 2021.

Jones, Ryan Tucker. *Empire of Extinction: Russians and the North Pacific's Strange Beasts of the Sea, 1741–1867.* Oxford UP, 2017.

Klein, Naomi. *This Changes Everything: Capitalism vs. the Climate.* Simon and Schuster, 2014.

Lent, Peter C. *Muskoxen and Their Hunters: A History.* U of Oklahoma P, 1999.

Lord, Nancy. *Early Warming: Crisis and Response in the Climate-Changed North.* Counterpoint, 2011.

Levihn-Kutzler, Karsten. "From Global Risk to Private Catastrophe: The Domestic and the Planetary in Daniel Kramb's *From Here* and Susannah Waters' *Cold Comfort*." *Open Library of Humanities*, vol. 4, no. 1, 2018, pp. 1–24.

Markon, Carl T., Steve T. Gray, Matthew Berman, Laura Eerkes-Medrano, Thomas Hennessy, Henry P. Huntington, Jeremy Littell, Molly McCammon, Richard Thoman, and Sarah Trainor. "Alaska." *Impacts, Risks, and Adaptation in the United States: Fourth National Climate Assessment.* Vol. 2, US Global Change Research Program, 2018, pp. 1186–1241.

Mitchell, Donald Craig. *Take My Land, Take My Life: The Story of Congress's Historic Settlement of Alaska Native Land Claims, 1960–1971.* U of Alaska P, 2001.

Moore, Jason W. "The Rise of Cheap Nature." *Anthropocene or Capitalocene?: Nature, History, and the Crisis of Capitalism*, edited by Moore, PM Press, 2016, pp. 78–115.

Napoleon, Harold. *Yuuyaraq: The Way of the Human Being*, edited by Eric Madsen, Alaska Native Knowledge Network, 1996.

Nelson, Edward. *The Eskimo about Bering Strait.* Government Printing Office, 1900.

Pierrot, Briggetta and Nicole Seymour. "Contemporary Cli-Fi and Indigenous Futurisms." *Departures in Critical Qualitative Research*, vol. 9, no. 4, 2020, pp. 92–113.

Rearden, Don. *The Raven's Gift.* Penguin, 2011.

Sakakibara, Chie. *Whale Snow: Iñupiat, Climate Change, and Multispecies Resilience in Arctic Alaska.* U of Arizona P, 2020.

Sharp, Suzanne, and Diane Hirshberg. *Thirty Years Later: The Long-Term Effect of Boarding Schools on Alaska Natives and Their Communities.* Center for Alaskan Education Policy Research, 2005.

Tidwell, TiaAnna. "Settler Colonial Belonging and Indigenous Erasure in *The Snow Child* and *The Raven's Gift*." 2017. University of Alaska Fairbanks, MA Thesis.

Trexler, Adam. *Anthropocene Fictions: The Novel in a Time of Climate Change.* U of Virginia P, 2015.

Tuck, Eve. "ANCSA as X-Mark: Surface and Subsurface Claims of the Alaska Native Claims Settlement Act." *Transforming the University: Alaska Native Studies in the Twenty-First Century,* vol. 1, 2014, pp. 240–72.

Vizenor, Gerald. *Manifest Manners: Narratives on Postindian Survivance.* U of Nebraska P, 1999.

Waters, Susannah. *Cold Comfort: Love in a Changing Climate.* Doubleday, 2006.

Whyte, Kyle. "Indigenous Science (Fiction) for the Anthropocene: Ancestral Dystopias and Fantasies of Climate Change Crises." *Environment and Planning E: Nature and Space,* vol. 1, nos. 1–2, 2018, pp. 224–42.

Black
A Speculative Almanac for the End of the World

KIMBERLY BAIN

It might be best to attend to the silhouettes of my vexation this way: What forms of anti-Black weather are imagined, crafted, manifested, and insured in the present moment? In what follows, I am preoccupied with anti-Black speculative forms (including financial speculation, climate and weather forecasting, insurance underwriting, and speculative technologies). These speculative forms are the sinews connecting climate change and racial capitalism; they are especially significant as they shape racial capitalism's (weather-dependent and -determinant, and not-so-distant) speculative futures.

My inquiry is, of course, a climatological one. This is in no small part for the ways we have seen (and some of us—too many of us—have lived through) the accumulative brutality of the climate crisis that defines the global contemporary moment. Weather, as we have seen time and again, kills.[1] And weather kills overwhelmingly in the communities most vulnerable to racial capitalist exploitation: those who are incarcerated, working class, disabled, low-income, racialized, living in the Global South, unhoused, or undocumented migrants, among others. The climate crises that have accelerated and increased in magnitude have been shaped in no small part by the anti-Black logics and practices of racial capitalism, which is ever expanding the class of people available to the violence of climate collapse.[2] As Christina Sharpe writes in *In the Wake: On Blackness and Being,* "The weather is the totality of our environments; the weather is the total climate; and that climate is anti-black" (104). A transitive law undergirds her statement here: through genocide, enslavement, dispossession, colonization, and so forth, the contemporary moment is run through with anti-Blackness. For that matter, so too are the responses, rhetorics, and technologies surrounding climate crises and climate change. In other words, the convergence of climate (as sociopolitical atmosphere and affect) and climate (as weather conditions in a given geographic locale over long durations) that we see now are nothing less than the amplitudes of modernity—which is to say, anti-Blackness.

In my attending to the many forms of anti-Black weather that are imagined, practiced, and insured in the present moment, I am unable to leave behind the question of reading. Anti-Blackness both produces and is a product of the way we read the world. This is especially so in arenas where speculative modes of reading—such as forecasting—determine not only what is possible in the now but how we imagine and secure what is possible in the future. For example, as Sharpe articulates later in *In the Wake,* the almanac (as a lexicon for the weather, dependent upon past precedent to predict future forecasts) was a climatological technology that shaped daily movements on the plantation and the slave ship and, in extension, the very shape, rhythms, and rituals of racial capitalism as it developed and perfected its logics in the system of chattel slavery in the Americas (112). Racial capitalism, in this way, has historically deployed speculative forms (part prediction, part proof) alongside climate toward its goal of abstracting the Black person into the Black body (rending flesh from body) to render Black bodies into commodities, resources for extraction, and laboring things.

As we search for new ways to read for and forecast crisis, catastrophe, and change—whether via the atmosphere, the ocean's tides, or the stock market—it is not out of hand to state the following baldly: an attention to climate and capitalism is by necessity preoccupied with anti-Blackness and anti-Black speculative forms. This, in turn, demands an attention to Black arts and letters, with especial attention to speculative genres. Black arts and letters have long taken up—explicitly, subversively, subtly—the anti-Black foundation of the world. As Aimee Bahng writes, speculative fiction is a genre "wherein cultural producers from the global financial undercommons have refused to relinquish the terrain of imagined futures [and] reconfigure speculation as a modality more fundamentally rooted in inconclusive reflection . . . The term 'speculation' has also been helpful in that it obliquely and bleakly resonates with discourse of venture capitalism. It tethers financial speculation to other forms of capitalist expansion" (8). Speculation and speculative genres, then, are intertwined, with the latter sometimes operating in tandem with the former, even as it provides a horizon for resistance. The anti-Black speculative nature of climate crisis produces its own kind of speculative genre, which includes financial speculation, climate and weather forecasting, insurance algorithms, mathematical models for infrastructural collapse, and speculative technologies for "escape." Nonetheless, Black cultural productions have theorized and transubstantiated the logics that have historically sutured race, capital, and weather together, instead turning those very abstractions into almanacs for another way of being and other ways of living across past, present, and future.

Given the centrality of speculation to racial capitalism and the nigh impossibility of demarcating any distance between the violent practices of racial capitalism and the climate crises we increasingly face, I am intrigued by the work of Black creatives who imagine the crisis of climate and capital. Thus, to theorize the question of anti-Black speculative forms at the intersection of climate and capitalism, I turn to a single (though not singular) text: the final episode of Terence Nance's 2018 HBO series *Random Acts of Flyness*.[3] Though a single text, the citational praxis of the show—embedded in its fragmented, palimpsestic, and speculative structure—invites a broader engagement with Black texts beyond the show, providing something approaching a partial almanac of Blackness. In particular, it succeeds in narrating the logics of capitalism, which preserve the structural position of Blackness as containing surplus value essential to a host of economic, social, and political functions, even as Black people remain disposable.

It is through the metaphors and materialities of the analytic *the cloud* that I enter my exploration of the convergence of climate change and capital. The cloud is a climatological phenomenon—produced by, producing of, and indicative of weather—as well as a technological one that echoes the logics of capitalism. I turn to the cloud as my analytic precisely because I am preoccupied by the question of how "the weather" and speculative racial capitalism become intimately entangled in the moment of catastrophe—catastrophes that leave strange fruit suspended upon the air. In the end, using the episode as a speculative case study to attend to cloud, climate, and capital, I find another way to articulate my preoccupation—which is to say, my vexation: When anti-Black speculative forms have shaped capitalism and climate, is there a method by which we can refuse these totalities? Are there climates where we can—finally—be? And if there aren't to be other climates until the end of the world, is there an almanac for surviving the end of the world while Black?

CATASTROPHE

Random Acts of Flyness is a compendium of Black thought. While the show has been variously defined as a sketch show, the more appropriate taxonomy might be *citational,* as the show orients each episode around a conceptual critical theme that takes viewers across various narratives, images, sounds, and so forth. The show's Black citational method makes it a rich text for engaging with the praxis of Black critical thought. This is especially true for the final episode of its first season, entitled "They Won't Go When I Go."[4] In this episode, viewers are introduced to Nina, a young Black woman who lives in New York City. The first shot of Nina is as she clocks out from her job as a waitress at a club, a montage of Nina ending her shift and making her way to the subway to return home (00:05:48–00:06:41). As Nina descends into the subway, the station announcer warns of an impending Category 5 hurricane. Passengers are warned that the approaching Hurricane Zelda is slated to hit New Drexciya, the "unmapped, underwater, autonomous zone" that has been excluded from evacuation.

New Drexciya is a direct invocation of the aquatic mythology first dreamed by the Detroit-based, '90s electronic duo (comprised of James Stinson and Gerald Donald) by the same name. Drexciya was a duo that, to use the language of Saidiya Hartman, sought to critically fabulate a past future-conditional history for Black persons via experimental and cryptic soundscapes that they produced on the Roland TR 808 drum machine.[5] As they explored in the album entitled *The Quest,* their collection of experimental sonics, Drexciya developed a mythology of Black persons who could breathe underwater. Drexciya (the name shared by both the duo and their speculative world) was the name for Black persons, descended from captive Africans, able to breathe the oceanic unbreathable by virtue of learning to breathe in their mother's wombs. They are the oceanic descendants of the children birthed underwater when their pregnant mothers were thrown overboard for being rebellious during the Middle Passage. This sonic fiction—or differently said, alternative Black history and present—of a Black society, born from pregnant captive Africans who resisted their enslavement by being destructive, disruptive, and rebellious, is the Black mythography-turned-geography upon which the show's diegetic hurricane will strike.[6]

The atmosphere, the weather, and the climate of Nina's world are full of impending catastrophe. On one level, we are faced with the catastrophe of the diegetic Category 5 Hurricane Zelda. Category 5 hurricanes (such as Hurricane Maria in 2017) are labeled as "catastrophic" on the Saffir-Simpson scale, which categorizes hurricanes specifically based upon potential damage to human-made structures in the Western hemisphere.[7] Even in cases where hurricanes get downgraded to tropical storms, the damage can be and is significant. Hurricane Sandy, which hit New York City in late October 2012, flooded the city's coastal neighborhoods and subway and roadway systems, destroyed thousands of homes and businesses, and shut down US stock trading on October 29 and 30. Meanwhile, in July 2021, Tropical Storm Elsa (which was downgraded from a Category 1 hurricane several times over the course of its duration) hit New York City, flooding significant parts of the Bronx and Harlem (which are predominantly Black neighborhoods), leaving folks stranded in their cars or struggling to board subway trains as they sloshed through waist-deep water (Shanahan and Wong).[8] The weather repeated itself when, in September of the same year, Hurricane Ida flooded basements, trapped people in their cars, and shut New York City down due to hours of nonstop rain. There's an obvious connecting line drawn between the (increasing) appearance of tropical storms and hurricanes in the northeastern parts of the United States—especially in a city like New York, which is threatened by the sea-level rises (particularly the city's financial center)—and the appearance of Hurricane Zelda in the episode. With climate change rewriting the textures of weather, it also rewrites the weather forecasts that are possible to imagine—and how we respond to those forecasts. In our current moment, for example, the MTA (Metropolitan Transportation Authority) has repeatedly announced plans to spend $2.2 million per month to hire more law enforcement. Rather than spend the funds to update the subway's crumbling infrastructure—infrastructure that is increasingly incapable of handling the wild weather changes due to climate change—the solution chosen by the corporate-state governing nexus (represented by then Governor Cuomo) was one of further policing and the further creation of populations and communities vulnerable to climate disaster.

This brings us to the other side of catastrophe: who remains excluded from the protections of the corporate-state governing nexus and who, as part of their exclusions, are included in the speculative economies of disaster capitalism. New Drexciya is declared both "unmapped" and "autonomous." Used here, the language of "autonomous" asserts New Drexciya as existing outside of the purview and therefore aid of governing bodies;

"autonomous" also asserts the unruly, disruptive, and rebellious—indeed, *racialized*—character of New Drexciya (which, within the world of the show, is located in proximity to the Bronx and Harlem). The racialized—and classed—natured of New Drexciyan residents is made overwhelmingly apparent in the changing composition of the subway riders. As we see later in the sketch, white and wealthy (read: mobile) passengers board and depart from the train early in its journey, the last white passengers exiting not so ironically at the Michelle Obama International Airport (00:06:25–00:07:00). Black passengers are aware of exactly what the airport signifies: as the last white travelers leave the train, a white couple gives Nina an awkward, pitying smile, to which Nina grimaces and shares a look with a fellow Black woman on the train. It's a look full of mockery, shade, and disdain.

Residents of New Drexciya, unlike the white and wealthy, are unable to flee the city in the face of disaster. Marked as displaceable, disposable, and sacrificial, New Drexciya becomes the site of the violent enactment of the force of the hurricane, which preys upon already preexisting social and political structures. Or better said, it is not the hurricane per se that preys on these formulations but rather the corporate-state governing nexus that continues to cement the abjection of Black people for the preservation of power. When responses to—and notably *preemption of*—disaster are orientated and organized toward "orchestrated raids on the public sphere in the wake of catastrophic events, combined with the treatment of disasters as exciting market opportunities," the question of whose bodies are valuable enough to save—and whose bodies are only worth saving when surplus value can be extracted—becomes the logic by which technologies meant to mitigate the climate crisis emerge (Klein 6). This is where CityDrive comes in.

CLOUDS

As Nina makes her way onto the 3 Train, the automated train announcer states that residents of New Drexciya will not be evacuated but instead are encouraged to "upload their consciousness to the CityDrive," a cloud-based service that stores the consciousness of a person in a nebulous, airy, white, virtual space (00:05:48–00:06:42). Rather than provide evacuation services to New Drexciya (Nina's home), lives are sacrificed for aesthetically pleasing neoliberal market imperatives that place the onus of surviving catastrophe upon the individual. Furthermore, survival is now couched in the market logics of a speculative technological process: namely CitiDrive and its ability to extract the consciousness of persons and place it—permanently—into the geography of the weather or what might be better called, here, "the cloud."

Digital information is material, both in the form of the server farms (which are little more than factories that host our digital lives) and the literal atoms that comprise the data all around us.[9] This is the case despite its ostensibly absent nature in places like the United States, where technological detritus and infrastructure are often exported to other nations via the nebulous rhetoric of "the digital." Maintaining data farms and their related infrastructure has become part and parcel of the oversized carbon footprints of a select few that drives the cycle of Anthropocenic weather that we see accelerating in our contemporary moment. In this way, the cloud is produced by and producing of the weather. And the cloud, as a digital and speculative geography (and much like all social, political, and economic geographies of our past, present, and future) is infused with the logics of modernity—which is to say that questions of extractive racial capitalism, anti-Blackness, and the long wake of reproducibility of enslavement remain.

As Charisse Burden-Stelly explicates, enslavement was a world-making project that sought to position Blackness within the structural location of containing surplus value "essential to an array of political-economic functions, including accumulation, dis-accumulation, debt, planned obsolescence, and absorption of the burdens of economic crises" while remaining worthless. It is the schism between containing value and remaining worthless that is important to my analysis here. In "Mama's Baby, Papa's Maybe: An American Grammar Book," Hortense Spillers outlines a crucial trajectory and logic that undergirded the violence of enslavement: "But I would make a distinction in this case between 'body' and 'flesh' and impose that distinction as the central one between captive and liberated subject-positions" (67). While a deeper attention to Spillers is not possible in the confines of this essay, what Spillers articulates for my thinking is the process by which the violent abstraction of personhood from embodiment is part of the replication of the grammars of racial capitalism. CityDrive is marketed as a technology capable of transporting one's consciousness to a different space—separating out the laboring self from the leisurely self. As the CityDrive headset itself states later in the episode: "CityDrive [is] your portal to virtual New York. Now you too can live a life of leisure while your avatar goes to work, walks your dog, pays your bills, checks your mail, eats your vegetables, comforts your child, cleans your house, goes to the bank, folds your laundry . . . waters your plant" (00:15:30–00:16:04). However, the CityDrive marketed to residents of New Drexciya is the promise of being digitally airlifted out of the path of a hurricane. Yet, given the long and entangled histories that trouble any easy relation between Blackness and the shipping of bodies (even digital shipping of one's embodiment, as it were) means that the act of storing Black embodiments—severing the relation between body and flesh—promises to reanimate the logics of enslavement.

As she rides the train home, Nina drifts to sleep. We too drift: between scenes of times and places we are unsure are past, future, or simply constructions of her (un)consciousness. In her dreams or memories, she waters plants under a grow light; she is suspended underwater; she rolls over in her bed. We cut to an empty train car, with Nina sitting in a different location and being crooned to by electro-soul artist, Moses Sumney. The scenes begin to repeat, but this time they are slightly askance: we see Nina's hands—the ones that previously watered the plants—extended outward, shaking, her bodily opacity failing (00:07:06–00:07:35). Nina's loss of bodily opacity—her increasing transparency—is a destructive process that comes with the terrifying erasure of Black personhood and severing of her ownership of her body. What Spillers names the "hieroglyphics of the flesh" are written into Blackness via the whippings, lacerations, brandings, and so forth on the plantation and in the hold of the ship; they are rewritten upon Blackness in other sites of capture—including soon-to-be-future ones like the cloud. Nina's increasing transparency—the seams of her data stream parted and bleeding—is, as we soon find out, Black flesh flayed open.

When we cut away from Nina's disintegrating embodiment, we land somewhere familiar. Later in the episode, we're made privy to the struggle of an elderly Black man (00:10:03–00:10:15). When we first apprehend the drowning Black elder—before we *know* the figure to be a drowning Black man—what we perceive is a curiously shaped blob: a singular, curled, and possibly mammalian life-form suspended in an oceanic surround. The *oceanic* character of the *surround* comes into being at the intersection of the visual (which fails to bring full understanding on its own) and the acoustic. The soundscapes signal the oceanic via the hydroacoustic sampling that tempers the scene. The electronic detailing evokes the textures of bubbles and bewilderment and curiosity; the acoustic compressions and rarefactions yield a pressure within the listener's ears that seems to verify and certify the state (that is, liquid) of the white, almost airy expanse.

The oceanic surround, too, is the oceanic that surrounds Blackness. As Spillers writes, "Those African persons in 'Middle Passage' were literally suspended in the 'oceanic,' if we think of the latter in its Freudian orientation as an analogy for undifferentiated identity . . . they were also nowhere at all. Inasmuch as, on any given day, we might imagine, the captive personality did not know where s/he was, we could say that they were culturally 'unmade,' thrown in the midst of a figurative darkness that 'exposed' their destinies to an unknown course" (72). The white, airy, oceanic expanse that Nina finds herself in is the same oceanic environment of the drowning elderly Black man from before. Except, we suddenly realize, it is not that Nina and the Black elder are trapped exclusively in the literal oceanic; they are, too, in the figurative oceanic. *This* oceanic is white and airy—the atmosphere, the climate, the cloud.

They are, in one way or another, being unmade in the cloud. For Nina, her body and existence have become *captive* data—captive *flesh*—held in the cloud. Trapped as she is in the cloud, Nina's body becomes white and transparent. When Blackness is understood to be a mode of relationality, it's an almost inevitable outcome that her captive digital flesh exists in a wide expanse of nothingness. This nothingness is a nothingness of antirelationality, where the status of kinlessness previously attributed to enslaved persons is reformulated through a digital, atmospheric, weather-filled geography that denies connection with another. In this way, the logics of the hold of the ship—the historical geography of captivity, forced migration, illness, and the apocalypse, a geography shaped by the weather that battered slave ships and provided captains and crews alike reason for throwing enslaved persons overboard—become transfigured into the logics of the cloud. The cloud is a future and contemporary geography of captivity, shaped by imagined invisibility and intangibility, but also shaped by the weather.

CAPITALISM

When we reemerge from the digital dreamscape, it is to Moses Sumney playing for Nina (00:07:35–00:09:30). Together, we—the viewer, Nina, and Sumney—traverse the deep, dark, sweet space of a subway tunnel, something like an underground railroad. But this space—away from the unrelenting whiteness and weathering of the cloud—offers only brief solace; his song lulls her to sleep a sleep of rest, a slight smile on her face. But once his song ends, her face twists into one of deep sadness, regret, and pain. In the end, it is unclear whether this dream montage is proof or prophecy: prophecy of what follows or proof that the future has already happened. Either way, it's too late: Nina, as we soon find out, has decided to upload her consciousness to CityDrive.

When Nina exits the train, it's with the few stragglers who remained on the train ride with her (00:09:30–00:10:02). Laden with food stuffs, her work bag, and a sleek white shopping bag, Nina walks out onto the surface of what is likely the Harlem River. Her neighbor exclaims, "Yo, Nina, don't let them fool you with that CityDrive shit." To which Nina replies, sleek white bag slapping against her leg: "Either way I gotta work." At home, when Nina boots up the CityDrive headset and begins uploading her consciousness, the process leaves her sleepy and unable to stay awake (00:15:08–00:18:30). We watch as Nina becomes unmade: the process of uploading her consciousness severs her relation to her physical body. Her synapses no longer correspond to speech and movement on the physical plane and instead become speech on the digital plane; she becomes unable to control her body, limbs flopping and posture collapsing. The upload is, as we find out only after Nina has already uploaded over 50 percent of her consciousness to the cloud, destructive. By the time Nina can consent to the upload, her home has sprung a leak: Hurricane Zelda has arrived (00:18:40–00:19:05). The weather of the external atmosphere has begun seeping into her Black home.

This is where we meet "Worry no. 4.3 Xextillion of Jungian Integer Worries that a Black Person Should Not Have to Worry About . . . Something that really happened" (00:19:05–00:19:15). As Nina narrates to us: "You arrive in the cloud, the singularity having just occurred." The singularity is, of course, Ray Kurzweil's articulation of it: "a future period during which the pace of technological change will be so rapid, its impact so deep, that human life will be irreversibly transformed" (16). The concept of the singularity has been taken up by Silicon Valley types (the most notable of them being Elon Musk), especially for the way it promises to assist humanity in transcending the bounds of the body. As Kurzweil writes, "The Singularity will represent the culmination of the merger of our biological thinking and existence with our technology, resulting in a world that is still human but that transcends our biological roots. There will be no distinction, post-Singularity, between human and machine or between physical and virtual reality" (17–18). With CityDrive, this singularity is not only possible, but in fact named as the solution to a crisis (climate change) that has come into existence precisely *because* of the unfettered accumulative logics that drive racial capitalism and—by extension—the singularity itself.

What Kurzweil and others cannot admit, let alone conceive of, is this: the singularity is an anti-Blackness which has no limit. The idea that the singularity (as the convergence of human and machine, real with the virtual) is ahead of us is false. This is least of all because enslaved persons were forced be both human and machine, real and abstract, in their very existence. Thus, the singularity as another instance of anti-Black racial capitalist logics—and in the show, its logics are amplified and accelerated by climate crisis. Both the Black elder and Nina have found their existences simultaneously fixed within the unbreathable space of the oceanic and the cloud. Despite uploading their consciousness to the cloud to escape the weather, they still must—as Nina says, one of her few pieces of dialogue in a noisy and speech-filled sketch—work. For the Black elder, the schism between person and body—"worthless" embodiment and commodity form—is finalized in his drowning. It is not difficult to imagine the same outcome awaits Nina, trapped in the cloud and unable to save her physical body. After all, does racial capitalism need the physical body when the commodity can be titrated out and retained? The Black body—already a container malleable enough to hold political-economic processes like accumulation, debt, dispossession, and so forth—is no longer needed when the virtual embodiment of the Black body can hold all this in perpetuity.

It is not incidental that the space of the cloud becomes a space for deploying weather and weathering to reproduce the captive Black body. Reproducing and renewing Black people's (whether as body or flesh) structural relation to capitalism—as commodity, as means of production, as raw material for extraction—has been one of the regimes of thought driving capitalism. As racial-capitalist futures are imagined, new grammatical structures are dreamed up to ensure that Black people remain as asymptotically close (near zero) to enslaved status as possible, finding their expression in new geographies, new temporalities, new mythologies, and new weather.

In our attending to the cloud as a speculative technology of and for capture, we must also turn to another crucial aspect of the histories of racial capitalism: the growth of insurance as a speculative financial tactic. As Ian Baucom writes, the spectre of capital functions "to convert history, for the most part, into a calculable matter of credits and debts, to reduce the vast business of empire to a column alternately labeled debt or misfortune and another labeled payment" (7). In *Random Acts,* the speculative economies that comprise insurance and underwriting do away entirely with the need for a physical body, needing only flesh to accomplish its goals. In this way, the cloud—much like the hold of the ship—becomes a site of dispossession, deploying the speculative logics of insurance.

This is not unlike the insurance practices of enslavers, which depended as much on the imagined and future conditional presence of Black enslaved persons and therefore the imagined and future conditional presence of profit. One such arena of the speculative technologies of insurance, intersecting with weather and Blackness, was the case of the slave ship Zong, where Captain Luke Collingwood and his crew threw 133 enslaved persons overboard after an ostensible bout of bad weather (Baucom 8–17). For the enslavers, the movement of Black cargo from the suffocating hold of the ship—in air thick enough to choke, wet and moist and sweet and sour with the stench of fear and sweat and death and afterbirth and pus—to the suffocating waves of the ocean was a change of little consequence. The captain, and his financial backers and prospectors in England, had already imagined the value of that Black cargo and speculated upon their worth. As part of the calculus of racial capitalism, the enslaved were dead weight and their lives only worth the insurance payout that the captain and crew would be guaranteed for the "lost" cargo.

Speculation and racial capitalism, even then, had already shaped the practice of insurance; it simply finds its continuation with Nina. As a television reporter announces in the aftermath of the hurricane: "Survivors of the Hurricane are caught in a legal limbo with insurance companies who are rejecting their claims on the basis that their so-called digital evacuation only requires settlement payments to be made in cryptocurrencies, only to be accepted in 'the cloud.' Several evacuees were only able to upload parts of their consciousness before their physical consciousness and subaquarium homes were all destroyed" (00:24:55–00:25:15). Unsurprisingly, insurers and insurance companies are among the first responders to the disaster, never, however, to assist those affected by catastrophe but rather to ensure that corporations can reap the profits of the weather. When the diegetic insurance companies in *Random Acts* attempt to provide "settlement payments" solely "in cryptocurrencies only accepted in the cloud," we are faced with something like an entire geography and entire climate of the world. Mining for cryptocurrencies, as is the case with mining for natural resources, produces such vast environmental burdens that we see the weather being replicated all over again (therefore further forcing disavowed communities into the digital "cloud"). The harmed residents of New Drexciya are left without means to—literally—buy themselves from the very corporate-state amalgamation that imagined their surplus value, underwrote it, and insured its existence. Blackness once again becomes stored, carted as cargo, and commodified.

In Nina's case, we are privy to a repeat of her dreamscape, a repeating of the flaying open of her flesh as her body becomes transparent. In her dream, her fading embodiment literally revealed the seams of the data streams that comprise her existence. To quote Marx, "all that was solid melts into air." In the montage of her existence postcatastrophe, digital Nina works nonstop. Hours upon days upon weeks pass by, with Nina trapped where we first saw her: in the kitchen of the club, cooking. There is no rest nor reprieve for Nina's existence—her body, as far as we know, is permanently severed from her person, in a medical facility after the water storm floods her apartment. The oceanic surround of the ocean; the oceanic surround of the cloud.

CARE

Thus far, I have moved through an analysis of the anti-Black climate and racial capitalism via the cloud and anti-Black speculative forms, using *Random Acts* as a case study to think the contradictions of capitalism. But as I close, I seek to find another way to articulate my sense of urgency around the intersection of climate and racial capitalism. As Jodi Melamed writes, capitalism can only "accumulate by producing and moving through relations of severe inequality among human groups" (77). Therefore, to imagine that as we face greater climate catastrophe, we are not at the core facing a deeply racialized phenomenon is to deny, once again, the ways that capitalism and its aftereffects are at their roots a project of and product of racialization. But because Blackness is both a structural position, a mode of relationality, and a structure of feeling, what it can *do* is more than replicate those violences: it can refuse, it can disrupt, it can heal. This is where I close: with the beginnings of an almanac for the end of the world.

Without the other half of herself, Nina is left to sit in her apartment, attempting to retrieve a response to her calls:

> I feel some type of way. I can't explain it.
> —No symptoms.
> I ask about the other 57 percent. Where it is?
> —Soon come.
> I asked about CitiDrive. Where is it?
> —Soon come.
> When can I go back to work?
> —Soon come.
> All I see is water.
> —Soon come. (00:24:32–00:25:30)

The "soon come" of Black being—the Black almanac for navigating the weather, living through disaster, and rewriting the end of the world as abolition—is the "soon come" of community. It's how Nina reunites with herself: through the Black folk who sit by her side and whisper to her, who groom her body, who care for her impossibly ravaged self. The end of the world had arrived, but those who were best equipped to help Nina breathe once again, in atmospheres different and no less or more breathable, were the community. A community already come. No speculation needed.

NOTES

1. Weather both in terms of the earth-based meteorological events of climate but also weather as climate (as in racial climate), weather as in *weathering*.

2. In my attention to the urgent question of anti-Black climate, I am compelled to turn to racial capitalism as my way of attending to the question of class. This has, in small part, to do with the way racial capitalism and whiteness have discursively arranged and assembled class along stratifications that serve whiteness. (Under this logic, the working class is always white and the "welfare queen" is always Black, whether or not this is materially or historically true.) In this way, class serves as a political and sociological shorthand that has unfortunately been trafficked as a phenomenon in a way that obscures more than it reveals, rendering opaque the violent contortions of abstraction and generalization that produce taxonomies of life under capitalism.

3. *Random Acts* is widely available for streaming via Apple TV, YouTube, Amazon Video, and HBO, among others.

4. Which is, of course, a citation of the eponymous song by Stevie Wonder, which has been covered by the likes of Chance the Rapper.

5. Though electronically composed and therefore strikingly *unlike* the actual sound of the drum, the board can sonically provide a transmuted practice of drumming throughout the Black artistic diaspora. The 808 is the sound of breaking,

chopping, screwing, remixing, and technological hacking for Black artists who could not afford the more expensive drum machines for music production. But it also produced a Black sociality that defined and continues to define what it means to listen with others and dance with others. The 808 is a Black soundscape that escapes the visual, escapes the single subject.

6. Drexicya as a sonic fiction is crucial—especially as this final episode of *Random Acts* is primarily a sonic one. This sketch has comparatively little dialogue compared to other core sketches in the show. Instead, we are keyed into Nina's world through its atmosphere: the sounds of the ambient life, the music she plays in her home once she arrives, the dire announcements by technology, etc.

7. Notably, the naming of Hurricane Zelda is contrary to hurricane-naming conventions of our contemporary moment, conventions that exclude names beginning with Q, U, W, X, and Z. This means there are twenty-five names per year available for naming hurricanes, with storms in excess of the twenty-fifth usually named using the Greek alphabet. The question, of course, is: how has the weather changed and altered in this future-present, such that hurricane naming conventions—the very grammars by which we identify and articulate climate catastrophe and natural disaster—have shifted to include that which was previously excluded for lack of need?

8. Elsa was not unique for flooding NYC—there have been numerous instances of tropical storms and hurricanes destroying and flooding predominantly Black neighborhoods for years, especially Hurricane Katrina.

9. It's estimated that by 2245 half the atoms on the planet could be digital data. This is because data consumes energy and, therefore, while considered to be "weightless," it does indeed have a kind of material form. While that mass is currently infinitesimally small, the rate at which we produce data means that before long, to reverse a much-quoted line from Marx, all that is air will become solid.

WORKS CITED

Bahng, Aimee. *Migrant Futures: Decolonizing Speculation in Financial Times*. Duke UP, 2018.
Baucom, Ian. *Spectres of the Atlantic: Finance Capital, Slavery, and the Philosophy of History*. Duke UP, 2005.
Burden-Stelly, Charisse. "Modern U.S. Racial Capitalism: Some Theoretical Insights." *Monthly Review*, vol. 72, no. 3, July 2020. https://monthlyreview.org/2020/07/01/modern-u-s-racial-capitalism/.
Hartman, Saidiya. "Venus in Two Acts." *Small Axe*, vol. 12, no. 2, 2008, pp. 1–14.
Klein, Naomi. *The Shock Doctrine*. Picador, 2008.
Kurzweil, Ray. *The Singularity Is Near: When Humans Transcend Biology*. Viking, 2005.
Melamed, Jodi. "Racial Capitalism." *Critical Ethnic Studies*, vol. 1, no. 1, 2015, pp. 76–85.
Nance, Terence. "They Won't Go When I Go." *Random Acts of Flyness*, episode 6, HBO, 8 Sept. 2018.

Shanahan, Ed, and Ashley Wong. "Heavy Rains Pound New York City, Flooding Subway Stations and Roads." *The New York Times*, 8 July 2021. https://www.nytimes.com/2021/07/08/nyregion/flooding-subways-nyc.html.

Sharpe, Christina Elizabeth. *In the Wake: On Blackness and Being.* Duke UP, 2016.

Spillers, Hortense. "Mama's Baby, Papa's Maybe: An American Grammar Book." *Diacritics*, vol. 17, no. 2, 1987, pp. 64–81.

PART III

Class Privilege and Climate Anxiety

Class and Revolution in the Climate Fictions of Kim Stanley Robinson
Transition to Postcapitalism

ANDREW MILNER

The Californian science fiction (SF) writer Kim Stanley Robinson is a declared ecosocialist and arguably the most distinguished acolyte of Fredric Jameson, America's leading Marxist literary critic. Robinson won the John W. Campbell Memorial Award for Best SF Novel for *Pacific Edge* in 1991, Hugo Awards for *Green Mars* and *Blue Mars* in 1994 and 1997 respectively, and Nebula Awards for *Red Mars* in 1993 and for *2312* in 2013. His work has thus enjoyed professional, fan, and academic legitimacy: the Nebula Awards are made by a professional writers association, the Science Fiction and Fantasy Writers of America; the Hugo Awards by a fan organization, the World Science Fiction Society; and the Campbell Memorial Award by a panel of experts appointed by the Center for the Study of Science Fiction at the University of Kansas. Jameson has dedicated two books to Robinson; in 2008 Robinson was named a "Hero of the Environment" by *Time* magazine; and in 2010 he was Guest of Honor at the 68th World Science Fiction Convention. In an article published in the journal *Utopian Studies*, Robinson tells of how a friend alerted him to the key flaw in his first utopian novel, *Pacific Edge* (1990): "Stan . . . there are guns under the table." This remark provided *Red Mars* (1993) with a chapter title, whilst the *Mars* trilogy as a whole developed a detailed account of three political revolutions. Robinson explains that this was a deliberate choice on his part, because "I felt that in *Pacific Edge* I had dodged the necessity of revolution" (4). In the same article, he also elaborates on the special significance of science and scientists in his SF: "I had . . . come to feel that many people, and especially many of my leftist colleagues, thought of science as merely the instrument of power. . . . To me it seemed that we actually exist in a situation that can better be described as 'science versus capitalism': a world in which smaller progressive concepts . . . were going to be defeated . . . unless they were aligned with the one great power that might yet still successfully oppose a completely capitalist future, which was science" (6).

The content of scientific research can indeed operate thus and will perhaps tend increasingly to do so as late capitalism proves increasingly destructive of the preconditions for organic life. But research findings are not in themselves a social force or "power." To become such, they need to be socially organized, as for example in the April 2017 Marches for Science in the US and elsewhere, in opposition to the Trump Administration's "War on Science." These marches were organized by professional associations, community groups, and labor unions. The involvement of professional associations and labor unions serves to remind us that the vast majority of scientific researchers are in fact employees, or what Marx would have termed proletarians, which, in turn, reminds us that organized labor has historically been the one great social power to resist capital. Yet recent climate fictions, even those by avowed socialists like Robinson, hardly ever depict the organized working class as a social force capable of preventing anthropogenic—or should it be capitalogenic?[1]—global heating. This essay will explore how Robinson negotiates the transition to postcapitalism in his later work, from *Forty Signs of Rain* (2004) through to *New York 2140* (2017) and *The Ministry for the Future* (2020).

THE *SCIENCE IN THE CAPITAL* TRILOGY AND *GREEN EARTH*

On Robinson's own reading, the *Mars* trilogy is a revolutionary utopia. His next two utopian novels, he explains, were *Antarctica* and *The Years of Rice and Salt* ("Remarks" 4–5). It could, however, be argued that these also dodge the "necessity of revolution," the first by substituting science for politics, the second by projecting an alternative history of the past into an alternative future. But in Robinson's next novel, *Forty Signs of Rain*, as in the whole of the *Science in the Capital* trilogy and its eventual omnibus edition as *Green Earth*, politics once again becomes paramount, albeit politics of a kind that is deliberately nonrevolutionary. Robinson's work is often described as "hard SF" and is justly famous for the quality of its scientific research. In the *Science in the Capital* trilogy, however, where the subject matter appears closest to its author's deepest concerns, the reader is almost overwhelmed by the details, not only of the science but also of the internal mechanisms of scientific policy-making. Indeed, remarkably little actually happens in the first volume, *Forty Signs of Rain,* until the spectacular flooding of Washington, DC, at its conclusion (326–56). *Fifty Degrees Below,* which deals with the stalling of the Gulf Stream, and *Sixty Days and Counting,* which recounts the opening stages of the Presidency of the environmentally activist former Californian senator, Phil Chase, are more fast-moving but still often overburdened with scientific and technical detail. Moreover, the whole trilogy suffers from a preoccupation with American internal politics that might not excite much international interest, even if the US were still the only global superpower. The trilogy's central protagonist, Frank Vanderwal, is a Californian biomathematician and rock climber whose initial cynicism about science policy is eventually superseded by active enthusiasm for a Chase administration. Chase himself is an idealized amalgam of an Al Gore who managed to get elected and a Barack Obama who managed to get things done. It is easy to see why American readers might find both Vanderwal and Chase plausible and attractive, but non-Americans neither. This is surmise, of course, but nonetheless only the first volume has as yet been translated into Spanish, none into German, Italian, Czech, Polish, or Russian (or, for that matter, Japanese or Chinese).

In *Green Earth,* the trilogy's 1,632 pages are reduced by about three hundred pages and much of the political and scientific policy detail is cut back (xiii). In his author's introduction, Robinson explains that he had intended to write a "realist novel" as if it were SF, "describing Washington D.C. as if it were orbiting Aldebaran," but concedes that "afterward it seemed possible that occasionally I might have gone too far" (xii). The key institutions it depicts—the Presidency, the Senate and the Pentagon, the Republican and Democrat political parties, the National Oceanic and Atmospheric Administration, the National Science Foundation, and the University of California San Diego—are indeed each recognizable from contemporary American society. But in the novel they are confronted by a series of climate crises that might well occur in the near future but have not done so as yet. These are each, thus, examples of what Darko Suvin would describe as a "novum" (63), that is, a novelty or innovation absent from extratextual reality that nonetheless drives a fictional narrative, and they thereby give Robinson's realist novel a distinctly science-fictional character. In "Part One: Forty Signs of Rain," the melting Arctic ice cap causes coastal California to be plunged into the "June Gloom" of "a permanent El Niño," while extensive and excessive rains beset the entire country and eventually transform an inundated Washington, DC, into a "city floored with water" (*Green Earth* 21, 256). In "Part Two: Fifty Degrees Below," meltwater from the collapsing ice caps causes the Gulf Stream to stall, which in turn results in much colder temperatures, bordering on a new Ice Age, all around the North Atlantic: "It was one of the ironies of their time that global warming was about to freeze Europe and North America" (456). In "Part Three: Sixty Days and Counting," sea levels rise very rapidly as carbon emissions cook the planet, culminating in near-catastrophe in China: "the Chinese have trashed China itself, and . . . entered a major ecological crash. . . . The cumulative impacts were going to kill entire regions and endanger the lives of one-sixth of humanity" (1044).

Climate mitigation is a recurrent theme in the novel, from Yann Pierzinski's algorithmic calculation that the introduction of genetically altered lichen into temperate forests will result in a carbon dioxide drawdown of billions of tons (147), through Diane Chang's proposals for carbon capture and sequestration (370), to the Quibler family's installation of solar panels in their own home (1064). But the single most spectacular act of mitigation occurs as climate engineering in Part Two, when the United States Navy is put to work on an international project to disperse billions of tons of salt into the Arctic and Atlantic Oceans in order to raise salinity levels and thereby restart the Gulf Stream (652–53). Negative adaptation, or harm minimization, is also a recurrent theme. The central motif here is Khembalung, a fictional low-lying island state near the Bay of Bengal, at immediate risk from rising sea levels and extreme weather (102). As the Khembali ambassador, Drepung, explains to Anna Quibler, "Over the years we have built a nice town. . . . The whole island has been ringed by dikes. Lots of work. Hard labor. . . . Dutch advisors helped us. Very nice" (48). But even Dutch engineering proves ultimately insufficient: just as Vanderwal and the Quiblers are visiting, Khembalung is finally overwhelmed by catastrophic floods (400–401). This means the demise of the island itself, but not of its Buddhist culture, which the Khembalis carry with them into resettlement in Maryland (650, 657). In ancient Tibetan scripture, Khembalung is one of the mythical "hidden lands" created by the Indian Buddhist master Padmasambhava. Both Robinson's use of the name and the novel's more general tendency to romanticize Khembali Buddhism are instances of a primitivist trope common in contemporary Western climate fiction. But there is nothing romantic about the fictional island's fate, which is very likely to be shared by real-world islands such as Tuvalu and Kiribati:

"it looked like a shallow green bowl, submerged in brown water until only an arc of the bowl's rim remained in air" (404).

Insofar as *Green Earth* toys with the notion of a positive outcome from climate change, this is centered around Chase's election to the US presidency. When we first meet him, Chase is caught up in the routine frustrations of the practical politics of combating global warming, busily presenting climate bills, sanguinely taking what he can from the senatorial committee and Congress, always under pressure to do more from Charlie Quibler, his environmental policy advisor. "So Phil! Are you going to do something about global warming now?" Charlie shouts from a launch sailing along the Mall, at the end of Part One. "I'll see what I can do!" Chase replies (282). In Part Two, Chase announces his intention to run for the presidency very spectacularly, from a hot air balloon at the North Pole: "This beautiful ocean, free of ice for the first time in humanity's existence, is sign of a clear and present danger" (454). He wins the election and takes the oath, pledging to explore all peaceful means "to hand on to the generations to come a world that is as beautiful and bountiful as the one we were born into" (752). This implies more than mere climate mitigation, however: it turns out to offer the promise of a distinctly positive form of quasi-utopian adaptation. So, in a "Cut to the Chase" blog, written shortly after he survives an assassination attempt, the president writes that:

> empires are one of the most evil and destructive of human systems. . . . America . . . was so successful that we became an empire by accident. Then we had to stand down. . . . Capital is created by everyone, and should be owned by everyone. . . . And the Earth is owed our permanent care. And we have the capability to care for the Earth and create for every one of us a sufficiency of food, water, shelter, clothing, medical care, education, and human rights. . . . Eventually I think what will happen is that we will build a culture in which no one is without a job, or shelter, or health care, or education, or the rights to their own life. Taking care of the Earth and its miraculous biological splendor will then become the long-term work of our species. We'll share the world with all the other creatures. It will be an ongoing project that will never end. (478–79)

This passage is from *Sixty Days and Counting*, but it is omitted from *Green Earth*. It's difficult to know why exactly Robinson chose to delete those lines, whether he considered them "telling readers things they already knew," "extraneous details," or "excess verbiage" (*Green Earth* xii). But it strikes me as likely to be none of these. Rather, I suspect the decision arose from a growing awareness, based in the empirical experience of contemporary American realities, of just how implausible it would appear to many readers, perhaps most, that any Democrat president could ever write such things.

2312 AND *AURORA*

Robinson's account of his utopian novels ends here, but his utopian practice continued thereafter, most immediately with *2312*, set in the twenty-fourth century, and *Aurora*, set between the twenty-sixth and thirtieth centuries. Both are what Raffaella Baccolini and Tom Moylan would call a "critical dystopia," that is, a dystopia containing within itself utopian elements that hold the promise of an eventual utopian outcome; both are concerned with climate change; in both, Mars, Venus, Mercury, the Jovian and Saturnine moons, and many of the asteroids are already inhabited by humans and thereby subject to some degree of terraforming; in both, Earth is depicted as ravaged by the negative consequences of anthropogenic extreme climate change; and in both, serious attempts are made to mitigate those consequences. These are at their most spectacular in *2312*, where the protagonists and eventual lovers, the Mercurian artist Swan Er Hong and the Titanian diplomat Fitz Wahram, help to return thousands of extinct or near-extinct species to Earth from the asteroid terraria—artificial ecosystems built in the hollowed-out interiors of asteroids—in which they've been preserved. Robinson's description of the resultant landings is simultaneously inspirational, surreal. and vaguely comic: "It looked like a dream, but . . . it was real, and the same right now all over Earth: into the seas splashed dolphins and whales, tuna and sharks. Mammals, birds, fish, reptiles, amphibians: all the lost creatures were in the sky at once, in every country, in every watershed. Many of the creatures descending had been absent from Earth for two or three centuries. Now all back, all at once" (395). Earth itself, "the planet of sadness" (303), is still trapped in a system of predatory late capitalism—hence the scale of the environmental damage—but the rest of the solar system is run along socialistic lines, in a future version of the Mondragon system of workers cooperatives currently operating in Euskadi.

Aurora's main storyline is the attempt to establish a human colony on Aurora, an Earth-like moon of Tau Ceti's Planet E. This is ultimately unsuccessful because, as a dying settler observes, "any new place is going to be either alive or dead. If it's alive it's going to be poisonous, if it's dead you're going to have to work it up from scratch" (178). The colony is abandoned, and a minority of the would-be settlers decide to return to Earth. They nearly starve en route but are saved by the novel's primary narrator, the wonderfully intelligent "Ship," a quantum computer AI, which puts them into hibernation and finally sacrifices itself in order to send 616 survivors back to Earth. Their home planet, they have already learned, has been seriously damaged by global heating: "on Earth the sea level was many meters higher than it had been when their ship had started its voyage, and the carbon dioxide level in Earth's atmosphere was around 600 parts per million, having been brought down significantly from the time Ship had left. . . . That suggested carbon drawdown efforts" (271).

The scale of environmental catastrophe only becomes fully apparent, however, after their return. Sea levels have risen by twenty-four meters during the twenty-second and twenty-third centuries, all Earth's beaches are drowned, and, despite the attempts at carbon drawdown, sea levels have thus far barely fallen: "Yes, they are terraforming Earth. . . . They are calling it a five-thousand-year project. . . . It'll be a bit of a race with the Martians" (436). *Aurora* subverts the conventions not only of the generation starship subgenre but also of almost all space travel and first contact SF. But its very pessimistic estimate of how long it would take to terraform Earth or Mars—thousands of years—also subverts, or at least runs contrary to, the original expectations of the *Mars* trilogy. In the novel's denouement, Freya, the colonists' informal leader, leads the survivors into an alliance with the "Earthfirsters," a group working on landscape restoration, specifically beach return, who are opposed to the deep space exploration still advocated by the "space cadets." As one Earthfirster explains to Freya: "We don't like the space cadets. . . . This idea of theirs that Earth is humanity's cradle is part of what trashed the Earth in the first place" (439). Desperately damaged though Earth undoubtedly is, the still-dominant late-capitalist mode of production is subject to clear and effective challenges by utopian enclaves and communities: the latter-day Mondragon cooperators in *2312*, the Earthfirsters in *Aurora*. And in both novels, the utopians are firmly on the side of science and scientists, as they had been in the *Mars* trilogy.

FROM *NEW YORK 2140* TO *THE MINISTRY FOR THE FUTURE*

New York 2140 is the first of Robinson's novels to depict a specifically utopian outcome from global climate crisis. Initially, climate change appears to function only as a dystopian setting: by the early to mid-twenty-second century, sea levels have risen by fifty feet, so that the whole of Lower Manhattan has long since been flooded. But the buildings that remain standing are still inhabitable, their lower floors transformed into dockyards, the streets that once ran between them into canals traversed by vaporettos and water taxis. Mise en scène established, the main plot seems to be a detective mystery about the disappearance of two "coders," Ralph Muttchopf and Jeffrey Rose, or "Mutt and Jeff," from their temporary home on the "farm floor" of the Met Life tower on Madison Square. Jeff has already explained to Mutt and to the reader why "the world is fucked": "It's not just that there are market failures. It's that the market is a failure. . . . Things are sold for less than it costs to make them. . . . We've been paying a fraction of what things really cost to make, but meanwhile the planet, and the workers who made the stuff, take the unpaid costs right in the teeth" (4). The mystery narrative turns out to be the trigger for a more important political narrative, which moves the novel toward its eventual utopian climax. And that too is a result of climate change: Hurricane Fyodor batters the city so badly as to prompt what amounts to a popular constitutional revolution.

The novel is divided into eight parts, each subdivided into eight sections, each devoted to a particular character or characters: Mutt and Jeff, the two kidnapped coders; Inspector Gen Octaviasdottir, a New York Police Department detective called in to investigate their disappearance; Franklin Garr, a market trader for the aptly named WaterPrice; Vlade Marovich, the superintendent, or manager, of the building from which Mutt and Jeff disappeared; an anonymous New York citizen who explains periodically how the city works; Amelia Black, a "cloud" star, famous for taking off her clothes, who heads an internet show about wildlife survival; Charlotte Armstrong, a lawyer defending the rights of immigrants who calls in Inspector Gen to investigate Mutt and Jeff's disappearance; and Stefan and Roberto, two twelve-year-old "water rats," orphaned scavengers with their own scavenged boat, busily involved in their own submarine explorations. Inspector Gen, Franklin, Amelia, and Charlotte are all Met Life tower tenants, Vlade also lives in the tower, and Stefan and Roberto scavenge around its periphery. The legal status of such property in the "intertidal" is open to dispute, since it has in effect become a new commons. The Met building itself is a cooperative, but some anonymous entity wants to buy it for twice its declared value and is apparently also willing to sabotage the building by drilling holes that will let water into the basement floors. As the citizen observes, "wherever there is a commons, there is enclosure" (210).

If *Green Earth*'s Phil Chase had been an Al Gore figure, then the various inhabitants of the Met building turn out to be a composite Bernie Sanders. Vlade plays a crucial role in rescuing Mutt and Jeff from the sunken container in which they've been imprisoned (*New York 2140* 314–16). Franklin advises Charlotte that a "financial general strike" organized by the Householders' Union, could prevent a Government bailout of the banks (348–49). After the hurricane, Inspector Gen faces down the armed private security forces "protecting private property" in Upper Manhattan (515). Amelia announces on camera that "it's democracy versus capitalism, we the people have to band together and take over. . . . Anyone who stops payment on their odious debts . . . immediately becomes a full member of the Householders' Union" (528). Charlotte persuades her ex-husband, Larry Jackman, now head of the Federal Reserve, that bank nationalization should be the price for a financial bailout, and runs for Congress as a Democrat, campaigning against the banks: "Make that whole giant leech on the real economy into a credit union, and squeeze all that blood money we've lost back into us" (554). She is elected (574), the banks are nationalized (601), Congress passes a "Piketty tax" on income and capital assets (602), and "a leftward flurry of legislation" is "LBJed through Congress" (604). Whereas in *Green Earth* a charismatic Democratic president had saved the world, in *New York 2140* Robinson's hopes are vested in radical Democratic congresswomen and the good fortune that the Federal Reserve might be headed by one of their ex-husbands.

The novel's utopian conclusion is complemented by a whole series of individual happy endings: Stefan and Roberto really do discover sunken treasure, British gold from the Revolutionary War aboard the remains of *HMS Hussar*; Vlade and his ex-wife, Idelba, really do get back together; Charlotte really does strike up a successful sexual relationship with Franklin, who is sixteen years her junior; the political battle for New York really is "a Pyrrhic defeat" in which "the losers of a Pyrrhic victory . . . are really the winners. . . . They lose, then they say to each other, Hey we just lost a Pyrrhic victory! Congratulations!" (598). The key weakness, however, is that all this happiness is far too easily bought, most especially at the political level.

The notion that either of America's two pro–Big Business parties can ever be converted to ecosocialism is surely radically improbable. As Gore Vidal famously observed: "There is only one party in the United States . . . and it has two right wings: Republican and Democrat" (268). And at one level, Robinson knows this to be the case: "We can't imagine the bridge over the Great Trench, given . . . the massively entrenched power of the institutions that shape our lives—and the guns that are still there under the table, indeed right on the table" ("Remarks" 8). The improbability level is expanded, moreover, by the fact that in the novel neither any significant changes to the American constitution nor any significant changes to the banking system will have been achieved between now and 2140. Given institutional arrangements as resistant to change as these—arrangements that have survived, and indeed prospered during, a fifty-foot rise in sea levels—how realistically likely is it that all this could be effectively challenged as a result of one hurricane, no matter how devastating? Ultimately, the novel's utopia turns out to be "utopian" in the pejorative sense of being hopelessly impractical.

This utopianism is genuinely Robinson's own, not merely that of the novel. As he has recently explained: "We could use the Democratic Party . . . to elect a majority in Congress to enact a New Deal flurry of changes. Corporations could squeal but they couldn't make the army go onto the streets against the people. In this country the corporations can't do that" (Robinson and Feder 97). Equally improbably, in Robinson's 2018 novel *Red Moon*, he projects similarly utopian aspirations onto the Chinese Communist Party. Strictly speaking, *Red Moon* is not a climate fiction, but it does nonetheless explore environmentalist thematics, especially in the reflections on "Green Beijing" by Ta Shu, a famous Chinese poet and travel journalist (147, 199). It is also very much a novel about revolutionary—or, at least, quasirevolutionary—social change. *Red Moon* is set in 2047–2048, the year in which Hong Kong is due to be fully absorbed into the People's Republic of China, at a time when China has already become the dominant force in lunar exploration and colonization. The eponymous red moon thus refers literally to a solar eclipse that bathes the lunar surface in dusky red light but metaphorically to the extensive Chinese presence on the moon. The main plot concerns the internal Chinese power struggles in the run-up to the Twenty-Fifth Congress of the CCP: President Shanzhai is working to secure the succession for Huyou, minister of state security, the worst of the current rightist careerists, whilst Finance Minister Chan Guoliang and head of the Central Commission for Discipline Inspection Peng Ling are sympathetic to the "New Leftists," who hope to continue Xi Jinping's attempt to steer towards "socialism with Chinese characteristics" (131–34).

The novel's three main characters, who meet each other on the moon, are Ta Shu, the American Fred Fredericks, a technical officer at the Swiss Quantum Works, and Chan Guoliang's daughter Chan Qi, a leading dissident who also happens to be five months pregnant. In different ways, all three are involved in the bloodless revolutions that engulf both the USA and the PRC: "In the US, Congress had finished nationalizing the major banks. . . . Demonstrators and some legislators were demanding a universal basic income . . . supported by progressive taxation on . . . income and capital assets. . . . People were in the streets, but mainly to celebrate a return to democracy. . . . It was hard to shoot such crowds. . . . In that fundamental sense, it was the same in China. The army and security forces were so far holding off." (432). And once again it all ends happily: Peng is elected president and Chan premier, Qi has the baby aided by Fred, and everyone escapes repeated assassination attempts by the PLA's reactionary "Red Spear."

Like *New York 2140*, Robinson's most recent novel, *The Ministry for the Future*, perhaps his most impressive climate fiction to date, depicts a specifically utopian outcome from climate crisis. But where *New York 2140* pursued a fundamentally constitutionalist political resolution and *Red Moon* a quasirevolutionary option, *The Ministry for the Future* attempts an interesting combination of both. The constitutional option revolves around the eponymous Ministry located in Zurich, which is established in 2025 as a Subsidiary Body for Implementation of the Paris Agreement. Its Irish head, Mary Murphy, is the nearest the novel has to a protagonist. The revolutionary terrorist option is represented by the Indian "Children of Kali," who use drones to bring down sixty passenger jets in a matter of hours and, later, to infect millions of cattle with bovine spongiform encephalopathy (BSE), or mad cow disease (229). The novel moves backwards and forwards between personal narratives, factual summaries of climate science, and "objective" slices of future history. It opens with an unprecedented heat wave in India that kills twenty million people, viscerally described from the point of view of an American aid worker, Frank May, who becomes the sole survivor of a mass death, subsequently suffers post-traumatic stress disorder (PTSD), and later becomes a comparatively ineffectual ecoterrorist. Robinson's use of the word "poached" in this chapter, to describe the deaths of people fleeing the heat to shelter in a nearby lake, is powerfully disturbing (12).

Subliminally, the catastrophe changes everything, to borrow a phrase from Naomi Klein: "The culture of the time was rife with fear and anger, denial and guilt, shame and regret, repression and the return of the repressed.... The Indian heat wave stayed a big part of it" (227).

By comparison with Robinson's earlier fictions, *The Ministry for the Future* is much more sympathetic to ecoterrorism and also, incidentally, to vegetarianism: "Of course many people were quick to point out that these Children of Kali were hypocrites and monsters, that Indians didn't eat cows and ... that coal-fired power plants in India had burned a significant proportion of the last decade's carbon burn.... Then again those same Indian power plants were being attacked on a regular basis" (230). Robinson is clear, however, that ecoterrorism really works: "in the forties and ever after, less beef got eaten. Less milk was drunk. And fewer jet flights were made" (229–30). More significantly, he also suggests that the Children of Kali might actually be an offshoot of the Ministry itself. Murphy's Indian chief of staff, Badim Bahadur, admits to having established a "black wing" and warns her that "there might be some people who deserve to be killed" (115). Later, an anonymous narrator, who might well be Bahadur, tells of an encounter with the Children, in which he announced: "I understand you. I've helped you, I've helped work like yours all over the world.... I've done more to stop the next heat wave than anyone you have ever met. You've done your part, I've done mine.... I am Kali" (390–91). This combination of constitutionalism and terrorism leads directly to the novel's utopian outcome. But neither of these options owes very much to anything remotely resembling working-class self-activity. And, as with *New York 2140* and *Red Moon*, the price of utopia is bought far too cheaply to be entirely credible: "Aircraft carriers? Sunk. Bombers? Blown out of the sky. An oil tanker, boom, sunk in ten minutes. One of America's eight hundred military bases around the world, shattered.... The war on terror? It lost" (347).

LEARNING FROM WILLIAM MORRIS

Robinson's visions of the United States and the People's Republic, the American Democratic Party and the Chinese Communist Party, the Ministry for the Future and the Children of Kali, seem ultimately implausible. This is primarily a textual matter, not a question of whether or not these or similar ideas would or would not work in the real world but rather a statement that there is little intratextual plausibility to the mechanisms by which utopia is achieved within the novels. Comparison with William Morris's *News from Nowhere* serves to make the point. Whatever we make of Morris's utopia—and even if we positively prefer Edward Bellamy's *Looking Backward*—the processes by which it is brought about are eminently plausible, unsurprisingly so perhaps, insofar as they rehearse the real history of the Paris Commune and in some respects anticipate that of the Russian Revolutions of 1905 and 1917. The key issue here is what V. I. Lenin dubbed "dual power," that is, the creation of alternatively legitimated alternative institutions with their own alternative armed forces. For Lenin and most subsequent Leninists, this was a uniquely Russian phenomenon pertaining to the immediate struggle between the Provisional Government and the Petrograd Soviet during 1917 (48). But in reality almost all major revolutions have been predicated on similar such institutions: the Commons and the London Trained Bands, later the New Model Army, in England; the Provisional Congresses and the Continental Army in America; the National Constituent Assembly and the National Guard in France. Here, Morris's Marxism turns out to be oddly astute. So, in *News from Nowhere,* the ruling class's parliament and government are directly challenged by the working class's "Committee of Public Safety." And Morris's Old Hammond is at pains to remind William Guest that: "One claim . . . was of the utmost immediate importance. . . . This was the claim of recognition and formal status for the Committee of Public Safety, and all the associations which it fostered under its wing" (312).

Dual power in this extended sense is almost certainly a necessary corollary of the sad truth that there are guns under the table. The *Mars* trilogy had acknowledged this, but, as Robinson's focus shifted from Mars to New York and thence to Beijing and Zurich, the lesson seems to have been unlearned. Robinson's Jeff tells Mutt that the workers are exploited, but the sources of resistance in these later novels are never in any obvious sense proletarian, not the radical Democrats nor the Chinese New Left, not the NSF nor the US Navy, not the Khembalis, not the Earthfirsters nor the NYPD, not the Householders' Union nor the Federal Reserve, not the Ministry nor its black wing. There are thus no representations of characteristically working-class forms of struggle: no workplace sabotage, no slowdowns, no strikes, no picket lines, no union halls, no labor unions. The absence is particularly striking in *New York 2140,* which is set in what is in reality, after Hawai'i, the second most unionized state in the American Union (Bureau of Labor Statistics).

The obvious question to ask is why America's leading socialist SF writer, the protégé of America's leading Marxist literary critic, should evince so little interest in the politics of organized labor. My guess is that this is an effect of the persistence into the twenty-first century of the ideological residues of postmodernism, one of the twin hegemonic belief systems of twentieth-century late capitalism, the other being neoliberal economics. Certainly, there is nothing in empirically observable social reality to suggest the irrelevance of either class in general or organized labor in particular. No doubt, labor has been overwhelmingly on the defensive since the early 1980s across much of the Western world. Sociologists increasingly identify two distinct systems of hegemony operating during the post–Second World War period: the Keynesian or social democratic system, which lasted from the late 1940s until the late 1970s, characterized by the nationalization of key industries, an extensive welfare state sustained by progressive taxation, and strong labor unions; and the Friedmanite or neoliberal system, which lasted from the early 1980s until the Global Financial Crisis of 2007–8, characterized by the looting of the public purse through so-called privatization schemes, the redistribution of wealth and income from labor to capital and from the poor to the rich through increasingly regressive taxation policies and the weakening of labor unions through the imposition of legal restraints on their capacity to organize and act.[2] The central achievement of neoliberalism is thus, as Thomas Piketty has shown, that early twenty-first-century levels of global inequality are returning to the historical high attained in Europe during the period immediately prior to the First World War (438). But this does not mean that organized labor has somehow been definitively beaten, as both neoliberal economists and postmodern cultural critics are inclined to suggest. Short of perennial fascism—Jack London's *The Iron Heel*—organized labor cannot be definitively beaten, if only because the operation of labor on nature is ultimately the source of all value. This is a truism of classical political economy that would have secured the assent of Adam Smith and David Ricardo as well as Karl Marx. And, if the truism is true, it follows that capital needs labor in a way that labor does not need capital.

In contemporary political reality, but not in Robinson's fiction, the labor movement remains a significant actor in the collective effort to avoid climate catastrophe. So, at its founding congress in 2006 the International

Trade Union Confederation adopted the Canadian Labour Congress's "Just Transition" policy of "developing alternative employment in a sustainable economy." This program has been endorsed by a number of national labor congresses, including the British Trades Union Congress. In 2012, sixty-four trade union bodies from twenty-four countries came together to found the much more radical Trade Unions for Energy Democracy, organized around the slogan "Resist, Reclaim, Restructure" and supported financially by the New York office of the German Rosa Luxemburg Stiftung. No doubt, these aren't quite the "reforms so numerous and systemic that ultimately they will add up to revolution" that Robinson hopes for ("Remarks" 15), but they certainly point in that direction. It seems strange, then, disappointingly so in fact, that his climate novels should make so little effort to represent fictional movements analogous to these in the real world.

NOTES

1. If our era is defined as the "Capitalocene" rather than the "Anthropocene," as Jason Moore has argued in *Capitalism in the Web of Life*, then it would follow that global heating must be capitalogenic (173).

2. Since 2008 there has been no clear hegemonic order. Hence, the rise of populisms on the Right and on the Left.

WORKS CITED

Baccolini, Raffaella, and Tom Moylan, editors. *Dark Horizons: Science Fiction and the Dystopian Imagination*. Routledge, 2003.

Bureau of Labor Statistics. *Union Members in 2018*. US Department of Labor, 2019.

Canadian Labour Congress. *Just Transition for Workers During Environmental Change*. Canadian Labour Congress, 2000.

International Trade Union Confederation. *Programme of the ITUC*. ITUC conference, 1–3 Nov. 2006, Vienna.

Jameson, Fredric. *The Antinomies of Reason*. Verso, 2013, p. v.

———. *Archaeologies of the Future: The Desire Called Utopia and Other Science Fictions*. Verso, 2005, p. v.

Klein, Naomi. *This Changes Everything: Capitalism vs. the Climate*. Simon & Schuster, 2014.

Lenin, V. I. "The Dual Power," in *Selected Works* vol. 2. Progress Publishers, 1970, pp. 48–50.

London, Jack. *The Iron Heel*. Macmillan, 1907.

Moore, Jason W. *Capitalism in the Web of Life: Ecology and the Accumulation of Capital*. Verso, 2015.

Morris, William. *News from Nowhere* in *Three Works by William Morris*. Lawrence and Wishart, 1977, pp. 286–320.

Morton, Oliver. "Heroes of the Environment 2008: A Special Report on the Eco-Pioneers Fighting for a Cleaner, Greener Future: Kim Stanley Robinson." *Time*, 24 Sept. 2008.

Piketty, Thomas. *Capital in the Twenty-First Century*. Trans. Arthur Goldhammer. Harvard University Press, 2014.

Robinson, Kim Stanley. *2312*. Orbit, 2012.

———. *Antarctica*. HarperCollins, 1997.

———. *Aurora*. Orbit, 2015.

———. *Forty Signs of Rain*. HarperCollins, 2004.

———. *Green Earth*. HarperCollins, 2015.

———. *The Ministry for the Future*. Orbit, 2020.

———. *New York 2140*. Orbit, 2017.

———. *Red Moon*. Orbit, 2018,

———. "Remarks on Utopia in the Age of Climate Change." *Utopian Studies*, vol. 27, no. 1, 2016, p. 3.

———. *Sixty Days and Counting*. HarperCollins, 2007.

———. *The Years of Rice and Salt*. HarperCollins, 2002.

Robinson, Kim Stanley, and Helen Feder. "The Realism of Our Time: Interview with Kim Stanley Robinson." *Radical Philosophy*, series 2, no. 2.01, 2018, pp. 87–98.

Suvin, Darko. *Metamorphoses of Science Fiction: on the Poetics and History of a Literary Genre*. Yale UP, 1979.

Trades Union Congress. *A Green and Fair Future for a Just Transition to a Low Carbon Economy*. Touch Stone, 2008.

Trade Unions for Energy Democracy. *Resist, Reclaim, Restructure: Unions and the Struggle for Energy Democracy*. Rosa Luxemburg Stiftung and The Worker Institute, 2012.

Vidal, Gore. "The State of the Union." *Matters of Fact and Fiction: Essays 1973–76*, by Vidal, Random House, 1977, pp. 265–85.

Heartland of Darkness
Nostalgia and Class in the Climate Fiction of Paolo Bacigalupi

JEFFREY M. BROWN

The first lines of Paolo Bacigalupi's 2005 cli-fi short story "The Calorie Man" offer a surprising act of literary sleight-of-hand.

> "No mammy, no pappy, poor little bastard. Money? You give money?" The urchin turned a cartwheel and then a somersault in the street, stirring yellow dust around his nakedness.
>
> Lalji paused to stare at the dirty blond child who had come to a halt at his feet.... Around them, the town was nearly silent in the afternoon heat. A few dungareed farmers led mulies toward the fields. Buildings, pressed from WeatherAll chips, slumped against their fellows like drunkards, rain-stained and sun-cracked, but, as their trade name implied, still sturdy. At the far end of the narrow street, the lush sprawl of SoyPRO and HiGro began, a waving rustling growth that rolled into the blue-sky distance. It was much as all the villages Lalji had seen as he traveled upriver, just another farming enclave paying its intellectual property dues and shipping calories down to New Orleans. (Bacigalupi 391)

Opening with the pidgin English of an orphan beggar, the text immediately shifts perspective to the story's protagonist, who turns outward to take in the wider context of this encounter: a riverside village, stifling midday heat, the sagging shapes of prefab architecture, green foliage that obscures the horizon. This opening draws directly on the raced and classed discourses of imperialist fiction that provide an interpretive guide to readers, whose awareness coalesces only through the eyes of a colonizer. Bacigalupi would use a similar technique in the follow-up to this short story, set in the same near-future world: his seminal 2009 cli-fi novel *The Windup Girl*.

There, the text opens on a marketplace in postapocalyptic Bangkok, as the novel's American protagonist barters with a local peasant for genetically engineered fruit, thereby reaffirming the stability of colonial hierarchies even in the wake of a climate disaster. "The Calorie Man," however, folds in details that subtly rewrite this story. The "urchin," we discover, is blond-haired; the protagonist bears the Indian name "Lalji." By the end of the paragraph, we realize: this river is not the Chao Phraya nor the Congo but rather the Mississippi, and the dilapidated village Lalji passes through is just one tiny outpost on his journey deep into the heartland of an ecologically and economically devastated United States.

The purpose of this challenge to literary expectations is clear: "The Calorie Man" sets out to show how, in a world left fundamentally altered by anthropogenic climate change, global class and racial hierarchies have been similarly rearranged. But the success of this tactic depends upon the assumptions of Anglophone readers, whose facility with the English language is contrasted with that of the American beggar child. The shock of recognizing the US heartland is produced by readers' understanding of genre tropes in colonialist literature, forcing such readers to grapple with the classist foundations of their own reading strategies. Bacigalupi's critique thus depends upon a historical paradox: just as rising sea levels threaten to wipe out coastal territories, devastate global infrastructure, and destroy or reset the technological grounds and positivist fixations of Western civilization, so too does climate change exert a kind of tidal force upon narrative possibility, as Bacigalupi's work is borne backward into the formal and epistemological strategies of late-Victorian colonialist fiction. Reading Bacigalupi, one is drawn back in time one hundred years, continually haunted by the strategies of ambivalent commentary that defined the realist and modernist traditions.

In "The Calorie Man," the vehicle of class and climate critique is a specific act of literary nostalgia: Bacigalupi's story—about a trader's journey upriver in search of a mysterious figure whose exceptional mind bears equal potential for destruction and salvation—neatly echoes and revises that canonical text of modernist uncertainty, Joseph Conrad's *Heart of Darkness*. Yet Bacigalupi's dependence upon Conrad bears with it a poisoned skepticism; his story's characteristic mode is anxious and self-critical, disturbed and undone by the symmetries and equivalences that form its foundation and its ending. Bacigalupi's tale ultimately depends upon a conception of the American heartland as the homeland, a place defined by a version of middle-class domesticity that emerges "naturally" from American soil. By returning to a home defined equally by ecological and class imbalance—and one founded in an abiding cultural fixation on anachronism—Bacigalupi forces us to question the complicity of narrative itself in the effort to address (neo)colonial racism, environmental despoliation, and economic inequality.

NOSTALGIA AND KNOWLEDGE: COLLECTIVE MEMORY, CLASS IDENTITY, AND THE GROUNDS OF CLIMATE CRITIQUE

The nostalgic critique of Bacigalupi's "The Calorie Man" operates on two levels. First, the story's narrative and its focal character both attempt to critique the ways in which nostalgic undercurrents reproduce the catastrophic violence of climate disaster: effecting a critical distance that deliberately rejects nostalgic self-delusion in favor of realist vision, Bacigalupi's story exposes how the desire to restore trauma is often built upon the same fictions that create that devastation. This critique itself, however, is then undermined by Bacigalupi's citation of Conrad: by recognizing the discursive foundation of this critique in the modernist ambivalence of *Heart of Darkness*, "The Calorie Man" implies that its own critical potentials are already foreclosed.

The narrative perspective of "The Calorie Man" is defined by Lalji's ability to defamiliarize the American heartland: his sensibility is rooted in a class identity and racial experience that contests a stable, normative understanding of geography, history, and climate. The shock of recognition in those opening paragraphs shows how imagery of the postapocalypse maps uncomfortably onto that of the premodern, suggesting an ironic continuity not only between past and future but also between the self and the other: between exploiter and exploited, colonizer and colonized, upper and lower class. Throughout the remainder of the tale, Lalji continues both to enact and to disrupt such continuities, indicating how the collective experience of climate change likewise threatens both to erase and to reinscribe various inequities. "The Calorie Man" interrogates this experience via the operations of *nostalgia*: a bittersweet sentiment that provides an affective reconnection to a time, place, and identity only through a simultaneous reminder of irrevocable loss. The critical insight afforded by Lalji exists in tension with the operations of nostalgia, and this tension often drives the plot of the story.

Lalji's investment in nostalgia is quite literal. Ostensibly, he makes his living trading goods on a postapocalyptic Mississippi River, but, as a freelance transporter operating a "swift, inconsequential boat," he has maintained his independence primarily as a salvager and a smuggler, selling antiques from the "Expansion," Bacigalupi's term for the world that existed prior to the exhaustion of fossil fuels and the ensuing "Collapse" (395). In this sense, Lalji recognizes that a desire to restore the past is also, itself, a collective resource—and one that can be exploited for personal gain by those like him, whose "inconsequential boat" allows him to navigate the pervasive cultural currents of nostalgia. Lalji's greatest score was the salvage of an enormous sign for a gas station, which he'd sold to an executive of an agribusiness interest. He reminisces about this sale:

> The AgriGen woman had laughed at the sign. She'd mounted it on her wall, surrounded by the lesser artifacts of the Expansion: plastic cups, computer monitors, photos of racing automobiles, brightly colored children's toys. She'd hung the sign on her wall and then stood back and murmured that at one point, it had been a powerful company . . . global, even.
> Global.
> She'd said the word with an almost sexual yearning as she stared up at the sign's ruddy polymers.
> *Global.* (403–4)

Nostalgia is here conceived in directly economic terms. It is defined and quantified by the sale of this sign, an overt symbol for the relationship between economic power and ecological despoliation: it not only refers to the consumption of fossil fuels but is also an embodiment of that consumption, composed of "ruddy polymers" and mounted alongside "plastic cups."

But if Lalji's salvage of this antique thereby signals a bitter reflection on the source of climate change, this reflection immediately pivots toward the delusions of class identity. Crucially, the executive's collection belies her class position: though she stands at the apex of the present class hierarchy, her yearning for the past is nevertheless invested in objects of mass-cultural consumption and middle-class identity, "lesser artifacts"—cups, computers, toys—that provide a tangible link to a sense of twentieth-century American domesticity. And if nostalgia is traditionally rooted in a sense of homecoming, here that desire is also turned inside out: the executive's yearning is for a home that also was the entire world, embodied in that essential term *global*. Her exile from this home is a reduction to merely local influence. We detect, therefore, an essential tension in the text's manner of characterizing her. If she is, as Lalji regards her, "a representative of the most powerful energy company in the world," that idea of the world is no longer knowable, for the communications and transportation technologies that substantiate that power—or that permit acts of political and aesthetic "representation"—have been lost. The executive's nostalgia is an epistemic contradiction rooted in the illusions of class (404).

Bacigalupi's story thereby draws a direct connection between the forms of cultural consumption that precipitate climate change and those that absolve responsibility by fixating upon "inconsequential" actions associated with a nebulous middle-class identity. The executive desires to restore a world that would plummet once more into the abyss, but the imagery of this world is defined by reified icons that displace an awareness of global consequences with the memory of mundane personal experiences: drinking from a cup, operating a PC, driving a car, playing with one's children. The executive's murmured "Global" is merely a pretext for her sense of the local. Flooded with both pity and contempt for her, Lalji feels "a sudden sadness at how very diminished humanity had become" (404). He is drawn to universalize her experience, to disregard his own subject position and to see her as "representative" of a common humanity that extends beyond class and race. Even as he defamiliarizes her perspective, Lalji is caught within its nostalgic undertow.

This scene is essential but not entirely surprising. Bacigalupi simply connects the dots between the illusory social consensus of the culture industry and a unified "humanity" threatened by climate change, recognizing how the petrochemical industry and its byproducts materialize that connection. But the straightforwardness of the scene's critique is challenged by its medium: the experience of nostalgia, which tends to reverse the lines of causality that would otherwise explain the connection. To illustrate such problems, Bryan D. Price notes how contemporary nationalist nostalgia is rooted in its adherents' immediate contact with icons, monuments, or memorabilia: local, physical touchstones that promise an antidote to the abstractions of globalization and postmodernity (106). But the materiality of these fragmented icons—like the exhibits in the executive's office—blurs the divide between aesthetics and politics, taking on what Fredric Jameson has called a "curatorial" ephemerality that neutralizes their ability to provoke "lasting institutional consequences" (145–46). To speak of nostalgia in American culture today is, therefore, to utilize objects that invoke a "universal" brand of white middle- and working-class domesticity, an experience of class identity that also applies to a corporate executive and can be felt by an immigrant smuggler. Such nostalgia perhaps emerges as a rejection of neoliberal or globalist policies that shifted the centers of economic production away from the agricultural, manufacturing, and energy sectors that define the American heartland, but nostalgia's emotional experience is centered upon the very products that accelerated that dislocation: plastics and petrochemicals.[1] To "know" the American heartland is already to participate in its destruction; conversely, to destroy the entire world requires a peculiar form of nostalgic myopia, a deliberate unknowing that confuses the global for the local, the universal for the particular, the corporate for the individual.

Nostalgia therefore represents not only a problem of political affect or class identity but also one of epistemology. Though itself a consuming passion for origins, nostalgia fundamentally resists efforts to determine its own origins as it cuts across, combines, and resituates competing identities and narratives, understood across a multiplicity of interrelated disciplines and perspectives. In academic literature across multiple fields, the popular fixation on politicized nostalgia in recent years has been countered by a collective recognition that the terms by which we understand nostalgia—from history to psychoanalysis, rhetoric to medical ontology—are deeply overdetermined (Kurlinkus and Kurlinkus 87–109; Murphy 125–41; Novack 2–5). It is for this reason that nostalgia has long been anathema to a strain of thought dating back to Plato that imagines itself to be founded in objective fact and disciplined argumentation. As David Lowenthal has shown, nostalgia has been castigated as "ersatz, vulgar, demeaning, misguided, inauthentic, sacrilegious, retrograde, reactionary, criminal, fraudulent, sinister, and morbid," and Kimberly Smith has documented the history of antinostalgic rhetoric in positivist arguments for industrialization in the Progressive Era, which were often wielded against the nostalgia articulated by an oppressed working class (Lowenthal 27; Smith 505–27). If nostalgia produces false equivalencies in the experience of class, antinostalgic rhetoric often positions itself beyond class consideration—and therefore beyond politics, beyond perspective, and beyond the human.

It is therefore through the problem of epistemic indeterminacy that nostalgia becomes central to our understanding of anthropogenic climate change. To assess the effects of human action on a warming planet means simultaneously to occupy a position beyond any local orientation—to draw upon data that offers a totalizing vision of the biosphere—and also to acknowledge that access to that position is granted only by mechanisms that privilege specific forms of "progress" and knowledge. A sense of belatedness has always characterized climate discourse: atmospheric chemist Paul Crutzen, who popularized the term "Anthropocene" ("recent human") in 2000, recognized similar controversy even during the adoption of the term "Holocene" ("recent whole") in 1885, as contemporary scientists (such as G. P. Marsh or Antonio Stoppani) had already noted the role of humankind in fragmenting that "recent whole" (Crutzen and Stoermer 69). To set apart the Anthropocene from the Holocene is to create a vision of humanity as separate from the environment that produces and sustains it and to rewrite ecological history in terms of a historical moment when humanity began to intrude upon the "natural" world through industrialized carbon consumption. The forms of empiricism embedded in climate science are also, in this sense, nostalgic or backward-looking: they echo an attitude of disinterested objectivity that was only enabled at the same historical moment that precipitated environmental collapse.

The paradoxical antinostalgic strain in environmentalist discourse thus privileges a specific, not "universal," idea of human knowledge and action in the world. The problem is neatly outlined by William Cronon's "The Trouble with Wilderness," an essay that marks a significant point in the development of modern ecocriticism by subjecting the history of American environmentalism to postmodern tools of analysis. Cronon traces the American conception of nature back through a series of rhetorical touchstones in American transcendentalism and European Romanticism to show that nostalgia for nature is a direct product of the Industrial Revolution and the elaboration of global capitalism; it is a historically contingent rhetorical attitude, not an "authentic" or essential experience. And he implores readers to recognize an (im)personal nostalgia for nature in their reception of this idea: "Such memories may be uniquely our own, but they are also familiar enough to be instantly recognizable to others. Remember this?" (Cronon 8). It is no surprise, then, that the mainstreaming of Cronon's idea provoked a passionate rebuttal that rests on shaky metaphysical, historical, and political grounds. "Cronon may be correct that *ideas* of nature don't exist outside of cultural understanding, but Nature in all of its self-governing complexity most certainly does," declared environmental activist Bill Willers. "It is Nature in the form of internally regulated systems at a grand scale, free of human manipulation, that wilderness advocates are struggling to defend and to restore—regardless of whose culture happens to be preeminent at the moment" (Willers 61). The language here draws unironically upon contested Enlightenment ideals of "self-government"—ideals which, historically speaking, were often predicated upon mass violence, subjugation, enslavement, and the creation of a class system that fueled extractivist, unsustainable industry. Collapsing the entirety of human history and cultural difference to achieve environmental "restoration" sometimes means relying upon rhetoric that makes such restoration necessary in the first place.

In "The Calorie Man," Lalji grapples constantly with a second temptation that mimics this problem: a form of antinostalgic "realism" that directly counters the myopia of the corporate executive but that also feeds his cynicism and guilt. Though he facilitates a critique of the executive's American nostalgia, he too is haunted by his own past: his childhood in India, his family's collapse, and his flight to America. Lalji's personal tragedy was caused by his father's naiveté: a poor farmer, Lalji's father had insisted upon planting seeds that could have been used to ensure his sister's survival: "[Lalji] remembered planting. Squatting with his father in desert heat, yellow dust all around them, burying seeds they had stored away, saved when they might have been eaten, kept when they might have made Gita fat and marriageable." With a nostalgic faith in agrarian patterns of life, ecological stewardship, and divine protection, Lalji's father had failed to recognize that the seeds they squandered were genetically engineered to be infertile, produced to ensure an agribusiness monopoly. Lalji discovered the truth in an act of desperation one night: digging up the seeds, he "found them already decomposed, tiny corpses in his hand, rotted. As dead in his palm as the day he and his father had planted them." Shamefully eating the seeds alone, the young Lalji is thus given "his first true taste of PurCal" (Bacigalupi 411). The truth that "human manipulation" has already precluded nostalgic restoration—both ecological and economic—comes to define Lalji's memory as he vacillates between hope and cynicism.

From the start of the story, Lalji therefore works to disentangle his own sensibility from the calamitous correlatives of nostalgia: his knowledge of the truth is the product of a critical skepticism that disavows class-based ideologies, recognizing acts of self-deception that define a spectrum of reactions to inequality and oppression both past and present. When confronted by the beggar child discussed above, Lalji chases him away, reflecting: "No true beggar at all. An opportunist only—most likely the accidental creation of strangers who had visited the village.... AgriGen and Midwest Grower scientists and land factotums would be pleased to show ostentatious kindness to the villagers at the core of their empire" (391–92). Linking genetic, climate, cultural, and socioeconomic engineering, Lalji also aims this critique at himself, questioning his own motives as he embarks on another potentially "inconsequential" journey upriver to rescue a man who might restore the world: "Was it worth it? If [Lalji] thought too much, his businessman's instinct—bred into him through thousands of years of caste practice—told him no. But still, there was Gita" (399).

The epistemology of both class and ecology is challenged by memory, and Lalji is therefore guarded against the results of "thinking too much." Yet his mind is drawn back to his sister, Gita, because of his desire to complete her story. Lalji recognizes that his nostalgia is also a *narrative* trap, built upon a global class hierarchy that no longer exists and grounded in a tradition of storytelling that no longer applies: "For a long time he thought he would go back and find her. That he might feed her. That he would send money and food back to his blighted land that now existed only in his mind, in his dreams, in half-awake hallucinations of deserts.... But she was dead by now, whether through starvation or disease, and he was sure of it" (406). For Lalji, dreams of restoration follow a predictable arc: his imagined tale of emigration and salvation is no less limited than his father's faith in pastoral resurrection. He therefore rejects the structure of a traditional American immigrant story along with the ethical injunctions it embodies, in favor of a knowledge about the world that is rooted in the abstractions of global perspective and modernist forms of narrativity.

NOSTALGIA AND NARRATIVE: MODERNIST AMBIVALENCE AND THE LITERARY TRADITION IN "THE CALORIE MAN" AND *HEART OF DARKNESS*

Narrative remains an essential mode for rethinking problems like Lalji's, precisely because the recursive effects of the literary tradition itself mirror and critique the feelings of the characters caught within its net. As Aaron Santesso reminds us, understanding literary nostalgia is not merely a matter of attuning ourselves to matters of individual desire but also of recognizing nostalgia's indebtedness to formal literary effects and their historical and political justifications (Santesso 13, 16). A similar idea is central to Amitav Ghosh's argument about the relationship between the "unthinkable" results of ecological disaster and the "grid of literary forms and conventions" that prevent contemporary writers from adequately addressing climate change; these issues present a self-nullifying "feedback loop" that can be recognized both in the genre-coding and the cultural consumption of cli-fi (Ghosh 7). Lalji, concerned about "thinking too much," recognizes how narration can limit critique; Bacigalupi, equally ambivalent, draws upon a "feedback loop" that already shaped the foundation of modern literature: Joseph Conrad's *Heart of Darkness*.

Lalji's perspective on nostalgia, global/local identity, and class has a very familiar antecedent: the same discursive methods characterize Conrad's essential vessel of modernist vision and imperialist critique, Marlow. Scholars have long recognized that Marlow is a kind of synecdoche for the entire project of literary modernism as Conrad had famously defined it in 1897: "Art itself may be defined as a single-minded attempt to render the highest kind of justice to the visible universe, by bringing to light the truth, manifold and one, underlying its every aspect.... My task which I am trying to achieve is, by the power of the written word to make you hear, to make you feel—it is, before all, to make you *see*" (*Narcissus* 17, 19). In Conrad, sensual affect is both the opponent and vehicle of a totalizing critical knowledge and the "highest kind of justice," and these epistemic contradictions are neatly condensed in the language of Conrad's paradigmatic hero.

Scenes like the one between Lalji and the executive in "The Calorie Man" bracket the narrative of *Heart of Darkness:* the ignorance that precedes Marlow as he embarks upon his journey is a brand of nostalgia that he finds entombed within the "sepulchral city," and it is mirrored by the pathos of Kurtz's "intended," whose memory betrays the "horror" that Marlow had discovered on the Congo. Marlow attempts to counter the illusions of the imperial "vision" with his own actual experience on the river, but the journey to the Inner Station is not aimed at uncovering the material source of Kurtz's remarkable productivity—the forms of environmental and racial violence that result in a cascade of ivory downriver—but rather at Marlow's elaboration of models of psychological truth and metaphysical purity. As Marlow moves forward, Kurtz comes to symbolize a solution to the kinds of hypocrisy and delusion that characterize the economic underpinnings of imperialism. Thus does Marlow find himself "lumped with Kurtz as a partisan of methods for which the time was not ripe"; Marlow's vision is a form of realism that is overtly positioned as progressive rather than reactionary or nostalgic (Conrad, *Heart* 62).

But, of course, Conrad works to undermine this aspiration. This happens both through the disintegration of Marlow's verbal coherence and also through the paradoxical discovery that Marlow's efforts at revising nostalgia and replacing it with truth are, in fact, only a reinscription of the same problem. The journey upriver is not a journey forward but backward, and Marlow's story does not redeem Kurtz's but instead rewrites it, gaining "its meaning from its attachment to the prior journey" (Brooks 244). The end of this process is Marlow's dislocation, which is conceived in professional, racial, national, and economic terms. In an essential early passage, Marlow is defined as both homeless and classless: "The worst that could be said of [Marlow] was that he did not represent his class. He was a seaman, but he was a wanderer too, while most seamen lead, if one may so express it, a sedentary life. Their minds are of the stay-at-home order, and their home is always with them—the ship—and so is their country—the sea" (Conrad, *Heart* 5). Marlow's "homelessness" is what permits his critique, but it is also what allows him to discover his "home" in the practice of narration. Likewise, Marlow's "classlessness" is not only a sign of imperial privilege; such "classlessness" is also envisioned as an attitude hostile to material forms of nostalgia founded in ecological and economic concerns, even as it nostalgically reinscribes the structures of domination that justify its narratological transcendence. The same forces that give birth to Marlow's critique also neutralize it.

"The Calorie Man" mimics this doubled structure. Like Marlow, Lalji is purportedly realistic about the violence that characterizes the world he inhabits, and he recognizes that forms of ecological catastrophe have as their outcome and their source economic exploitation. And, like Marlow, Lalji quests upriver in search of a man whose unique abilities simultaneously embody and redeem that violence. When he finally encounters this man, Lalji shakes off the effects of nostalgia within his own cultural touchstones: "Hemp sacking covered his body, dirty and torn, and his eyes had a sunken, knowing quality that unearthed in Lalji the memory of a long-ago sadhu, covered with ash and little else: the tangled hair, the disinterest in his clothing, the distance in the eyes that came from enlightenment. Lalji shook away the memory. This man was no holy man. Just a man, and a generipper, at that" (Bacigalupi 405).

Charles Bowman—the "calorie man" of the story's title—is a geneticist who had a hand in designing the patented food crops that sustain humanity in the wake of the apocalypse. The centerpiece of this redesign is reproductive control: the "calorie companies" maintain their monopoly by rendering their plants both resilient and infertile—they drive out competition, but they cannot be grown by local farmers like Lalji's long-deceased father. As Bowman wryly puts it: "We now pay for a privilege that nature once provided willingly, for just a little labor" (413). The conditions of late capitalism are mapped directly onto those of climate change—and, indeed, are indistinguishable from them, via genetic engineering and IP control. What once was "natural" is now a matter of economics, Bowman quips—but the goal of this story is the restoration of these segregated spheres. Bowman is now a fugitive; he has secretly cultivated heirloom crops and reengineered them to be "unbelievably fecund"—to shatter the monopoly and restore the world. "I'm going to be the next Johnny Appleseed," he announces (414). Bowman therefore represents both the corporatized technological threats of twenty-first-century ecoterror and the hopes of nineteenth-century American individualism, pioneer spirit, and conservationist zeal. He promises to restore the heartland; the vehicle of this promise, however, is a vision of heartland planted more than two centuries earlier.

What is most provocative about "The Calorie Man," however, is its refusal to follow its forebear, *Heart of Darkness,* into the closed circuit of Conrad's modernist critique. Like Kurtz, Bowman comes to represent something equally attractive and deplorable in the heart of the imperialist vision; like Kurtz, he dies on the return trip (a victim, in this case, of a raid by corporate police). But unlike Conrad, Bacigalupi never fully undermines Bowman's mission, and Lalji is never forced to reflect upon his complicity in the events that continue to reinscribe violence in this devastated world. Part of the reason for this is the medium of Bowman's vision: while Kurtz remains, in Marlow's imaginary, a "voice" whose heritage is a textual "Report" and its scrawled postscript, Bowman's legacy represents the reembodiment of his story into an ecological medium. Lalji and Bowman's ward, Tazi, are the only survivors of the raid, but Tazi reveals that Bowman's dream is not dead: she carries several jars of corn, rice, soybeans, and wheat, each of them filled with hundreds of Bowman's reengineered seeds. "They're his Johnny Appleseeds," she explains (419). We witness an essential discursive replacement: the seeds are anthropomorphized; they are conceived of not just as an extension of Bowman but also of a long train of conflicted ideologies, policies, and myths that lead us back into the nineteenth century. Whatever promise they hold—to break monopolies, to restore ecologies, to re-enfranchise the dispossessed—is a nostalgic effect of both genetic and narratological engineering.

Bacigalupi encodes this message in the final lines of "The Calorie Man," which carefully rewrite the opening warning of *Heart of Darkness:*

> Lalji frowned and picked up a jar of corn. The kernels nestled tightly together, hundreds of them, each one unpatented, each one a genetic infection. He closed his eyes and in his mind he saw a field: row upon row of green rustling plants, and his father, laughing, with his arms spread wide as he shouted, "Hundreds! Thousands if you pray!"
>
> Lalji hugged the jar to his chest, and slowly, he began to smile.
>
> The needleboat continued downstream, a bit of flotsam in the Mississippi's current. Around it, the crowding shadow hulks of the grain barges loomed, all of them flowing south through the fertile heartland toward the gateway of New Orleans; all of them flowing steadily toward the vast wide world. (419)

We are given a vision of economic and ecological transformation. Lalji's formerly "inconsequential" boat threads swiftly between the barges of the calorie companies, carrying an ecological "infection" whose outcome lies in the redemption of Lalji's nostalgia: a memory of his father's failure transformed into the dream of a future his father never saw. The story's success—Lalji's smile—depends upon his father's class position. This image of environmental resurrection is also rooted in a conviction that such restoration can only be conceived in the material experience of the homestead farmer.

But Bowman's disease is then borne out of the American heartland through that essential artery of commerce, and we are suddenly aware of the story's final act of narrative engineering: these lines simply rephrase the vision of Conrad's frame narrator as he regards the Thames in the opening pages of *Heart of Darkness:* "What greatness had now floated on the ebb of that river into the mystery of an unknown earth! . . . The dreams of men, the seed of commonwealths, the germs of empires." The lines in fact prompt Marlow's necessary historical critique: "And this also . . . has been one of the dark places of the earth" (Conrad, *Heart* 5). Such noble visions—the spread of seeds and germs, all gushing from the hearts of the imperial West—are inextricable from the darkness they perpetuate. In both Conrad and Bacigalupi, there is no expression of ecological restoration that is not already a figuration of neoliberal expansion disguised within class critique.

THE LIMITS OF NARRATIVE

What makes "The Calorie Man" important to our understanding of climate fiction and class is a recognition that the problems it addresses are both epistemological and formal: just as Bacigalupi's conflicted resolution is entrapped by the literary tradition, so too are we tempted to perform acts of interpretive restoration that rest upon similarly troubling equivalences. "The Calorie Man" can be read, for example, as a postcolonial revenge fantasy: this is *Heart of Darkness*, but with an Indian trader in place of a British colonialist, with the Mississippi in place of the Congo. But this kind of swapping is enabled by the ecologics of late capitalism and globalization; in this case, we are simply rendering the American heartland "other" in service of an equally nostalgic conception of the home, of nature, and of class identity. A critical trap has therefore come to define the cultural legacy of *Heart of Darkness*, nearly fifty years after Chinua Achebe famously called into question whether it ought to be reread at all. For J. Hillis Miller, the answer to that question lies in the ways that Conrad's text embodies a "failed apocalypse" (Miller 372): an "endlessly deferred promise" that invokes an "unknown and unknowable future" (378, 379). *Post*-apocalyptic climate fiction that echoes this narrative deferral therefore seems to miss the point that it simultaneously rehearses.

Both *Heart of Darkness* and "The Calorie Man" trade upon the problematic homology of individual desire and collective impact, upon the identity of the present and the past, and upon modes of thought that aim to erase class difference or establish common interests beyond cultural divides. The conditions of climate change, however, demand a manner of conceiving human agency that is not rooted in such equations. Contemporary theorists have noted the ways in which the "seemingly indisputable, and crucially transcendental, alibi of climate change" has been used to target the poor by building austerity rhetoric upon normative images of the middle-class homeowner, or how the epiphenomena of climate change have driven conceptions of "biological invasions" whose pretexts and goals are forms of militarization and border enforcement that undermine immigration and refugee policy (Mitropoulos 78–79; Groves 194). Such work recognizes how philosophical interventions that define labor and working-class identity—from Aristotle to Hannah Arendt—have long relied upon "untenable" notions of environmental stability (Macauley 120). By interrogating how these equations articulate themselves in the literary tradition—including in both nostalgic and antinostalgic forms of class and racial subjectivity—"The Calorie Man" circumscribes, but does not resolve, a set of essential problems for climate fiction.

One response to these problems might involve the redefinition of nostalgic literature: Jennifer Ladino suggests that "re-placing" nostalgia—generating new articulations of nostalgia's material grounds rather than its "free floating" narratological dimensions—can help resolve this dilemma in environmental discourse (Ladino 7). Alternatively, Dipesh Chakrabarty has written that the conditions of climate change require an entirely new idea of subjectivity, one distinct from the controversial negotiation of agency rooted in Enlightenment values, class-consciousness, and postcolonial critique. We must think of the human not in terms of universal rights and capabilities, nor as defined by "anthropological difference," but rather as a collective force that is itself alien to any person within it. "The science of anthropogenic global warming has doubled the figure of the human," he writes; "you have to think of two figures of the human simultaneously: the human-human and the nonhuman-human" (Chakrabarty 2, 11). The same is true of the world itself: if ecological forces are anthropogenic, they are also potentially anthropomorphic, as we see in "The Calorie Man." To recast the world in the image of the human was, as the very title of *Heart of Darkness* teaches us, the unconscionable core of the imperial ideology. Now, however, such action operates in the other direction, as the world of the Anthropocene reinscribes environmental and economic alienation upon its subjects, a form of alienation that manifests most powerfully in the desire to return and restore the home: to redeem the historical trauma with which this all began and to return to structures of knowledge about the world that made sense of such temporal, ecological, and economic dislocations. So long as this home is rooted in dreams of class identity that are likewise the products of that trauma—like the executive's delusions, Lalji's guilt, Marlow's "classlessness," or Bowman's "Johnny Appleseeds"—narratives of homecoming can only produce what they already know.

But the world today is both human and nonhuman; it is both home and not-home; it is both known and unknown. The Holocene—the "recent whole"—is already displaced by the Anthropocene. Any idea of wholeness, restoration, or unity is disturbed by the intrusion of the human and the ecologics through which humanity divides, mystifies, and narrates the world and itself: essential divisions of class and race that bisect the heartland like a river, tempting us constantly to ply those waters once more. And these acts of cleavage are, and have always been, equally invested in violence and in hope.

NOTE

1. For more on material culture and objects or things or commodities that are often relevant in many climate narratives, see Bill Brown's work on thing theory, such as his *Things* (U of Chicago P, 2004) and *Other Things* (U of Chicago P, 2019). See also Raymond Malewitz's *The Practice of Misuse: Rugged Consumerism in Contemporary American Culture* (Stanford UP, 2014).

WORKS CITED

Bacigalupi, Paolo. "The Calorie Man." 2005. *The Windup Girl,* Night Shade Books, 2015, pp. 390–419.

Brooks, Peter. *Reading for the Plot.* Harvard UP, 1984.

Chakrabarty, Dipesh. "Postcolonial Studies and the Challenge of Climate Change." *New Literary History,* no. 43, 2012, pp. 1–18.

Conrad, Joseph. *Heart of Darkness.* 1899. Edited by Paul B. Armstrong, Norton, 2017.

———. *The Nigger of the Narcissus.* 1897. Collier Books, 1962.

Cronon, William. "The Trouble with Wilderness: or, Getting Back to the Wrong Nature." *Environmental History,* vol. 1, no. 1, 1996, pp. 7–28.

Crutzen, Paul, and Eugene F. Stoermer. "The 'Anthropocene.'" 2000. *The Global Warming Reader,* edited by Bill McKibben, Penguin, 2011, pp. 69–72.

Ghosh, Amitav. *The Great Derangement: Climate Change and the Unthinkable.* U of Chicago P, 2016.

Groves, Jason. "Nonspecies Invasion: The Eco-logic of Late Capitalism." *Telemorphosis: Theory in the Era of Climate Change,* edited by Tom Cohen, Open Humanities Press, 2012, pp. 183–202.

Jameson, Fredric, Nico Baumbach, Damon R. Young, and Genevieve Yue. "Revisiting Postmodernism: An Interview with Fredric Jameson." *Social Text 127,* vol. 34, no. 2, 2016, pp. 143–60.

Kurlinkus, Will, and Krista Kurlinkus. "'Coal Keeps the Lights On': Rhetorics of Nostalgia for and in Appalachia." *College English,* vol. 81, no. 2, 2018, pp. 87–109.

Ladino, Jennifer. *Reclaiming Nostalgia: Longing for Nature in American Literature.* U of Virginia P, 2012.

Lowenthal, David. "Nostalgia Tells It Like It Wasn't." *The Imagined Past: History and Nostalgia,* edited by Christopher Shaw and Malcom Chase, Manchester UP, 1989, pp. 18–32.

Macauley, David. "Hannah Arendt and the Politics of Place: From Earth Alienation to Oikos." *Minding Nature: The Philosophers of Ecology,* Guilford Press, 1996, pp. 102–33.

Miller, J. Hillis. "Should We Read 'Heart of Darkness'?" *Heart of Darkness,* by Joseph Conrad, edited by Paul B. Armstrong, Norton, 2017, pp. 369–80.

Mitropoulos, Angela. "Oikopolitics, and Storms." *The Global South*, vol. 3, no. 1, 2009, pp. 66–82.

Murphy, Andrew R. "Longing, Nostalgia, and Golden Age Politics: The American Jeremiad and the Power of the Past." *Perspectives on Politics*, vol. 7, no. 1, 2009, pp. 125–41.

Novack, Stacey L. "The Politics of Nostalgia: Perils and Untapped Potentials." *Psychoanalysis, Culture & Society*, no. 22, 2017, pp. 2–5.

Price, Bryan D. "Material Memory: The Politics of Nostalgia on the Eve of *MAGA*." *American Studies*, vol. 57, nos. 1–2, 2018, pp. 103–15.

Santesso, Aaron. *A Careful Longing: The Poetics and Problems of Nostalgia*. U of Delaware P, 2006.

Smith, Kimberly L. "Mere Nostalgia: Notes on a Progressive Paratheory." *Rhetoric and Public Affairs*, no. 3, 2000, pp. 505–27.

Willers, Bill. "The Trouble with Cronon." *Wild Earth*, vol. 6, no. 4, 1996/1997, pp. 59–61.

Whose Odds?

The Absence of Climate Justice in American Climate Fiction of the 2000s and 2010s

MATTHEW SCHNEIDER-MAYERSON

Climate change is a physical fact, but humans comprehend it as a narrative via frames that are employed in everyday discourse, sublimated in popular culture, and highlighted by paraphrasers and tastemakers such as journalists, bloggers, filmmakers, celebrities, and politicians. The emergence of popular climate frames carries tremendous consequences, as these frames shape public and elite opinion and, through them, political and policy responses. In the 1990s and early 2000s, Americans conceived of climate change as a matter of contested science and gradual warming. In the 2010s the advent of the Anthropocene concept emphasized climate change as a looming catastrophe facing an undifferentiated humanity. The most important emerging frame—highlighted by every successive not-so-natural disaster—is that climate change is about justice for the already disadvantaged humans who bear the least responsibility and are least able to respond to its gradual transformations and pulsing cataclysms. This is the frame of climate justice.

Around the same time as this frame began gaining traction, cultural commentators and environmentalists heralded the arrival of a new genre of fiction, dubbed climate fiction, that "engage[s] with climate change as an important theme" (Trexler and Johns-Putra 187). Though storytellers have speculated about the consequences of climatic change for millennia, novels based on scientific evidence and plausible projections began appearing in large numbers in the 1990s. Works such as Octavia Butler's *Parable of the Sower* (1993) and T. C. Boyle's *A Friend of the Earth* (2001) were early examples, and by the late 2000s the trend was clear, with speculative fiction authors such as Kim Stanley Robinson, best-selling popular fiction novelists such as Clive Cussler, and mainstream literary heavyweights such as Barbara Kingsolver contributing groundbreaking and widely read novels focused on the environmental, psychological, social, cultural, and political dynamics of climate change. As this development gained recognition from literary critics and readers, climate fiction was welcomed as a sign of American artists and culture industries grappling with anthropogenic climate change.

This was undoubtedly true, and these literary pioneers deserve recognition. But especially in retrospect, it is clear that authors of this generation of American climate fiction chose to depict climate change through specific, limited, and surprisingly problematic frames. They primarily portrayed climatic destabilization as a problem for white, wealthy, educated, and privileged Americans, and secondarily gestured towards its consequences for human beings of all socioeconomic levels—the monolithic and flattened "we" of *homo sapiens*. In this way, they ignored climate justice, which many scholars, activists, and policymakers were emphasizing as the most appropriate framework for conceptualizing climate change so that responses do not exacerbate existing inequalities (Schlosberg and Collins 2014).[1] Ironically, then, these authors unwittingly mirrored the historical myopia of the American environmental movement itself (Gottlieb 307–346). The literary elision of climate injustice reflected and potentially reified a narcissistic tendency among many white American readers.

This chapter examines the absence of climate justice concerns in this critical first generation of American climate fiction (in the 2000s and early 2010s), which produced popular texts that created a template for future authors to follow. I focus on two representative texts that have been widely reviewed, assigned, and analyzed and are therefore likely to have reached a large number of readers: Nathaniel Rich's *Odds against Tomorrow* and Kim Stanley Robinson's *Science in the Capital* trilogy.[2] While we cannot expect a particular text, author, or genre to address every conceivable perspective, examining cli-fi novels on socioeconomic grounds is hardly a critical imposition. Works such as *Odds against Tomorrow* and the *Science in the Capital* trilogy owe a significant portion of their sales, critical attention, and reputation to the explicit centrality of climate change to their narratives. In interviews, Rich, Robinson, and other authors spoke with an admirable desire to expand their readers' environmental awareness and spheres of moral concern. Given that these authors consciously addressed climate change with an ethical and activist bent, it is worth asking which frames this consequential genre employed and which ones it largely avoided.[3]

FRAMING CLIMATE CHANGE

In 2009, geographer Mike Hulme identified six common narrative frames for climate change: scientific uncertainty, biodiversity, economics, national security, catastrophe, and justice and equity. To these we might also add two more recent frames: climate change as a public health concern and a patriotic challenge. Framing is an incredibly consequential matter, since the frames by which we individually and collectively apperceive any issue shapes our beliefs and subsequent actions (Nisbet)—or whether we take any action at all.

In the three decades that climate change has been an issue of public concern in the United States, particular frames have dominated media coverage and popular discourse. Until recently, most journalists stubbornly insisted on the scientific uncertainty frame, reflecting the modern American journalistic norm of "balance"; scientists and environmentalists tended to promote the catastrophe frame, mistakenly believing it the most persuasive; and corporations and well-heeled think tanks advanced the scientific uncertainty and economic frames. It is only recently that activists from and representatives of small and developing nations along with Northern environmentalists have succeeded in publicly advocating for the justice and equity frame, or what's commonly referred to as *climate justice*. Over the past decade, scholars and activists in the Global South and allies in the North have argued compellingly that climate change should be viewed through a moral lens, since it produces an unjust distribution of vulnerabilities and impacts not only between generations (intergenerational injustice) but between different groups in the present and future (distributive injustice), often reflecting and reinscribing historical cartographies of exploitation and colonialism.

The gulf between the responsibility for and current and expected suffering from climate change is staggering, and cannot be emphasized too frequently. Approximately 20 percent of the global population has been responsible for 75–80 percent of historical greenhouse gas emissions since the Industrial Revolution: historically wealthy nations like the United States (responsible for 27 percent of all emissions from 1850 to 2011) and Britain

(6 percent), with China (11 percent) catching up quickly (Ge et al). However, "75 to 80% of the damages will be suffered by the developing countries," according to one analysis (World Bank, *World Development Report*). A map of historical emissions is almost the inverse of expected vulnerabilities, losses, and casualties. Climate change, with its geographic ubiquity and temporal near-permanence, will constitute the greatest collective act of injustice in the history of our species.

The colossal injustice of global warming is illustrated by shining a spotlight on specific vulnerable countries. Take Bangladesh, which carries almost no responsibility for current climate change. This is true whether we calculate "responsibility" as a nation's total historical contribution or on a per capita basis—in 2013 Bangladesh ranked 210 out of 250 nations and territories in per capita greenhouse gas emissions, with the average American responsible for more than thirty-seven times more than the average Bangladeshi (World Bank, "CO2 Emissions").[4] As one of the lowest-lying, poorest, and most densely populated nations on the planet, Bangladesh is already suffering from climate change—as demonstrated by the devastating floods in May 2022, which left nine million people homeless (Paul and Hussain)—and it faces a catastrophic future. Even if warming is successfully limited to only 2 degrees (Celsius), nearly 20 percent of Bangladesh will be underwater—the equivalent of the entire East Coast of the United States—and twenty million people, or one out of seven Bangladeshis, are expected to be displaced by 2050 (CDMP II).[5] Agricultural regions will be inundated with saltwater, creating the conditions for famine. As the Syrian refugee crisis in Europe illustrated, even in the best of times other countries are not likely to welcome twenty million refugees, and Bangladesh's neighbors (such as India) will be dealing with their own climate-exacerbated problems, including drought and diminished agricultural yields (Guzman 2013). Epidemiologists caution that the expected conditions—rising seas, higher temperatures, unpredictable patterns of precipitation, people living in cramped and unsanitary spaces without access to water, and an overwhelmed medical infrastructure dealing with a mobile population—are ideal for the spread of disease.

Bangladesh is only one country. Similar stories can be told of every other country that is highly vulnerable to climate change, especially poorer ones, including India, Pakistan, the Philippines, Oman, Sri Lanka, Colombia, Mexico, Kenya, South Africa, and many others. Citizens of these nations will disproportionately suffer not only because they tend to be located closer to the equator and are often more dependent on local agriculture for survival, but because they will be unable to fund expensive adaptation measures. These include levees, seawalls, green infrastructure such as constructed wetlands and permeable pavements, mass relocation, and many other strategies currently in development and implementation. That wealthy nations will fund their adaptation (and build walls) with capital gained from decades (and in some cases centuries) of exploiting fossil fuels only adds a cruel layer of injustice to this dynamic.

WHOSE ODDS?

Given the reality of catastrophic climate injustice, it is worth asking, as cultural and literary historians will in the decades to come: how did art, literature, and media, including climate-change novels, represent this issue? As Antonia Mehnert notes in her study of climate fiction, fiction can "serve as a way for readers and viewers to empathize with people across time, and thus with future generations, as well as with people in different social, economic, and ethnic contexts" (Mehnert 88). In this sense, representational choices carry weight. While ecocritics have highlighted individual works that feature environmental justice and climate justice (e.g., Mehnert 183–220; Ziser and Sze), few have focused on whether these concerns appeared in some of the genre's popular and subsequently imitated works.[6]

Cli-fi novels in the late 2000s and early 2010s were heralded by environmental activists, critics, and scholars for their potential contribution to environmental politics. The liberal media was almost uniformly positive in its praise for the emergence of climate fiction, due to its perceived trickle-down impact on environmental consciousness and politics. Works such as Theroux's *Far North* and Kingsolver's *Flight Behavior* were praised not so much for their literary merit as their ecopolitical potential—their ability to persuade and mobilize readers to change their patterns of consumption, become more politically engaged, and support national and international agreements to limit greenhouse gas emissions (e.g., Evancie; Siperstein). Nathaniel Rich's *Odds against Tomorrow* floated on this wave of hype, earning praise from the gatekeepers of liberal intellectual and middlebrow magazines as well as popular websites. For years it was regularly assigned in climate fiction courses in the United States and referred to as one of the top cli-fi novels in magazine features and online listicles.

Odds against Tomorrow's focal character is Mitchell Zukor, a University of Chicago graduate and quantitative wizard who begins the novel as a junior analyst in an investment banking firm in New York. Zukor's lifelong obsession with the risk of catastrophic events quickly lands him a plum job in a new kind of financial firm, FutureWorld, whose consultations with large corporations allow them to claim active preparation for various disaster scenarios, from extreme weather events to nanobot attacks, and thereby indemnify themselves against future lawsuits. Once New York is flooded in a Superstorm-Sandy-like hurricane ("Tammy"), the exaggerated postmodern novel becomes an action-adventure story, with Zukor and his romantic interest, Jane, navigating the debris-filled canals of Manhattan. Hailed as a prophet for his prediction of the flood, Zukor reconsiders his vocation and relocates to the decimated and abandoned neighborhood of Flatlands, Brooklyn, where he stoically anchors a self-reliant community of similarly resilient survivors.

Most critics applauded *Odds against Tomorrow*, claiming that it describes and examines the "modern condition" (Evancie) and the future of "human communities" (Newitz) in the era of climate change. In reality it describes the condition and perspective of a small and lucky portion of our species. Zukor and Jane are white, highly educated (graduates of the University of Chicago, Princeton University, and the Wharton School of Business), young (in their mid-twenties) and highly mobile, having recently moved to New York City. Due to their success in exploiting financial loopholes, they amass the financial resources to survive Tammy with minimal hardship—for example, Zukor purchases a $28,000 canoe, which they use to escape downtown Manhattan after the storm. Indeed, when Jane first views the canoe she notes, "we're making enough money to buy almost whatever we want, when we want it" (151). As they leave New York, Zukor is able to ensure their easy passage with the $50,000 in cash he carries with him. Their financial resources and disentanglement from communities of place, which allows them to relocate easily and painlessly, is not representative of most Americans, people of color, Indigenous communities, or the vast majority of the 7.5 billion people who live outside the United States. This wealth is not just a material advantage in a time of crisis but shapes their outlook throughout the novel. For example, while eating rations at a post-Tammy FEMA (Federal Emergency Management Agency) camp, Mitchell whispers to Jane, "We're too rich for this" (259).

Where are poor people and people of color in *Odds against Tomorrow*? This is a question that should be asked of every climate-change narrative. The first nonwhite voice appears halfway through the novel, in a Native American epigram. Mirroring the cultural appropriations of previous generations of white American environmentalists, Rich mines Indigenous culture to provide a disembodied source of wisdom and a veneer of multiculturalism. When Zukor and Jane find themselves in a FEMA camp, their response to being placed alongside more socioeconomically average Americans is telling:

> Who were all these people? Waiting on line outside the food tent, taking fluids intravenously in the medical trailers, lingering by the administrative desk in the hope of hearing news, any news, the children racing wildly around the island in unsupervised games of tag, the babies screaming. It was clear what they weren't: Manhattanites. Many were first-generation immigrants. They didn't have friends with guesthouses in other parts of the country; they couldn't afford hotels or airfare. In many cases their entire family had lived on the same block. They were also stubborn: they didn't want to start over. (241)

This is the sole paragraph in the novel that focuses on poor people, people of color, or non-Americans, and it describes them in contemptuous terms by what they are not: residents of Manhattan. Elsewhere, descriptions of these outer-borough denizens frequently contain a hint of disgust. For example, a middle-aged woman who approaches Zukor's FEMA trailer is described as "a woman with a crumpled, washed-out face" who "smelled of detergent" (248).

While some critics have read the novel as a satirical critique of corporate capitalism and disaster profiteering (e.g., Siperstein), that element only describes its first third. As Tim Lanzendörfer notes, the rest of *Odds against Tomorrow* abandons its quasisatirical tone and establishes FutureWorld as a valuable and productive enterprise for both its clients and the world at large. Reader responses suggest the novel was not understood as a satire. In a survey of American readers of climate fiction, not one of the readers of *Odds against Tomorrow* appeared to view the novel as satire, and some reported that its primary lesson concerned the need for personal disaster preparedness. For example, a woman in her fifties wrote, "It made me very concerned about the effects of global warming. I also have thoughts of being more prepared for emergencies."[7] At least one reader seemed to view

Zukor as a model for climate adaption, saying, "It made me feel like I need to be smarter. I need to see things in different perspectives and angles." Similarly, an analysis of fifty randomly-selected reviews of the novel posted on the website Goodreads shows that while a minority of readers considered *Odds against Tomorrow* to be satire, most did not.[8] As a representative Goodreader put it, "The novel is a disturbingly *realistic* portrayal of the way things could go" ("Odds"; my emphasis).

Most of these readers seemed disappointed by the novel's conclusion. After escaping from the FEMA trailers, Zukor makes his way to the Flatlands neighborhood of Brooklyn, "just about the end of the earth . . . or as close as you can get without leaving New York City" (251). Renouncing the fortune he could earn through climate profiteering, Zukor takes up residence in an abandoned (but charmingly antiquated) former bank and develops the sense of masculinity and Emersonian self-reliance that comes from postapocalyptic gardening. Other stragglers trickle into the neighborhood. The novel ends with Jane—now running a new company, FutureDays—making regular deliveries of goods to support the budding community. In their eagerness to anoint *Odds against Tomorrow*, liberal critics, apparently unaware of the whiteness and problematic apoliticism of the North American back-to-the-land movement, praised this conclusion as a novel and radical proposal. Annalee Newitz of *Slate* even called Mitchell a "hero for the Occupy age," arguing that "there's a real sneakiness to Rich's story, which comes on like a deluge of disaster porn but then flows backward to reveal the fractured, reconfigurable landscapes of a David Graeber essay." In the leveled Flatlands, Zukor "forgot everything and decided he was exploring an abandoned world at the edge of the universe" (Rich 270), where he could finally put his neurotic obsession with risk and disaster behind him and embrace his (white) manhood: "Walking around the property, swinging the ax, he felt for the first time as if he owned the land. The Canarsie Bank Trust, as well as the adjacent plot, whatever it had been, was his domain" (290). This is a Lockean claim that by making of use of the land, Zukor now owns it.

This is deeply problematic from a justice perspective. While Flatlands might seem like the end of the Earth from the vantage point of Manhattan's Upper West Side, where Rich was raised (Holson), it is in reality a stable, middle-class neighborhood of sixty thousand. Home to African-Americans, Caribbeans, Latinxs, and Asian Americans, the neighborhood was not even flooded during Hurricane Sandy, when its denizens generously organized aid for their less fortunate neighbors in Brooklyn and Queens through organizations like the Flatlands Lions Clubs ("Superstorm"). To recapitulate: two white, wealthy, educated, twenty-somethings find a complicated financial means to profit off of climate disasters, then use these funds to settle a destroyed minority neighborhood, where they discover themselves by working the land. The familiar echoes of settler-colonial land appropriation and historical erasure are too loud to ignore. While we should not expect every climate-change novel to highlight specific perspectives, Rich's apparent ignorance of these settler-colonial reverberations and the absence of diversity and climate justice considerations constitute a deficient and pernicious framing of climate change.

WHITENESS IN THE CAPITAL

The absence of the climate justice frame was not isolated to *Odds against Tomorrow* but extends to other widely read and critically acclaimed American climate-change novels in this period. Let us consider from the same perspective Kim Stanley Robinson's *Science in the Capital* trilogy, *Forty Signs of Rain* (2004), *Fifty Degrees Below* (2005) and *Sixty Days and Counting* (2007). It is a fitting object of analysis, having received a great deal of attention by ecocritics as an exemplar of climate fiction. Rightly hailed as one of the most thoughtful and prolific environmentally engaged science fiction authors of the last three decades, Robinson also writes popular nonfiction essays on literature and environmental politics and has had a significant influence on contemporary environmental discourse.

Science in the Capital depicts a near future of abrupt climate change in which a carbon concentration of 400 parts per million leads to accelerated glacial melting, the stalling of the Gulf Stream, and dramatic temperature fluctuations and weather events. The focal character shifts from chapter to chapter, from Charlie Quibler, the environmental adviser to Senator-turned-President Phil Chase; to Anna Quibler, an administrator at the National Science Foundation; to Frank Vanderwal, a bioengineer and sociobiologist working at the same institution. The conceptual focus is on the relationship between science and politics in an era of abrupt climate change, expressing Robinson's utopian desire that science might someday become a kind of progressive political praxis (Canavan et al.). This wish is evident in his choice of a setting: Washington, DC, home of "big government," is flooded in the first novel and then frozen in the second, only to emerge as a global savior under enlightened leadership in the third. Robinson's primary goals are to depict potential political and technological responses to climate change and, secondarily, to investigate its psychological and philosophical implications.

Robinson gestures at an atmosphere of global cataclysms through short italicized interchapters that intermittently list weather events around the world even as the primary narrative focuses exclusively on Americans and the United States: "A tornado in Halifax, Nova Scotia; the third and catastrophic year of drought in Ireland . . . In Lisbon, a 60 degree drop in 7 minutes" (*Fifty* 369). However, as is the case in many American disaster films and novels, these descriptions are mere line items from a newsreel. They represent a nod towards planetary scope in which, as Ursula Heise has noted, "the narrative never develops any cultural," social, or political "perspective on the global" (Heise 207). Moreover, this gesture suggests, along with many American climate-change novels, that either climate change is ultimately a story that ought to be told through an American lens—the United States as axis mundi and global hero—or that climatic, social, economic, and political developments in the United States are a fitting synecdoche for parallel events worldwide. Neither is true.

In a novel set in Washington, DC, a "Chocolate City" whose population was approximately 30 percent white at the time of the trilogy's publication, all of Robinson's focal characters are not only white but educated, professionally secure, and financially well-off. In the trilogy's 1600 pages, the primary diegetic engagement with nonwhite experiences of anthropogenic climate change is the protagonists' serendipitous friendship with the displaced citizens of the fictional Khembalung. A Buddhist island nation of twelve thousand and a charter member of the (also fictional) League of Drowning Nations, the Khembalis have come to Washington because the rising seas will shortly drown their entire country. While Frank, Anna, and Charlie visit, that is exactly what happens. Every last Khembali abandons their home island in a stoic and orderly fashion while their white American visitors are whisked to safety in a helicopter, watching the ocean swallow the island from a safe distance. Resettling in Washington, all twelve thousand Khembalis somehow squeeze into a small property in Arlington, Virginia. When asked about his peoples' displacement, Rudra Cakrin, a Khembali leader, does not mourn the loss of his homeland or describe the difficulty of life as a refugee but merely says: "I do not mind it. It seems to be good for people. It wakes them up" (*Fifty* 213). Within the novel, Khembalung is a stand-in for other soon-to-be-drowned nations, such as Tuvalu and the Maldives, but also an opportunity for Robinson's Western characters to explore his synthesis of Buddhism and ecology. In seeking to develop connections between Eastern religion and resilience, Robinson sacrifices climate justice verisimilitude to use non-Western characters as stereotypical representatives of ancient and exotic wisdom.

The Khembalis' perspective could not be more different from the forceful and public activism of real island nations' citizens and leaders. At climate conventions, on social media, and through international environmental organizations, small island nations have been at the forefront of demands for rapid decarbonization and climate justice. For example, Tony de Brum, former president of the Marshall Islands, called climate change "a war for nothing less than the future of humanity" and asked, "in whose warped world is the potential loss of a country not a threat to international peace and security" (De Brum)? Mohamed Nasheed, former President of the Maldives, famously staged an underwater cabinet meeting and stated that if the 2009 Copenhagen COP (Conference of the Parties) were to fail, "We are going to die" (BBC). In *Science in the Capital*, the Khembalis have little trouble becoming permanent residents of the United States, purchasing land in Maryland, and constructing a utopic farm complete with treehouses for their guests. In the real world, climate refugees stand to lose their traditional homelands and cultures, there is no international legal recognition of the category of environmental refugee, and there are major obstacles to its emergence. Necessary land and funding for resettlement will be difficult to secure, especially as wealthy nations face their own challenges and find excuses to shirk their historical culpability.

Surprisingly few characters in *Science in the Capital* seem particularly troubled by its tremendous climate catastrophes. There is an exemplary level of individual and community resilience in Robinson's storyworld, which makes *Science in the Capital* one of the few positive (or even non-dystopic) popular visions of climate futures. At times, however, this rosy outlook obscures as much as it reveals. This is evident in *Fifty Degrees Below*, when a prolonged cold snap culminating in temperatures of fifty degrees (Fahrenheit) below zero is repeatedly deemed to be a "good thing" by his protagonists (456), because it will finally motivate conservative legislators to take action. Meanwhile, average Washingtonians jump at the opportunity to play in the snow:

> Late in the day Frank went back down to the Potomac to walk out on the ice. Scores of people had had the same idea. Now on the Potomac people were mostly standing around or skiing, playing football or soccer or ad hoc versions of curling.... When sunset slanted redly across the Potomac the light struck Frank like another vision out of Bruegel. One of his Flemish winter canal scenes, except most of the Washington, D.C., population was black.... It was like Carnavale on ice.... A giant steel drum added to the Caribbean flavor.... It seemed to him to be an extraordinarily beautiful populace, every race and ethnicity on Earth represented—the many black faces vivid and handsome, cheerful to the point of euphoria, laughing as they took in the scene. (421–22)

In reality most of these smiles would be frozen in place, since frostbite begins within five to ten minutes of skin exposure at such a low temperature. (Disorientation, slurred speech, and uncontrollable shivering, which might be mistaken for "euphoria," are also likely.) Retrospectively cringeworthy passages like this—a "giant steel drum" adding "Caribbean flavor" amidst the "laughing" "black faces"—should lead us to examine the portrayal of people of color within Robinson's work, especially given his stature within environmental literature and climate fiction in particular.[9] As one of the few appearances of people of color in these novels, this portrait of the impact of abrupt climate change on already disadvantaged minorities in the United States might be read as comic, if only his intentions in this work of "proleptic realism" (Luckhurst 173) were not so serious. Not even on the novel's wide radar, however, are the millions of poor, isolated, or elderly Americans for whom such an extreme and rapid temperature shift would prove fatal. Readers might well question whether his protagonists' admirable resilience is due to their indefatigable spirit or their racial and economic privilege.

Ecocritic De Witt Douglas Kilgore sees the role of race within the trilogy differently. Kilgore argues that Frank embodies an attempt to move beyond whiteness, constructing a new postcapitalist subjectivity in the face of climate change while using his racial privilege as a force for good, especially in his selfless friendship with the homeless "bros" who congregate in Rock Creek Park, where Frank lives in a treehouse for much of *Fifty Degrees Below.* "If the racial hierarchy sponsored by an extractive capitalism is splintering," Kilgore asks, "then what would replace it" (104)? Thus Kilgore explains Frank and Robinson's interest in sociobiology as a generative attempt to resuscitate distant subjectivities in the Anthropocene present.

However, as Jeanne Hamming notes, by the end of the trilogy Frank abandons his Paleolithic lifestyle, having achieved the heteronormative masculine American dream of marriage, fatherhood, and homeownership. Whether or not we agree with Kilgore's generous interpretation, Robinson's narrative proves unable to move beyond the concerns of his white, American, wealthy, educated protagonists, which has the effect of "backgrounding the environment" as well as people outside the cocoon of American whiteness and "foreground[ing] the floundering masculine subjectivity" that is threatened by global climate change (Hamming 27). Frank's blinding whiteness is manifest in an exchange that occurs during the titular freeze in *Fifty Degrees Below*, as Frank discusses winter clothing with city workers busily cutting down trees. "They were all black," the omniscient narrator notes. "They lived over in Northeast but had worked mostly Northwest when they had worked for City Parks. One of them went on about being from Africa and not capable of handling this kind of cold." At which point, Frank, the scientist and sociobiologist with the expensive down vest and nylon wind-jacket says, "We're all from Africa" (*Fifty* 427). This remark, simply passed over by the workers and narrator, seems to demonstrate Frank's ignorance (and Robinson's deprioritization) of the basic, critical claim of climate justice: that there are vastly different experiences of climate change according to race, ethnicity, gender, wealth, and nationality. At no point do we see Frank move beyond this ignorance, and at no point are the problematic dimensions of Frank's sociobiology—such as racism and social Darwinism (e.g., Ruse)—critiqued. However noble his intentions, Robinson ultimately uses climate change, the Khembalis, and the occasional appearance of Black characters as a means of reinvigorating the subjectivities and sensibilities of his white protagonists.

The overwhelming Americanness and whiteness of *Science in the Capital* inevitably influences the trilogy's recommendations for responses to climate change. In the final installment, *Sixty Days and Counting,* Charlie and Frank become consequential figures as Phil Chase is elected president on a platform of addressing climate change and transforming the United States' relationship with the world. While Charlie and Frank's friendship with the Khembalis and President Chase's anti-imperialist statements and blog posts are intended to demonstrate that the United States is opening itself to a less imperious and hierarchical relationship with other nations, the novel's large-scale geoengineering and bioengineering responses to climate change are not described as the product of a horizontal, democratic process. These interventions include unilaterally and haphazardly releasing a gene-edited carbon-sequestering lichen (developed by one of Frank's former students) into the Siberian forest, where it spreads at a perilously rapid and uncontrollable rate. Similarly, a massive amount of saltwater is pumped from oceans into glaciers and dry basins around the world, most of which are located in Asia and Africa. As Frank suggests in a meeting of top government officials, the "infrastructural value of property" is low in these regions and there are "statistically insignificant population to displace" (*Sixty* 243), which makes them ideal areas for terraforming. The justification for these experiments, sanctioned by the United Nations, is that "people were ready to try things," so that "even the more blatant interventions, like bioengineered bacteria or lichen, had the support of an admittedly smaller majority [of the population], like sixty percent" (*Fifty* 534). What's unstated is that this "sixty percent" refers to the American public and not the people whose lives are at stake. Robinson does not mention a mechanism for global decision-making about geoengineering, and these risky and consequential choices seem to be made by a small circle of American (and largely white) politicians, bureaucrats, and scientists.

As policymakers, ethicists, and scholars of international relations have noted, geoengineering presents a collective action and governance problem at least as complicated as climate mitigation. There is the distinct possibility that geoengineering will be carried out by wealthy and geopolitically powerful nations that consider grave risks to distant people to be acceptable. While these interventions are miraculously successful in the trilogy, they might just as easily go disastrously wrong at a planetary scale. For example, scientists note that the most popular candidate for geoengineering, solar radiation management, could disrupt the Indian monsoon, which could negatively affect billions of people and lead to the starvation of tens of millions (Brewer). Indeed, the growing interest in geoengineering has led to a field of research on geoengineering justice (e.g., Preston). In *Science in the Capital,* the exclusion of minority characters and climate justice considerations constitutes a structuring absence that enables Robinson's endorsement of potentially catastrophic and unjust technologies as commonsensical technosolutions.

AMERICA FIRST

This chapter has focused on two critically acclaimed works of American climate fiction of the 2000s and 2010s. While a thorough analysis of the framing adopted by all American climate fiction of this era is not possible in this space, we would come to a similar conclusion by examining the vast majority of it. Indeed, in Adam Trexler's *Anthropocene Fictions* (2015), the most exhaustive early survey of the novels of climate change and the Anthropocene, justice is not mentioned as a major or minor theme. Though literary critics have highlighted a number of important texts published during this period that did focus on socioeconomic, climate, or environmental justice, they are the exceptions. Despite the apocalyptic or dystopic focus of most American cli-fi, well-known authors generally shied away from depicting in detail the violence (both slow and spectacular) of climate injustice. Novels such as Marcel Theroux's *Far North* and Robert Charles Wilson's *Julian Comstock: A Story of 22nd-Century America*, like many cli-fi novels set decades or even centuries in the future, recall only vague periods of tribulation and hardship that time has transformed into legend. Especially as the resettlement of climate refugees from poorer countries becomes an increasingly urgent topic in the decades to come, these elisions constitute a missed opportunity to cultivate an awareness of climate justice and empathy in American readers.[10]

How do we explain this representational lacuna? Answers to this question are admittedly speculative, but important to consider. We might note, first, that these works were conceived, published, and received within an American political and cultural context in which colorblindness still held hegemonic power (Bonilla-Silva) and class, racial, and ethnic difference were invoked primarily as a contrast with normative wealth and whiteness. As a result, even well-intentioned texts by progressive authors tended to universalize or neglect race, leading to the erasure of differences that are due to race as well as ethnicity, class, gender, sexual identity, and nationality.

Second, we might view this failure of imagination as a tertiary consequence of the long history of organized and well-funded climate denial in the United States. The result of this coordinated campaign of confusion was a woefully low level of belief in anthropogenic climate change despite the scientific consensus—in a 2014 poll, 61 percent of Americans said there was "solid evidence the earth is warming," but only 40 percent believed it was due to human activities (Pew). As a result of the manufacture of doubt, the goals of concerned novelists were stunted, centered on the most basic questions of cause and effect, with less space to explore some of the second-order consequences that were not yet well understood by most Americans, such as infectious diseases, food security, mass migration from poor countries, and climate justice. So it is that the central drama of the most accomplished cli-fi novel of this period, Barbara Kingsolver's *Flight Behavior*, concerned the environmental awakening of a rural Tennessee woman who comes to accept the reality and gravity of anthropogenic climate change when millions of monarch butterflies, their established migration route disrupted, arrive in her backyard. Almost five decades after the first public reports on the consequences of greenhouse gas emissions, this was a principal goal of a major American novelist addressing climate change: to show that even poor, white, rural conservatives could accept a long-established scientific consensus.

Third, we might conjecture that the lack of interest that Americans seem to have in other peoples and places inevitably colors the stories that American authors choose to tell. In their quest for relevance and influence, Rich, Robinson, Kingsolver, and other authors attempted to meet their readers halfway, and most Americans remain squarely focused on the United States. Although globalization and digital technologies have allegedly shrunk the world, they have not appreciably expanded Americans' knowledge of and interest in other places and cultures. The stereotype of the American ignorant of global affairs is confirmed by cross-cultural polls that test Americans' knowledge of other countries. In a 2006 poll of eighteen-to-twenty-four-year-olds in Canada, France, Germany, Great Britain, Italy, Japan, Mexico, Sweden, and the United States, Americans placed second to last in knowledge of foreign countries and affairs (*National Geographic*). One reason for this relative ignorance is the lack of attention to foreign languages and international issues in American primary and secondary education (Devlin); another is the (often deliberate) spread of misinformation by some mainstream news networks (Fairleigh Dickinson). A more diffuse but perhaps more robust influence is what Rob Nixon called "superpower parochialism" (Nixon 35) combined with an imperial narcissism that accumulated during the long "American century," which leaves many Americans believing themselves to be firmly and eternally at the epicenter of most events of global and historical significance (Caldwell). Indeed, cultural myopia is part of what enabled support for the isolationism, unilateralism, and white supremacy of the Trump administration. Although prayers and small donations are always forthcoming to the victims of the latest not-so-natural disaster, many Americans fail to empathize with those beyond their borders or acknowledge the historical responsibilities generated by a near-century of fossil-fueled superpower status. Knowing this, many environmentally engaged American authors seem to have catered to their readers by featuring settings and characters with whom readers might readily identify.

WHITHER CLIMATE JUSTICE?

As empirical scholarship on the reception of climate fiction demonstrates, these works can have a potent impact on the way that readers conceive of anthropogenic climate change (Schneider-Mayerson, "Influence"; Schneider-Mayerson et al., "Environmental"). Given the influence of these novels on subsequent framings, and given the temporal lag of climate change, climate justice delayed is climate justice denied.

Due to the negative consequences of thinking about climate change, including anxiety and depression, even concerned Americans often avoid detailed reflections on our potential climate futures. In this context, climate fiction, and environmental media in general, can play a powerful role in influencing the frames that readers perceive, prioritize, adopt, and share with family, friends, coworkers, and others. The novel in particular has great potential to encourage and cultivate transnational empathy for the already disadvantaged victims of climate change, due in part to the extended temporal engagement that the form requires.

As we see in *Odds against Tomorrow* and the *Science in the Capital* trilogy, American climate fiction in the 2000s and early 2010s tended to emphasize particular climate frames: the catastrophe frame and, secondarily, the biodiversity, national security, and patriotic challenge frames. The justice and equity frame is important and necessary, because it constitutes the only frame that is likely to motivate a program of individual and collective mitigation and adaptation that will address and not exacerbate existing inequalities. As we move deeper into an era in which socioenvironmental concerns will be defined by adaptation, triage, and migration in addition to mitigation, keeping justice firmly in mind will be critical.

As such, scholars and critics ought to ask of *every* climate-change narrative, in literature and other media: whither climate justice?

NOTES

1. To identify the frame employed by a novel, critics must examine a text holistically, with attention to some combination of content, form, and structure. In some

sense, then, the identification of a particular frame (or combination of frames) is subjective, though critics familiar with these two texts are unlikely to disagree with my claim that the climate justice frame is largely absent.

2. Both texts have been widely reviewed and either won or were nominated for numerous awards. *Odds against Tomorrow* was named an NPR Best Book of the Year, *New York Times Book Review* Editors' Choice, and a *New Yorker* Book to Watch Out For, while *Forty Signs of Rain* (the first novel in the *Science in the Capital* trilogy) was nominated for the British Science Fiction Award and the Locus Award. Anecdotal data gathered at ecocriticism conferences supports the claim that these two works have been regularly assigned in college (and even some high school) classes. As of this writing, *Odds against Tomorrow* and *Forty Signs of Rain* have been cited in 86 and 179 scholarly articles, respectively. Whether a text is representative is largely subjective, but, as I note in this essay, surveys of the genre or category of "cli-fi" rarely include a mention of climate justice, suggesting that this theme has indeed been largely absent from most American climate fiction.

3. Studying absences and silences is an increasingly critical approach in the humanities and social sciences, due to the growing acknowledgment of the importance of selection, representation, and diversity. However, it seems to be less common within literary criticism (outside of psychoanalytic criticism, African American studies, and ethnic studies), perhaps because of the traditional focus on individual works or authors and the general tendency for critics to write about works that they enjoy or support, aesthetically or politically—a focus on absences is in some ways an inherently critical perspective. Studying absences and silences seems to be more common within some social scientific disciplines, such as communications. In this sense, importing the concept of "framing" from media studies enables us to evaluate the framing of American climate fiction, demonstrating the value of mobilizing concepts from multiple disciplines.

4. In other indices the United States' per capita carbon footprint is much higher. The emissions involved in the production and transportation of consumer goods from outside the United States are not counted in this data, allowing Americans to outsource their pollution to other countries.

5. This assumes no population growth. If Bangladesh's population doubles, as many demographers expect, the number of internally displaced persons and emigrants could be twice as high.

6. A related question is whether the themes and arguments that ecocritics see in particular texts are picked up by readers. Such questions are critical to assessing the influence of environmental literature on its readers and demonstrate the need for more empirical research. See Schneider-Mayerson, Weik von Mossner, and Małecki.

7. Survey conducted via Amazon's Mechanical Turk in September 2016, with 161 respondents. See author for more information.

8. As of April 20, 2017, *Odds against Tomorrow* had 254 ratings on Goodreads, which crowdsources literary reviews. Every fifth review was selected for analysis.

9. In *Science in the Capital* these examples abound. For example, in *Forty Signs of Rain*, Frank describes an Asian American character as an "Asian dragon lady" (27) who is "good-looking in an exotic way" (23).

10. The term "climate refugees" is used deliberately, even though "climate migrants" has become more common amongst scholars of the climate-migration nexus. From the perspective of climate justice, "refugee" acknowledges that those forced from their homes and homelands are, in a sense, victims of climate change, whereas for some scholars "migrant" signals agency—migration as a form of neoliberal adaptation. See Dreher and Voyer.

WORKS CITED

BBC. "Maldives Cabinet Makes a Splash." *BBC News*, 17 Oct. 2009. news.bbc.co.uk/2/hi/8311838.stm.

Bonilla-Silva, Eduardo. *Racism without Racists: Color-Blind Racism and the Persistence of Racial Inequality in America*. Rowman & Littlefield, 2018.

Butler, Octavia. *Parable of the Sower*. Four Walls Eight Windows, 1993.

Brewer, Peter G. "Evaluating a Technological Fix for Climate." *Proceedings of the National Academy of Sciences*, vol. 104, no. 24, 2007, pp. 9915–16.

Caldwell, Wilber W. *American Narcissism: The Myth of National Superiority*. Algora Publishing, 2006.

Canavan, Gerry, Lisa Klarr, and Ryan Vu. "Science, Justice, Science Fiction: A Conversation with Kim Stanley Robinson." *Polygraph*, no. 22, 2010, pp. 201–17.

Cussler, Clive. *Arctic Drift*. Berkley Books, 2009.

De Brum, Tony. "A Call to Arms on Climate Change." *The Drum*, 30 July 2013. www.abc.net.au/news/2013-07-30/de-brum-climate-change-marshall-islands/4852760.

Devlin, Kat. "Learning a Foreign Language a 'Must' in Europe, Not So in America." *Pew Research Center*, 13 July 2015. www.pewresearch.org/fact-tank/2015/07/13/learning-a-foreign-language-a-must-in-europe-not-so-in-america.

Dreher, Tanja, and Michelle Voyer. "Climate Refugees or Migrants? Contesting Media Frames on Climate Justice in the Pacific." *Environmental Communication*, vol. 9, no. 1, 2015, pp. 58–76.

Evancie, Angela. "So Hot Right Now: Has Climate Change Created A New Literary Genre?," *NPR*, 20 Apr. 2013. www.npr.org/2013/04/20/176713022/so-hot-right-now-has-climate-change-created-a-new-literary-genre.

Fairleigh Dickinson. "What You Know Depends on What You Watch: Current Events Knowledge across Popular News Sources." PublicMind, 3 May 2012. publicmind.fdu.edu/2012/confirmed/final.pdf.

CDMP II. *Trends and Impact Analysis of Internal Displacement due to the Impacts of Disasters and Climate Change*. Comprehensive Disaster Management Programme (CDMP II), Ministry of Disaster Management and Relief, Dhaka, 2014.

Ge, Mengpin, Johannes Friedrich, and Thomas Damassa. "6 Graphs Explain the World's Top 10 Emitters." *World Resources Institute*, 25 Nov. 2014. https://www.wri.org/insights/6-graphs-explain-worlds-top-10-emitters.

Gottlieb, Robert. *Forcing the Spring: The Transformation of the American Environmental Movement.* Island Press, 2005.

Guzman, Andrew. *Overheated: The Human Cost of Climate Change.* Oxford UP, 2013.

Hamming, Jeanne. "Nationalism, Masculinity, and the Politics of Climate Change in the Novels of Kim Stanley Robinson and Michael Crichton." *Extrapolation*, vol. 54, no. 1, 2013, pp. 21–45.

Heise, Ursula. *Sense of Place and Sense of Planet: The Environmental Imagination of the Global.* Oxford UP, 2008.

Hulme, Mike. *Why We Disagree about Climate Change: Understanding Controversy, Inaction and Opportunity.* Cambridge UP, 2009.

Holson, Laura M. "The Family Franchise." *The New York Times*, 4 Jan. 2013. www.nytimes.com/2013/01/06/fashion/nathaniel-and-simon-the-brothers-rich.html.

Kilgore, De Witt Douglas. "Making Huckleberries: Reforming Science and Whiteness in *Science in the Capital*." *Configurations*, vol. 20, nos. 1–2, 2012, pp. 89–108.

Kingsolver, Barbara. *Flight Behavior.* HarperCollins, 2012.

Lanzendörfer, Tim. "Commercializing Risk and Facing Disaster: Nathaniel Rich's *Odds against Tomorrow*." Presentation at the conference America After Nature, 61st Annual Conference of the German Society for American Studies (DGfA), University of Würzburg, 12–15 June 2014.

Luckhurst, Roger. "The Politics of the Network: The *Science in the Capital* Trilogy." *Kim Stanley Robinson Maps the Unimaginable: Critical Essays*, edited by William J. Burling, McFarland, 2009, pp. 170–80.

Mehnert, Antonia. *Climate Change Fictions: Representations of Global Warming in American Literature.* Springer, 2016.

National Geographic–Roper Public Affairs 2006 Global Geographic Literacy Survey. National Geographic Education Foundation, 2006. https://media.nationalgeographic.org/assets/file/NGS-Roper-2006-Report.pdf.

Newitz, Annalee. "End Times." *Slate*, 3 May 2013. www.slate.com/articles/arts/books/2013/05/nathaniel_rich_s_the_odds_against_tomorrow_reviewed.html.

Nixon, Rob. *Slow Violence and the Environmentalism of the Poor.* Harvard UP, 2011.

Nisbet, Matthew C. "Communicating Climate Change: Why Frames Matter for Public Engagement." *Environment: Science and Policy for Sustainable Development*, vol. 51, no. 2, 2009, pp. 12–23.

"*Odds against Tomorrow* by Nathaniel Rich." *Goodreads.* https://www.goodreads.com/book/show/15759484-odds-against-tomorrow.

Paul, Ruma, and Zarir Hussain. "Bangladesh Military Scrambles to Reach Millions Marooned after Deadly Flooding." *Reuters*, June 20, 2022. https://www.reuters.com/world/asia-pacific/millions-bangladesh-india-await-relief-after-deadly-flooding-2022-06-20/.

Pew Research Center for the People and the Press. "Section 7: Global Warming, Environment and Energy." *Pew Research Center*, 26 June 2014. http://www.people-press.org/2014/06/26/section-7-global-warming-environment-and-energy.

Preston, Christopher J., editor. *Climate Justice and Geoengineering: Ethics and Policy in the Atmospheric Anthropocene*. Rowman & Littlefield, 2016.

Rich, Nathaniel. *Odds against Tomorrow*. Farrar, Straus and Giroux, 2013.

Robinson, Kim Stanley. *Forty Signs of Rain*. HarperCollins, 2004.

———. *Fifty Degrees Below*. HarperCollins, 2005.

———. *Sixty Days and Counting*. HarperCollins, 2007.

Ruse, Michael. *Sociobiology: Sense or Nonsense*. Springer Science & Business Media, 1984.

Schlosberg, David, and Lisette B. Collins. "From Environmental to Climate Justice: Climate Change and the Discourse of Environmental Justice." *Wiley Interdisciplinary Reviews: Climate Change*, vol. 5, no. 3, 2014, pp. 359–74.

Schneider-Mayerson, Matthew. "The Influence of Climate Fiction: An Empirical Survey of Readers." *Environmental Humanities*, vol. 10, no. 2, 2018, pp. 473–500.

Schneider-Mayerson, Matthew, Abel Gustafson, Anthony Leiserowitz, Matthew H. Goldberg, Seth A. Rosenthal, and Matthew Ballew. "Environmental Literature as Persuasion: An Experimental Test of the Effects of Reading Climate Fiction." *Environmental Communication*, 2020, pp. 1–16.

Siperstein, Stephen. "Climate Change in Literature and Culture: Conversion, Speculation, Education." 2016. U of Oregon, PhD dissertation.

"Superstorm Sandy: One Year Later." *Lions Club International Foundation*, 28 Oct. 2013.

Theroux, Marcel. *Far North: A Novel*. Farrar, Straus and Giroux, 2009.

Trexler, Adam. *Anthropocene Fictions: The Novel in a Time of Climate Change*. U of Virginia P, 2015.

Trexler, Adam, and Adeline Johns-Putra. "Climate Change in Literature and Literary Criticism." *Wiley Interdisciplinary Reviews: Climate Change*, vol. 2, no. 2, 2011, pp. 185–200.

Wilson, Robert Charles. *Julian Comstock: A Story of 22nd-Century America*. Macmillan, 2009.

World Bank. *World Development Report 2010: Development and Climate Change*. World Bank, 2010.

———. CO2 emissions (metric tons per capita). https://data.worldbank.org/indicator/EN.ATM.CO2E.PC?view=map&year_high_desc=false. Accessed 23 Aug. 2017.

Ziser, Michael, and Julie Sze. "Climate Change, Environmental Aesthetics, and Global Environmental Justice Cultural Studies." *Discourse*, vol. 29, nos. 2–3, 2007, pp. 384–410.

Cli-Fi and the Crisis of the Middle Class

MAGDALENA MĄCZYŃSKA

Climate change is a social crisis. As Nancy Tuana argues in her denouncement of "climate change apartheid" (a term she borrows from Desmond Tutu), racist patterns of capitalist extraction have allowed a small minority of humans to pursue middle-class aspirations while devastating communities and environments worldwide (5). The consumerist American Dream, whose postwar exuberance drove the Great Acceleration, has never been accessible to all. "Every family in the world cannot have two cars, a washing machine, and a refrigerator," as Amitav Gosh points out, for the simple reason that humans would "asphyxiate in the process" (92). Today, as neoliberal capitalism continues to widen the wealth gap within and between nations, and as atmospheric carbon dioxide levels continue to climb, it is clearer than ever that the promise of middle-class comfort for all has materialized only for a narrow elite, leaving the rest of the human and nonhuman family to pay the price.

How does climate fiction respond to this crisis within the novel's traditional class territory? In *The Great Derangement,* Ghosh laments the dearth of climate-themed literary fiction and attributes this shortage to the incompatibility of realism's "rhetoric of the everyday" (which he links, via Franco Moretti, to the "regularity of bourgeois life") with the larger-than-life scale and drama of climatic events (19). But, as Ghosh's critics point out, such pro-realism bias obscures the abundance of recent genre (and genre-bending) fiction concerned with climatic transformations. As Stephanie LeMenager notes, in the era of climate crisis, "artistic genres are fraying, recombining, or otherwise moving outside of our expectations of what they ought to be because life itself is moving outside of our expectations of what it ought to be" (477).

The fast-expanding archive of cli-fi is generically diverse, including speculative, fantasy, detective, noir, postapocalyptic, dystopian, romance, zombie, and science fiction. Unlike literary realism, most of these genres do not traditionally center "bourgeois life." Nevertheless, climate narratives set in radically altered worlds often rely on middle-class repertoires. Familiar settings (single-family homes, apartment buildings, cafés, shopping malls, gas stations, airports) and objects (personal electronics, domestic appliances, furnishings, branded foodstuffs) return—with a difference—as ruins, remnants, or *natureculture* fossils. These transformations signal a pervasive anxiety about late capitalist middle-class life, foregrounding its unsustainability, its manifest contribution to the global environmental crisis, and its systemically exclusionary premises.

My reading focuses on four narratives that recombine the apocalyptic with the quotidian. Maggie Gee's *The Ice People* (1998) depicts a rapidly advancing ice age; Margaret Atwood's *Oryx and Crake* (2003) traces the origins and aftermath of a bioengineered plague; Cormac McCarthy's *The Road* (2006) follows a father and son across a postcatastrophe wasteland; Colson Whitehead's *Zone One* (2011) imagines Manhattan besieged by zombies. Not all authors reference climate change to the same degree. McCarthy never mentions climatic disruption, although his damaged landscapes and skyscapes suggest it. Whitehead juxtaposes his zombie plague with the "less flamboyant, more deliberate ruination altering the planet's climate" (240) and repeatedly likens the zombies to weather and flooding. Atwood and Gee name specific climatic effects: global warming and cooling (Gee), drought, rising ocean salinity, and permafrost melt (Atwood). All four endgame narratives lend themselves to interpretation as metonymic stand-ins for climate apocalypse. What makes this quartet especially useful for examining the interface of climate and class is that their stories are told through the lens of middle-class, precatastrophe-bred protagonists, whose sense of "the normal" aligns with that of (presumed) middle-class readers. The effect is a palimpsestic superimposition of the readers' present onto projected future(s). As Marco Caracciollo notes in his discussion of postapocalyptic climate fiction, such dyadic narrative structures "evoke the post-world as a negation of the pre-world" (226). This absence/presence effect can generate nostalgia (Caraciollo's focus), but also disgust, regret, mockery, and horror—both at the monstrosity of the postcatastrophe future and at the monstrous injustice inherent in the consumerist middle-class ideal within a neocolonial world system.

THE VANISHING CENTER

Canonical cli-fi dystopias imagine societies bifurcated into elites (in control of resources and adaptation technologies) and precarious underclasses (bearing the brunt of climate impacts). As postcatastrophe societies reorganize themselves, the center of the social spectrum becomes less and less robust. In George Turner's *Sea and Summer* (1987), Sydney is split between home-owning "Sweets" and unemployed "Swills" housed in dilapidated, flood-prone developments. In Octavia Butler's *Parable of the Sower* (1993), corporations erect powerful company towns, while the dwindling middle classes face a choice between indentured labor and destitution. In Paolo Bacigalupi's *Water Knife* (2015), dehydrated masses struggle to buy water by the sip in the shadow of lush private oases.[1] Such "vanishing center" tales expose the limits of the capitalist promise in face of environmental catastrophe. Not only does the hoped-for prosperity fail to materialize, but political and economic power congeals in the hands of militarized corporate interests. Projecting this pattern onto "relatable" middle-class communities makes visible the inequities already present, globally and intranationally, in a world controlled by advanced capitalist interests.

Atwood's *Oryx and Crake* shows a stark class divide between biotech families housed in luxury compounds and those in unsafe, polluted "pleeblands." As the novel progresses, the boundary between the two realms firms. Middle grounds shrink as peripheral workers move into compounds, pleeblands become "ultra-hazardous," and compound security grows "tighter than ever" (251). Atwood gives us glimpses of pleebland landscapes via train windows and TV screens, as the protagonist, Jimmy, observes "endless dingy-looking streets" (27) filled with "rows of dingy houses" (196) and the decaying infrastructure of "vacant warehouses, burnt-out tenements, empty parking lots" (185). This bleak terrain is, unsurprisingly, a site of environmental degradation, marred by smoking factories, gravel pits, and garbage incinerators (196). Pleeblanders suffer higher infection rates, more injuries by runaway organisms created in compound labs, and higher levels of pollution: "more junk blowing in the wind, fewer whirlpool purifying towers" (287). Their communities are exploited through internal tourism, as the rich, protected by security guards and state-of-the-art vaccines, go "slumming" in search of entertainment and sex.

The spatial organization of Atwood's dystopia records the entrenchment of a new, neofeudal order. Jimmy's father happily admits this: "Long ago, in the days of knights and dragons, the kings and dukes had lived in castles, with high walls and drawbridges and slots on the ramparts so you could pour hot pitch on your enemies" (28). The Compounds, the father goes on, "were the same idea," designed "for keeping you and your buddies nice and safe inside, and for keeping everybody else outside" (28). Under the guise of dystopian projection, Atwood registers the global reality of gated compounds (some state-sized) surrounded by depressed territories that provide labor, bear the environmental costs of development, absorb waste and toxicity, and serve as exoticized playgrounds for the rich.

In Gee's *Ice People,* class divides established before the apocalypse widen and morph as society grapples with catastrophic impacts. The protagonist, Saul, initially ignores climatic shifts because his privilege insulates him from their consequences: "In wealthier areas, life went on as usual. I didn't let the newscasts upset me" (12). After the brief period of warming gives way to a rapidly advancing ice age, Europeans become climate refugees, vying for entry into more habitable regions. Those who remain sort themselves into two groups: the protected Insiders and small groups of rebel Outsiders, who weather the new conditions without the protections of "civilization."

In Whitehead's *Zone One,* American society struggles to reestablish itself amidst a zombie pandemic. The protagonist (known only by his nickname, "Mark Spitz") works as a "sweeper" preparing lower Manhattan for rehabitation. His job is to find, kill, and dispose of zombie stragglers lingering in city buildings. The novel's sweeper crews represent a cross-section of lower middle-class America: "erstwhile cheerleaders, salesmen of luxury boats, gym teachers, food bloggers, patent clerks, cafeteria lunch ladies, dispatchers from international delivery companies" (39). Instead of adequate protective equipment, these exhausted frontline workers are offered swag promoting "reconstruction's first official sponsors" (38) and a branded vision of rebirth ("American Phoenix")—evidence of capitalist logic reestablishing itself in the aftermath of disaster.

The restoration of New York is engineered by the elites for the elites. "You think we're going to end up here?" asks a fellow sweeper, "We ain't special. They're going to put the rich people here. Politicians and pro athletes. Those chefs from those cooking shows" (89). The gulf between on-the-ground crews and their sponsors becomes painfully apparent when Zone One is visited by a sleek government representative: "She was a meteor crashed from another part of the solar system, or a place even more remote, life before the agony" (201). The desperate push to make Manhattan great again is part of a longer historical pattern: as Andrew Stombeck argues, *Zone One* is a novel about real estate and zoning, referencing both the finance-capital takeover of New York City in the 1970s and 1980s, and the more recent takeover of neighborhoods by gentrifiers. More than any other novelist under discussion here, Whitehead makes it apparent that his dystopian vision is a look within as much as a look ahead—and that the horrors of the zombie plague are not a negation of the current "normal" but its consummation.

FUTURE RUINS

Cli-fi's future landscapes draw on the infrastructure of modern middle-class life, reflected back to the reader in the form of ruins. Ruins, in art and life, have long served as reminders of nature's triumph over human endeavor or as sites of nostalgia for lost ancestral grandeur. In the eighteenth and nineteenth centuries—the European heyday of ruin obsession—decaying ancient and medieval structures provided a metonymic link to the past: to their devotees, these remnants offered not only the pleasures of the picturesque (or the sublime), but also the possibility of tracing—or, more often, fabricating—genealogies of ethnonational and class identity. The anxieties and disruptions of the early industrialial era bred nostalgia for a more orderly, hierarchical past; as the capitalist middle class (along with the modern novel) rose to dominance, the remains of castles, churches, and chapels pointed synecdochally to a vanished, "noble" social order.

The semiotics of cli-fi ruins differ dramatically from this familiar script of social nostalgia. At the tail end of middle-class triumphalism, the ruined anthroposcapes of climate fiction invite not a look back but a horrified glance into the future. The Anthropocene "future ruin" offers contemporary readers a deformed but recognizable version of their own middle-class quotidian: not grand monuments to a noble past, but suburban homes, city apartments, convenience stores, supermarkets, gas stations, motels, and highways. Such familiarity prompts (alongside an unwelcome recognition), a sense of temporal unhomeliness, a psychic displacement that disturbs the logic of the American Dream and its class aspirations. Superimposed on the familiar infrastructure of everyday life, future ruins force a recognition of the violence inherent in late capitalism's consumerist lifestyle, disrupting the capitalist narrative of futurity as a site of never-ending progress.[2]

Climate fiction's ruins signify not historical continuity but disruption, a rift in the narrative of civilizational growth sponsored by the era of fossil-fuel optimism. Commerce and transportation, the twin pillars of modern carbon economy, are especially pervasive in cli-fi's ruinscapes. Atwood's Jimmy traverses streets piled with "multi-vehicle crashes" and flanked with "gutted" shops (221). McCarthy's protagonists travel along disintegrating highways, under ghostly advertisements: "Farther along were billboards advertising motels. Everything as it once had been save faded and weathered" (8). McCarthy's evocation of familiar buildings and objects as they "once had been" turns the reader into a macabre archaeologist of late capitalism: "Cars in the street caked with ash, everything covered with ash and dust. Fossil tracks in the dried sludge. A corpse in the doorway dried to leather" (12). Gee's survivors literally burn through the vestiges of carbon civilization as they seek shelter in an abandoned airport: "the fires that keep us warm are steadily burning their way through the airline's abandoned fixtures. Old desks and partitions collapsing like foam, carpets unravelling in thick, black fumes" (4). The material products of fossil-fuel extraction transform from familiar fixtures to reminders of disastrous unsustainability.

Descriptive close-ups of future ruins draw attention to the takeover of human infrastructure by nonhuman agents: organisms as well as physical processes of decomposition. Cli-fi's use of the "world without us" trope is not new: Richard Jefferies's late-Victorian precursor, *After London; or, Wild England* (1885), envisions southern England overgrown with lush vegetation. A more recent nonfiction iteration of the trope, Alain Weisman's *The World without Us* (2007), presents detailed projections of infrastructural collapse. In McCarthy's *The Road*, the protagonist repeatedly enters buildings in various stages of degeneration, swollen from water damage or desiccated from exposure. Factory-made surfaces disintegrate, the paper "swollen and sodden," the linoleum "stained and curling" (7). No longer utilitarian, objects reclaim their materiality. In Atwood's *Oryx and Crake*, the resettlement of urban landscapes by plant life reverses the efforts of human husbandry: "The buildings that didn't burn or explode are still standing, though the botany is thrusting itself through every crack. Given time it will fissure the asphalt, topple the walls, push aside the roofs. Some kind of vine is growing everywhere, draping the windowsills, climbing in through the broken windows and up the bars and grillwork" (221–22). Such images of decay and overgrowth align with the traditional function of poetic ruins as reminders of civilizational fragility—but this time the reader is situated not at the safe vantage point of a future (more successful) civilization, but in the midst of a world system birthing its own destruction.

Colson Whitehead's *Zone One* abounds in images of physical disintegration, but the novel's most powerful invocations of "the world without us" take on the less tangible form of visions and dreams. The protagonist imagines Manhattan as "an uninhabited city, where no one lived behind all those miles and miles of glass . . . and all the elevators hung like broken puppets at the end of long cables" (7). This apparition is not a prophesy but a revelation (the true meaning of "apocalypse") of New York City's essence: "The city as a ghost ship on the last ocean at the rim of the world. It was a gorgeous and intricate delusion, Manhattan, and from crooked angles on overcast days you saw it disintegrate, were forced to consider this tenuous creature in its true nature" (7). Another variation on the posthuman city comes in the protagonist's anxiety dreams, where familiar spaces (pizza joints, yoga studios, the subway) are populated by the dead. The daily affairs of these necrocitizens—"paralegals, mohels, resigned temps, bike messengers, and slump-shouldered massage therapists" (133)— are framed by the equally lifeless iconography of capitalist advertising: "In the advertisements lodged just above eye level, airbrushed heads of the dead hawked trade schools and remedies" (133). Whether as posthuman polis or necropolis, the city defies triumphalist narratives of urban progress, reminding readers of the finitude inscribed in Manhattan's "true nature."

WASTE-SCAPES, TRAILS, BARRICADES

The ruined landscapes of climate fiction are strewn with objects: the debris of an unsustainable way of life that now sustains the scarce survivors. Cli-fi scavengers sift through the remnants of carbon civilization in search of food, clothing, tools, and fuel. As Véronique Bragard observes in her discussion of apocalyptic waste-scapes, those who "used to be producers of waste, are reduced to their basic materiality and become garbage collectors" (479).[3] Climate fiction's garbage obsession marks a shift away from the novel's traditional investment in the material texture of middle-class life. Since the emergence of novelistic realism, loving descriptions of everyday domestic spaces helped confirm the centrality of the middle-class experience within a modern capitalist society. In climate fiction, the same fixtures and furnishings that once served as metonymic stand-ins for social class affiliation now expose the socioenvironmental crisis wrought by late capitalism's rapacious logic.

The plot of McCarthy's *The Road* is a long log of scavenging: a garage yields a hand drill (16–17), an old smokehouse yields a ham (17), a supermarket a can of soda (23), an abandoned house a packet of grape juice powder (119), a garden shed gasoline and flower seeds (132), and so on. This trickle of goods occasionally turns into a river, such as when the protagonists discover a bunker filled with food: "chile, corn, stew, soup, spaghetti sauce. The richness of a vanished world" (139). Ironically, the novel's few moments of pleasure (a can of Coke, a flavored drink) are provided by an industrial food complex that precipitated Earth's ecological devastation. Also ironically, the protagonists push their scavenged goods in a shopping cart—an icon of consumerism but also homelessness, rampant in today's vastly unequal "advanced" societies. These encounters with familiar goods and objects within postcatastrophe wastelands defamiliarize the "normal" of contemporary middle-class life, suggesting new teleologies for late capitalist development.

Apart from their obvious function as means of survival, cli-fi's material objects form visual assemblages that serve as powerful condemnations of runaway consumerism. Severed from their original contexts, banal articles of middle-class existence resonate in new ways, reminiscent of the trash-to-art poetics of twentieth-century Dadaism (another end-of-the-world aesthetic). Atwood's protagonist in *Oryx and Crake* registers the visual cacophony of his ruined city: "overturned golf carts, sodden, illegible printouts, computers with their guts ripped out. Rubble, fluttering cloth, gnawed carrion. Broken toys" (351). Sometimes, these object catalogues cohere into visual tropes, like the *trail* of abandoned items. Atwood's protagonist stumbles upon such a "trail of objects people must have dropped in flight, like a treasure hunt in reverse," including "a suitcase, a knapsack spilling out clothes and trinkets; an overnight bag, broken open, beside it a forlorn pink toothbrush. A bracelet; a woman's hair ornament in the shape of a butterfly; a notebook, its pages soaked, the handwriting illegible" (226). McCarthy's father and son find several such trails. One features barely recognizable items: "Boxes and bags. Everything melted and black. Old plastic suitcases curled shapeless in the heat. Here and there imprints of things wrestled out of the tar by scavengers" (190). Another is more legible: "Odd things scattered by the side of the road. Electrical appliances, furniture. Things abandoned long ago by pilgrims enroute to their several and collective deaths" (199–200). The trail trope invokes the *vanitas* (still life as reminder of impending mortality), but instead of reflection on the impermanence of material beauty, it offers a critique of consumerism's business as usual.

Another common trope in climate-disaster fiction is the *debris barricade*—either constructed by humans or left behind by violent flooding. Examples of the latter can be found in Kim Stanley Robinson's *New York 2140* (2017) and Nathaniel Rich's *Odds against Tomorrow* (2013), both set in postdiluvian versions of New York City.[4] Whitehead's *Zone One* abounds in barricades, a stock zombie narrative motif. As the protagonist checks Manhattan residences for stragglers, he comes across elaborate constructions erected from household detritus: "He became a connoisseur of the found poetry in the abandoned barricade. The minuscule, hardscrabble wedge of space between the piled-up furniture and the apartment door the departing had squeezed though" (165). In some cases, residents transform into zombies before they can escape their apartments, entombing themselves behind piles of possessions: "groping their way toward expensive security locks but incapable of reaching them for the passel of splendid contemporary furniture they'd piled against it" (41). Whitehead offers further details of the "splendid" furnishings: "particle-board media centers laden with layaway plasmas, limited-issue replicas of Danish-modern wardrobes" (41). By imagining the macabre afterlives of familiar consumer items, such moments of defamiliarization force a confrontation with the material legacies of capitalist accumulation. Whitehead's descriptions of material objects reference—but also upend—their traditional novelistic function as markers of class belongings: no longer relevant to their undead possessors, the former signs of middle-class prosperity stay behind as void signifiers pointing to a self-annihilating social order.

HOME SWEET HOME

The affective center of the American Dream is the (heteronormative, white) nuclear family, ensconced within a single-family house complete with pets, furnishings, and time-saving appliances. In futuristic cli-fi, this sacred locus of consumer capitalism is subject to violent transformation. As Adam Trexler points out in his survey of Anthropocene fiction, many recent narratives "take up the question of contemporary domesticity as such: the fitness of twentieth-century homes, food, family arrangements, work, and shipping in the Anthropocene" (171). Cli-fi's abandoned, decaying domiciles reveal a crisis at the heart of modern capitalism's domestic ideal—and, by extension, at the heart of the unsustainable, resource-hoarding world order that continues to uphold it.

While constructing his apocalyptic landscape in *The Road,* McCarthy pauses to illuminate intimate domestic objects scattered against a background of destruction: "Trash on the floor, old newsprint. China in a breakfront, cups hanging from their hooks" (21–22); "Cheap plywood paneling curled with damp. Collapsing into the room. A red formica table" (119); "a living room partly burned and open to the sky. The waterbuckled boards sloping away into the yard. Soggy volumes in a bookcase" (130). In face of this ubiquitous disintegration, McCarthy's protagonist strives to recreate moments of middle-class normalcy for himself and his child: "He dragged a footlocker across the floor between the bunks and covered it with a towel and set out the plates and cups and plastic utensils. He set out a bowl of biscuits covered with a handtowel and a plate of butter and a can of condensed milk. Salt and pepper" (145). The narrative's dominant affect is nostalgia—the father continues to pine for the comforts of his marriage as well as his childhood, both represented by single-family homes straight out of the American Dream playbook. But the young son's relationship with domesticity is one of mistrust. The boy refuses to enter houses and implores his parent to avoid them. This generational split signals a crisis of domesticity in face of environmental collapse (even if the novel ends with an affirmation of normative family structures). Against his father's attempts at upholding the middle-class model of domestic life, the young boy intuits a rift between modern domesticity's professed innocence and its ecological and social consequences.

In extreme instances, cli-fi homes become sites of violence and horror. Unlike modern ecogothic fiction, which foregrounds natural settings and "monstrous" environmental forces to condemn extractive capitalism or express ecophobic anxieties (Deckard 174), the climate novels considered here center a more traditional gothic locus: the haunted house. Despite the differing spatial focus, cli-fi shares ecogothic's defining preoccupation with the longitudinal consequences of (ecological) slow violence (Deckard 180). Cli-fi's preoccupation with domestic infrastructure illuminates, yet again, how middle-class private life and its accoutrements (the traditional terrain of novelistic discourse) cannot be extricated from the global harm produced by modern consumer society.

In Maggie Gee's *Ice People*, the protagonist and his family find themselves squatting in a French country house, enjoying bourgeois pleasures like "tins of chestnut purée or vacuum packs of *langue de chat* biscuits or apple *compôte* or great wheels of cheese" (159). The idyllic respite ends abruptly when the travelers are overpowered and threatened with sexual violence at the hands of the homeowner and his companions. As the grim confrontation progresses, the humans are, in turn, attacked by a posse of mutant domestic robots. The rogue AI devices enact a bloodcurdling scene of slaughter by shredding and gobbling up all human bodies within their reach. This classic robot-revenge scenario offers a domesticated twist on the traditional sci-fi script. The aggressors are not humanoid replicants or military assets. Innocuously named "Doves," they are cute household helpers designed to dispose of organic trash while winning human affections with their soft feathers and baby-like visages. The juxtaposition of the Doves' adorable appearance and murderous behavior highlights the hidden horrors of capitalist domesticity and its obsession with ever newer and cuter consumer gadgets. Gee's smart appliances literally devour their makers, just as runaway consumerism, centered around the manufactured needs of nuclear families, threatens to devour the Earth's environmental and human resources.

A different site of violent consumption appears in McCarthy's *The Road*: a columned, dilapidated "grand house" that once belonged to white enslavers (105–6). Immediately upon approaching the mansion, father and son are enveloped in an unnerving gothic atmosphere: "wind rustling the dead road-side bracken. A distant creaking. Door or shutter" (105). The splendid interiors of the house are in the process of disintegration: "fine Morris paper on the walls, waterstained and sagging. The plaster ceiling was bellied in great swags and the yellowed dentil molding was bowed and sprung from the upper walls" (107). The palimpsest of decaying Victorian wallpaper points to the layers of historical horror entombed in the building. The dreadful visit culminates in the discovery of a hidden "pantry" where bound, mutilated humans await to be eaten—a scene of extreme brutality that links the current moment with the brutality of enslavement, further implicating the ideal of American domesticity in histories of violence and domination.

Cli-fi's remix of the domestic and the monstrous involves the most intimate spaces. Whitehead's *Zone One* features a lengthy narration of the protagonist's encounter with the zombie virus in a marital bed. The scene begins with a description of a generic suburb—the bucolically named "New

Grove" subdivision—where the protagonist's parents had moved decades ago in in pursuit of the American Dream. New Grove represents this Black American family's middle-class aspirations, evident in the parents' ongoing obsession with home remodeling.[5] As the protagonist approaches his childhood home, he zooms in on iconic items of suburban domesticity: a lawn sprinkler and a TV glowing through "powder-blue curtains" (81). Once inside the house, he walks past "high-definition enhancements and twin leather recliners equipped with beverage holsters" (85). At the center of this familiar suburban geography lies the bedroom, where the protagonist discovers a horrifying tableau: his (zombiefied) mother in the process of disemboweling his father. This gruesome primal scene echoes an earlier childhood incident of witnessing parental fellatio, collapsing Freudian anxieties about the nuclear family and late Anthropocene anxieties about consumer capitalism into a single vision of horror.

Atwood's *Oryx and Crake* features a similar moment of morbid intimacy. When scavenging a "Queen Anne" home, the protagonist experiences an anticipatory feeling of "claustrophobia and bad energy" (228–29), followed by a repulsive odor "like a thousand bad drains" (229). In the bedroom suite, he finds a dead woman in "a leopard-skin nightie" (230) and the corpse of a man (presumably her partner). The horror of the scene is enhanced by the intimate details of the couple's accessories: "The vanity table holds the standard collection of firming creams, hormone treatments, ampoules and injections, cosmetics, colognes" (231). Having inferred, from the contents of another bedroom, that the couple had a child, Atwood's protagonist inserts himself into the macabre family unit: "The back of his neck prickles again. Why does he have the feeling that it's his own house he's broken into? His own house from twenty-five years ago, himself the missing child" (233). By layering memories of middle-class childhood onto scenes of current trauma, *Zone One* and *Oryx and Crake* construct temporal palimpsests that link apocalyptic climate destruction with the primal site of the modern nuclear family.

BOURGEOIS UTOPIAS?

Climate fiction's unhomely ruins compel a reconsideration of the present (and the past) in terms of a projected futurity—what Srinivas Aravamudan calls *catachronism* (8). Atwood, Gee, McCarthy, and Whitehead encourage catachronic thinking by interweaving their postcatastrophe wastelands with images of precatastrophe consumerism. This splicing invites readers to draw a line between the reckless materialism inherent in the late capitalist middle-class way of life and its apocalyptic consequences. The planetary-level obliviousness of cli-fi's characters, whose attention is captivated by technological gadgets and consumer conveniences, is directly and inextricably linked with the devastation that follows.

Atwood's Jimmy remembers buying "new toys" as soon as he could afford them: "a better DVD player, a gym suit that cleaned itself overnight due to sweat-eating bacteria, a shirt that displayed e-mail on its sleeve while giving him a little nudge every time he had a message, shoes that changed color to match his outfits, a talking toaster" (250). Whitehead's "Mark" recollects his uncle's sleek Manhattan pad filled with the latest electronics, already imbued with an anticipatory ghostliness: "wireless speakers *haunting* the corners like spindly wraiths"; "a *mausoleum* of remotes in the storage inside the ottoman" (4; emphasis added). Gee's Saul recalls his generation's collective obsession with ever-new iterations of personal robot "Doves." McCarthy's father cherishes rare finds of consumer items that link him to memories of precatastrophe life. These references to consumerist abundance invoke a range of affective responses, from melancholy and longing to shame and regret. On one end of the spectrum, McCarthy's *The Road*, with its tender invocation of a lost world, offers what Adam Trexler calls "an impassioned paean to the preservation of the current order" (199). On the other end, the biting satire of Whitehead's *Zone One* draws a direct line between the logic of "the good old days" (40) and the spectacular damage of the final catastrophe.

Like many cli-fi characters (and readers), Whitehead's protagonist is not immune to the allure of bourgeois nostalgia. He enjoys hearing his colleague Kaitlyn recount her charmed life of shopping-mall outings, horseback riding, and curated parties, each "transcending the last and approaching a kind of birthday-party perfection that once accomplished would usher in an exquisite new age of bourgeois utopia" (58). But the pleasures of nostalgia give way to a chilling realization that the current plague might be the direct endgame of Kaitlyn's privileged lifestyle: "Maybe, he thought one night, it wasn't utopia that they had worked toward after all, and it was Kaitlyn herself who had summoned the plague: as she cut into the first slice of cake at her final, perfect birthday party, history came to an end. She had blown out the candles on the old era, blotted out the dinosaurs' heavens, sent the great ice sheet scraping forth, the blood counts zooming up into madness"

(58). Kaitlyn's (and America's) bourgeois utopia is revealed as a site of class and racial exclusion, always threatened by "the rabble who nibbled at the edge of her dream: the weak-willed smokers, deadbeat dads and welfare cheats, single moms incessantly breeding, the flouters of speed laws, and those who only had themselves to blame for their ridiculous credit-card debt" (266). Kaitlyn's dream belongs to a select group of citizens who "graduated with admirable GPAs, configured monthly contributions to worthy causes, judiciously apportioned their 401(k)s across diverse sectors" (31). This elite continues to keep out fellow Americans through a preoccupation with "good school districts" and "best Quality of Life" rankings—code words for ongoing segregation (31). Through an accumulation of hints and references, Whitehead exposes middle-class America's lifestyle choices as "postracial" mechanisms of white supremacist exclusion.[6]

Margaret Atwood's biotech apocalypse, Maggie Gee's great freeze, Cormac McCarthy's wasteland, and Colson Whitehead's zombie takeover disrupt the bourgeois aesthetics of novelistic realism while appropriating its visual and spatial vocabularies. Rather than recording the granular materiality of everyday life, climate fiction defamiliarizes and disrupts our constructions of the normal, rebuffing readerly desire to settle into familiar, comfortable storyworlds. Cli-fi reminds its readers that the modern pursuit of middle-class happiness has come at an exorbitant cost to the planet and to fellow beings, human and nonhuman. That the bourgeois utopia has never been accessible to all and is becoming less accessible by the minute as global disparities increase and income gaps widen. That the resource-intensive single-family home should never have become a universal model for organizing domestic life. That our focus has been ill-directed in quest of never-ending material progress. That the comfortable quotidian of advanced capitalist life is underpinned by violent exploitation, past and present. In staging the destruction of middle-class infrastructure, cli-fi rejects the novelistic apotheosis of bourgeois life, redirecting attention to the structural problems at the roots of the climate crisis.

In climate fiction's futuristic scenarios, the accessories of middle-class domestic life return as trash heaps, barricades, and trails of broken objects, while spaces of domestic intimacy transform into sites of horror and haunting. In staging these transformations, cli-fi draws attention away from the sanitized trappings of the American Dream and toward the out-of-sight landscapes that make the dream possible: racialized urban wastelands, overseas extraction sites, and global terrains of environmental toxicity. These sacrifice zones, essential to the capitalist project (and fueled by middle-class consumer demands) impose themselves upon the quotidian spaces of novelistic imagination to force a reckoning with the true cost of modern progress. Climate dystopias are, on a most literal level, imaginative warnings about a world yet to come; but they can also be read, with or against the grain of authorial intention, as accounts of ecosocial nightmares already in progress.

NOTES

1. Cinematic adaptations tell a similar story. In Bong Joon-ho's *Snowpiercer* (2014), human survivors travel on a train divided into a rear section whose cramped passengers subsist on ground insects and a luxurious front section complete with greenhouses and sushi bars. Similarly, Francis Lawrence and Gary Ross's *The Hunger Games* trilogy (2012–15) contrasts decadent urban elites and masses of exploited labor.

2. For an overview of the recent cultural phenomenon of "ruin porn," see Lyons.

3. Bragard's focus, informed by material ecocriticism's emphasis on the vitality and agency of matter, is the "reconnection with the materiality of things" (480). She sees McCarthy's protagonists as "Romantic heroes" who rediscover "texture and tactile materiality" (485). This approach becomes the source of Bragard's positive reading of *The Road* as an affirmation of the "vibrancy and agency of matter" (485). See also Bill Brown's work on thing theory, such as his *Things*, the sequel *Other Things*, and *A Sense of Things: The Object Matter of American Literature*. See also Raymond Malewitz's *The Practice of Misuse: Rugged Consumerism in Contemporary American Culture*.

4. For analysis of urban landscapes in Rich and Robinson, see Mączyńska.

5. On Whitehead's protagonist as "a Black everyman whose survival becomes allegorical for the lived experiences of Black men in the U.S. today" (62), see Heneks.

6. For discussion of Whitehead's critique of the postracial, see Saldívar and Hurley.

WORKS CITED

Aravamudan, Srinivas. "The Catachronism of Climate Change." *Diacritics*, vol. 41, no. 3, 2013, pp. 6–30.
Atwood, Margaret. *Oryx and Crake*. Nan A. Talese, 2003.
Bragard, Véronique. "Sparing Words in the Wasted Land: Garbage, Texture, and Écriture Blanche in Auster's 'In the Country of Last Things' and McCarthy's 'The Road.'" *Interdisciplinary Studies in Literature and the Environment*, vol. 20, no. 3, 2013, pp. 479–93.
Caracciollo, Marco. "Negative Strategies and World Disruption in Postapocalyptic Fiction." *Style*, vol. 52, no. 3, 2018, pp. 222–41.

Deckard, Sharae. "Ecogothic." *Twenty-First-Century Gothic: An Edinburgh Companion*, edited by Maisha Wester and Xavier Aldana Reves, 2019, pp. 174–88.

Gee, Maggie. *The Ice People*. Richard Cohen Books, 1998.

Ghosh, Amitav. *The Great Derangement: Climate Change and the Unthinkable*. U of Chicago P, 2016.

Heneks, Grace. "The American Subplot. Colson Whitehead's Post-Racial Allegory in *Zone One*." *The Comparatist*, no. 42, 2018, pp. 60–79.

Hurley, Jessica. "History Is What Bites. Zombies, Race, and the Limits of Biopower in Colson Whitehead's *Zone One*." *Extrapolation*, vol. 56, no. 3, 2015, pp. 311–33.

LeMenager, Stephanie. "The Humanities after the Anthropocene." *The Routledge Companion to the Environmental Humanities*, edited by Ursula K. Heise, Jon Christensen, and Michelle Niemann, Routledge, 2017, pp. 473–81.

Lyons, Siobhan, editor. *Ruin Porn and the Obsession with Decay*. Palgrave Macmillan, 2018.

Mączyńska, Magdalena. "Welcome to the Post-Anthropolis: Urban Space and Climate Change in Nathaniel Rich's *Odds against Tomorrow*, Lev Rosen's *Depth*, and Kim Stanley Robinson's *New York 2140*." *Journal of Modern Literature*, vol. 43, no. 2, 2020, pp. 165–81.

McCarthy, Cormac. *The Road*. Vintage International, 2006.

Saldívar, Ramón. "The Second Elevation of the Novel: Race, Form, and the Postrace Aesthetic in Contemporary Narrative." *Narrative*, vol. 21. no. 1, 2013, pp. 1–18.

Stombeck, Andrew. "*Zone One*'s Reanimation of 1970s New York." *Studies in American Fiction*, vol. 44, no. 20, 2017, pp. 259–80.

Trexler, Adam. *Anthropocene Fictions: The Novel in a Time of Climate Change*. U of Virginia P, 2015.

Tuana, Nancy. "Climate Apartheid: The Forgetting of Race in the Anthropocene." *Critical Philosophy of Race*, vol. 7, no. 1, 2019, pp. 1–31.

Whitehead, Colson. *Zone One*. Anchor Books, 2012.

Homelessness in Lauren Groff's Florida Fiction

Climate Change and Displacement

TERESA A. GODDU

A yearning for home, signifying shelter, safety, and belonging, runs throughout contemporary US climate fiction, even as the loss of home, figured by the destruction of the house as well as geographical, communal, and cultural dis-placement, symbolizes the climate crisis's rapid transformation of the planet. From the washing away of Dellarobia's house by an immense flood at the end of Barbara Kingsolver's *Flight Behavior* and the reduction of Frank's former house, blown sixty yards inland by Hurricane Sandy, to a vacant cellar in Richard Ford's *Let Me Be Frank with You*, to the estrangement the man experiences when entering his childhood home in Cormac McCarthy's *The Road* and the trauma Esch and her family endure escaping their hurricane-ravaged house in Jesmyn Ward's *Salvage the Bones*, the home in contemporary US climate fiction registers both the physical and psychic dislocations of the climate crisis. To be unhoused in climate fiction is also to be ontologically unmoored. Arguing that "we have now entered the 'age of solastalgia,' where our emotional compass is pointing in the direction of chronic distress at the loss of loved 'homes' and places at all scales" due to climate change (10–11), Glenn Albrecht maintains that a sense of homelessness—the uncanny and desolate feeling that a familiar place is becoming "unrecognizable" if not outright "hostile" (71)—is the Anthropocene's defining condition. The homelessness—both material and metaphorical—that haunts contemporary US climate fiction registers this larger unease: that we are no longer at home in the altered and deeply precarious landscape of the climate crisis.

Lauren Groff uses her home state of Florida throughout her short fiction, but most particularly in her story collection *Florida*, to represent the nation's—and at times the world's—sense of climate dis-ease and dis-placement. Having consistently written climate fiction about Florida over the course of the last decade (her earliest stories were published in 2011), Groff has created a connected canon of works—many collected in her award-winning volume *Florida*—that reflect and refract climate dread through the lens of her ecologically vulnerable and socially unrooted state.[1] As the nation's harbinger for climate change and environmental degradation (heat and hurricanes along with rising seas and habitat loss) and a Sunbelt state with a surging population and influx of visitors from elsewhere (tourists as well as retirees), Florida symbolizes the unstable terrain of a warming world. In Groff's rendering, Florida is a swampy—not sunny—space, steeped in darkness, desolation, and dread. A "state in the union as well as a state of mind," as Katy Waldman puts it, Florida symbolizes the "psychogeography" (Waldman) of climate distress: the existential fear of being planetarily unhomed. Groff materializes this psychic insecurity through both the alien nature of Florida's lush landscape and the economic fragility of its built environment. Houses are not only invaded by snakes and battered by storms but sold due to debt and abandoned because of eviction. The line between the housed and unhoused—the white middle-class homeowner and the transient homeless person—blurs in the economically perilous world of Groff's Florida fiction. Class precarity entwines with ecological collapse to haunt these stories.

Groff uses the psychogeography of Florida—its dank landscape thick with economic as well as environmental dread—to puncture the American fairytale of upward mobility and middle-class stability. Depicting the climate crisis as a housing crisis, Groff's Florida fiction demonstrates a widespread displacement from the safety and comfort of home as the planetary habitat degrades. While Groff's stories illustrate how all classes are vulnerable to being unhoused from climate change, they underscore the unequal distribution of those effects. In Groff's rendering, Florida is populated not only by the affluent but the abandoned, the "human flotsam" (3)—the poor, the disposable, the homeless—who portend America's climate future. Most specifically, Groff's stories are interested, like so much contemporary US climate fiction, in white middle-class anxiety about becoming unhomed.[2] They both probe this dread and critique the class privilege that creates it. Mapping the class divide that undergirds the climate crisis onto Florida's built environment, they expose how class boundaries threaten to dissolve under climate change and underscore the difficulty of bridging them in solidarity for survival.

Groff's Florida fiction charts the climate geography of class precarity through real estate. Storms—both environmental and economic—hit the stone manors of the European aristocracy, the gentrified houses of the middle class, and the cars of the unhoused. Her characters, across the class spectrum, are imperiled by weather events as well as economic stress. Bankrupted barons sell their family castles in the Alps and rent out their fifteen-thousand-square-foot houses in Sarasota for cash to stay afloat; the middle class, which cannot afford family vacations, finds sinkholes beneath its homes' foundations; and the working poor struggle to survive in tent cities. All, including the nonhuman, are vulnerable to losing their place.

Groff's stories, however, also make clear how the climate crisis is simultaneously an inequality crisis. According to Rob Nixon, there remain "immense disparities in human agency, impacts, and vulnerability" in the Anthropocene: we may all be navigating the same stormy sea, but we are not in the same boat. Groff notes the class "divergence" that lies at the heart of the Anthropocene's "great acceleration" through the markers, named in one of her story's titles, of above and below (Nixon). Everyone may be in danger of being put "out" from the shelter of home in the climate crisis, but those that live below the poverty line are most at risk. The frame of the upper-class house hit by a hurricane in "Eyewall" holds while the carousel lady's trailer, located at the bottom of the hill on the beach in "Yport," is defenseless against a tsunami. The first-world Miami tourist in "Salvador" imagines herself "soar[ing] over" (148) the Third World's hurricane wreckage, "dry and safe when all the rest of the world was vulnerable" (139), while the poor young girls of "Dogs Go Wolf," abandoned on an island during a storm, their fishing cabin "rock[ing] on [its] stilts" (46), almost die of hunger. The suicide that occurs in the bathtub on the fifth floor of an apartment building in "The Midnight Zone" is felt not by the fourth, third, and second floors, whose occupants are "away somewhere with beaches and alcoholic smoothies" (69), but by the first-floor renters, who discover the problem when "the water of death" (69) seeps into their carpet. Though death comes even to those who live above, it is those below—on lower ground and in the lower class—who bear the brunt of the devastation in these stories.

Groff foregrounds white middle-class precarity in these stories through her recurring unnamed female narrator, a writer with two young sons, who serves as the author's uncanny double. This narrator, who appears in five of the collection's eleven stories as well as the spin-off story, "Dusk," is suicidal with climate dread, "sad to the bone" (208) as she ponders the "midnight of humanity" (267), and troubled by economic insecurity. A homeowner on a street of renters in a neighborhood that is "imperfectly safe" (2), she finds things "fraying in [her] hands" (68). Not only is the peach tree in her yard dead from climate change, but she fears the doom lurking around every dark corner—there have been three rapes in her neighborhood—and death by lightning strike. Her climate dread is materialized in the sinkhole she finds next to her house when she is home alone on Halloween contemplating "climate change, this summer the hottest on record, plants dying all around" (161). Located near her house's southeast corner, a symbol of Florida in the national geography, the sinkhole represents a home—and nation—built on unstable ground, the porous limestone that undergirds Florida's "liquid landscape" (Navakas). Frightened that the baby sinkhole, which opens in the pouring rain, may be the sign of a much larger cavity "right there beneath her feet" (166), the narrator imagines herself falling to the "very black bottom of the limestone hollow" (168) from which "nobody could get her out" (168). A physical manifestation of her psychic state—her black hole of climate depression—the sinkhole becomes her new home: she imagines her family visiting her there, their "heads peering once in a while over the lip" (168). Having fallen below, she is exiled from both her family and her home.

The narrator's economic anxiety, which mirrors her climate dread, is manifested most explicitly in the homeless doubles that populate Groff's stories. In "Ghosts and Empties," a "homeless lady, a collector of cans" (5), inhabits the narrator's neighborhood, and an unhoused couple sleeps beneath her home: "at dusk, they would silently lift off the lattice-work to the crawl space under our house and then sleep there, their roof our bedroom floor" (3). Living in the space of the sinkhole, the unhoused couple represents the narrator's dual dread: her fear of being put outdoors by the climate crisis and of falling below due to economic distress. Her wakefulness—she tries to outrun her dread by taking long walks each night—registers her recognition that only a thin floorboard separates her from their fate. Her fear of becoming unhoused is further manifested in the story "Above and Below," where a white graduate student, who lives in the same university town as the narrator and travels the same landscape as the homeless couple, is evicted from her apartment and "fall[s] from safety" (183). Having used education to climb in class status—she comes from a home with cockroaches and "dirt-crusted linoleum" (187)—she finds herself abandoned by her rich boyfriend, who gave her etiquette books and took her to Sunday brunches. Like so many of the women in these stories, who lose their economic foothold through divorce or their partner's death—with gender enhancing class precarity—the graduate student struggles to subsist after her boyfriend departs: she has a "mountain of debt" (170), and her teaching assistant's stipend is "barely enough for her half of the rent, let alone groceries" (174). Giving up her dreams of a "sabbatical in Florence," along with "the gleaming modern house at the edge of the woods" (171), and discovering her books are monetarily *"Worthless"* (170) when she tries to sell them, she becomes itinerant, moving between beach, library, motel, tent encampment, and squat house. Haunting the margins of the university town as a ghost, she becomes invisible to her former students and her "funded friends" (174). Dis-placed in place, she experiences a type of social death. Estranged and unrecognized, she represents the grim truths that underlie the class structure of the university town: how many in the professional class are already the working poor, how cultural capital has become almost worthless, how difficult it is to gain class position, and how easy to lose one's place. Exiled from her former life, the graduate student, like the homeless couple, who the narrator can sense beneath her in the dark, symbolizes how fragile class status is and how close the middle class is to becoming unhoused and unhomed.

The economic instability that forms the foundation of the white middle-class home is also depicted in Groff's additional work, "Boca Raton," part of Amazon's *Warmer Collection* of climate stories, where the protagonist's little white cottage, ringed by overgrown citrus trees and rotting fruit, is threatened to be swallowed by the sea. A fallen and vulnerable Eden, the two-bedroom bungalow, whose heart pine is being eaten away by termites, represents the growing impossibility of homeownership—both in terms of existential security and economic ability. Located in a part of Boca Raton were "old people" cling "to houses they'd bought in the seventies for a whistle and a fistful of peanuts," the house is only within Ange's reach, and then just barely, because of another family's tragedy: a murder-suicide committed in the home allows Ange to buy it, using "every penny" of her savings plus two hundred dollars borrowed from a coworker, for what is left on the mortgage. A librarian, "paid very little," and single mother who relies on free lunches provided by a coworker, Ange barely makes enough money to get by and only then because she lives mortgage-free. Her house is not only her nest, the place where she wraps herself in the afghan her dead mother crocheted for her and tucks her daughter into bed, but also her nest egg. Ange's sleepless visions of her "little house" swallowed by rising seas, like her imaginings of Boca Raton being reduced to "a thin spit of land between dying ocean and dead sea" and the planet coming to a "full stop" from "plastics," "drought," and "hunger," manifest her existential, environmental, and economic terror of becoming unhomed. Suffering, like the unnamed narrator, from climate dread, Ange is awake to how her house—which holds her child and her money—is in the ocean's path: the only thing between it and the seeping sea a mile of street and the gentle hill it is built upon. In Groff's Florida fiction, the middle class survives on luck and slight advantages.

While Groff's stories probe this class anxiety, much as the recurring narrator "prods and prods the sinkhole in her mind" (165), they also hold the middle class responsible for its part in creating the conditions of its own—and others'—precarity. In "The Midnight Zone," the narrator, vacationing on spring break with her family at a free hunting cabin in a dark forest of "ancient sinkholes" (68) rather than at the expensive beach in the sea and sun, falls while changing a hot light bulb, hitting the floor with her head and blacking out. Here, the home is not a safe space—the floorboards injuring rather than protecting the narrator from what lies beneath—due to her consumption of electricity, which, as exemplified by the burning bulb, is making the world hot. The white middle-class gentrification of the narrator's neighborhood in "Ghosts and Empties," fueled by air-conditioning that drowns out "the night birds and frogs" (11), creates not just environmental but social harms. The renovation of "one of the oldest Cracker houses in north central Florida" (9), hollowed out except for its facade, collapses, almost killing a worker. Leaving nothing but a hole, over which the narrator contemplates the uncertainty of her own marriage, the collapsed house exemplifies the middle-class's narcissism (the reframing of dangerous labor practices as a family drama); its destruction of vernacular styles of architecture adapted to the environment (the Cracker house is "all porches and high ceilings" [9]); and its preservation and, hence, continuation of a white, southern, racial history. The overbuilt landscape of white gentrification not only creates the conditions for sinkholes but also displaces people of color and makes individuals homeless. The "black people have mostly withdrawn" (3) from the narrator's neighborhood, while the unhoused, who once stayed in Bo Diddley Plaza or in tent encampments among the trees, have been burned and fenced out. The "controlled burn" of the "old turpentine pine forests that ring the city" (11), which blackens the great oaks and sears birds in their sleep, also destroys dozens of acres where "the homeless had been living in a tent city" (11). The "six-foot fences" that go up the same night around the Plaza "for construction, or so the signs say" belie the city's "larger plan" (12) to rid itself of the homeless population. The blackened oaks and high fences reference the deeper history of this landscape: the state's use of forced Black labor, in the forms of "convict leasing and debt peonage" (Shofner 14), to scar the pine trunks and extract their sap for the turpentine business. The town's history of racial capitalism, which injured the environment and the Black laborers, extends to the current moment of white gentrification. The narrator, who first experiences the fires as producing "a pleasant smell like campfires in the air" (11), exposing her historical ignorance, is presented as complicit in this process. While she may have moved into the neighborhood when it was poor and Black and before it was "frenzied with renovation" and "infected" by "white middle-classness" (2), she participates in its gentrification: she can afford her house because it is "cheap" (2), and she works to scrape the "rotting paint off the oak moldings" (6) when she first moves in. Moreover, while she looks for "her" homeless couple in the aftermath of the fires, imagining herself taking "their arms" (12), making them sandwiches, and offering them a place to live under her house, she cannot find them, nor can she imagine them as anything other than her benevolent possessions, reliant on her very limited largesse. Unwilling to invite them in or even serve them a hot meal, the narrator is ineffectual in righting the wrongs that she helps to create. White middle-class collusion in the structures that produce environmental and economic homelessness is voiced throughout these stories.

Besides suggesting the middle class's complicity in its own downfall—injuring the nonhuman world, workers, people of color, and the poor in the process—Groff's stories critique the white middle class for dismissing its dread by taking comfort in being situated high above. The British tourists in "Yport," a cliffside town in France, console the narrator's son, who is worried about a tsunami coming in the middle of the night, by explaining "that most of the houses are well above the average sea-surge level and that in all likelihood, only the boardwalk and carousel and some of the restaurants would be underwater" (249). Saying that "nobody lives at sea level . . . So nobody would be hurt" (249), they disappear the carousel lady and her "six or so" (266) children who live in a trailer behind their boardwalk business. In "Salvador," the American tourist survives a stormy night by imagining herself not just soaring in a plane over the hurricane wreckage but leaving it all behind: "It would not be her mess to clean up. She was a visitor only; she could be absolved" (148). Once more, Groff's writing uses the spatial imagery of above and below to intimate that the white middle class fails to take responsibility for the ruin its consumption creates, leaving the devastation to others. The recurring narrator may be exhausted by "living in debt" (70) to her husband, who makes up for her deficits as a mother, but she has "no intention of repaying" (70) him. She may refuse any "easy absolution" (13) for herself—she leaves the drugstore, whose abundant aisles are full of "gaudy trash" (12), without the salts that will soak away her anxious aches—but she never has to pay a price in these stories. The mother who loses her son to a tsunami while vacationing in Florida in Groff's standalone story "Under the Wave," is a renter and Black; the child she adopts, who also survives the wave coming up "through the ground in the night," is white but poor. The narrator may roam the dark night trying to outrun her climate dread, but her exile is self-imposed: she has a home to which she can return.

Despite being awake to climate catastrophe, the recurring narrator, Groff shows, remains cocooned in her class privilege. The narrator stereotypes the "subhuman" as nonhuman, seeing the homeless couple as "a papaya tree bent over a rain barrel" (6) or the "dirty blond children" (266), who play on the seawall in Yport, as "urchins" (267). She also misreads class relations. Blinded by her own benevolence, she offers the seemingly destitute children, who turn out to be the carousel owner's, her own children's tickets. Insulated by her white privilege, she downplays the dangers that surround her: she hears "the gunshots splatter[ing]" in the air in her neighborhood, resulting in a murder, as "fireworks lit by the kids who lived a few houses down" (6). Moreover, her privilege paralyzes her. Her wish to help the homeless couple ends with her relief that she never found them, since "it is not a kind thing to tell human beings that they can live under your house" (12). Simultaneously sympathizing with and dehumanizing the homeless couple, the narrator feels both "too much and too little" (13).

She empathizes with their plight but is unable to imagine how, by inviting the couple into rather than under her home, she might begin to dissolve the structures that separate them. Throughout these stories, Groff underscores how the narrator feels too much and does too little.

The narrator's lack of solidarity with both human and nonhuman highlights the failure of community that runs throughout Groff's Florida fiction. "Alone," "isolated," and "sunbattered" (42), her characters have a difficult time connecting to each other under the scorching skies of climate change. Characters "hunger for touch" (192) that is rarely bestowed, despite hugs "just being human" (70). While the stories offer fleeting connections—a bereft husband putting his head in the crook of his wife's neck and breathing in her love, a homeless shelter volunteer "briefly" laying her cheek atop an unhoused lady's head as both "closed their eyes and leaned closer in" (182)—they dwell in dread and aloneness. The narrator's complex misanthropy, not the husband's simple belief in humanity's goodness, dominates the collection: she "loves humanity almost too much" (162), which makes her constantly disappointed at how awful human beings can be. "Bad thoughts" lead to "new, worse actions" in a world where "terrible things" (205) happen, leading her to believe that "humanity can't even save itself" (162). If Rebecca Solnit's nonfiction focuses on how disasters—climate and otherwise—strengthen solidarities between people, Groff's fiction shows how the climate crisis exposes "how delicate the ties that bind us to another" are (203).

Groff's stories foreground the difficulty of creating solidarity specifically in class terms. Political movements, like Occupy, roll into Bo Diddley Plaza like the tide, claiming "the right to sleep there," and then, growing "tired of being dirty" (3), roll out again, leaving the homeless behind. Male partners not only cheat on their mates but plot, as Grant does in "For the God of Love, For the Love of God," to leave their spouses and a life of scrimping and "shitty linoleum" in Florida's "soul-sucking heat" for law school and a life of "old linen and crystal" (121) in Michigan's cooler realms. Women also fail to create solidarity either within or across class positions: the mother in "Dogs Go Wolf" calls her fellow prostitutes "backstabbing bitches who'd rob you sooner than help you" (49); the mutual aid that the homeless graduate student shares with the unhoused mother, Jane—the graduate student watches Jane's children as Jane works for food—ends with the graduate student abandoning Jane's children when Jane is jailed for prostitution; and the narrator's best friend breaks up with her rather than listen to any more of her middle-class climate catastrophizing.

The stories' insistence that even the solidarity of sisterhood is impossible is most evident in "For the God of Love, For the Love of God." Here, the Swiss baron's wife, Genevieve, who has upgraded her American name of Jennifer and her middle-class status through marriage, invites her childhood friend, Amanda, who grew up lower-class and now works with homeless people, on a working vacation to France. Once a French major at the University of Florida, where she worked "three jobs just to survive" (110), Amanda is finally able to visit France in exchange for watching Genevieve's son, Leo. Only there for a week, Amanda in turn pays for a plane ticket for Mina, her niece, so that Mina can watch Leo in her stead. Back in Florida, Mina is also the one who bears the brunt of the domestic work. Living in her family's "spare room to save money" as she attends college, she does "all the dishes" and "takes care of the garden" (111). Despite describing each other as sisters—Amanda loves Genevieve "like a sister" (106) and describes Mina as "basically my sister" (105)—the relationships are transactional and exploitative. The white upper-class woman, who recognizes her class privilege even as she dismisses it with a wave of her hand, passes the responsibility for her young child, who already suffers from climate dread, burying dead birds that fall out of stormy skies, to her white lower-middle-class friend, who in turn dumps it on her Black college-age niece. This class hierarchy, in which responsibility for the most vulnerable is handed down to those below, exposes not just the class but also the racial and generational inequities of the climate crisis. Despite the complex family substitutions of the story—Amanda acts as Mina's mother when her sister abandons Mina, and Leo is a substitute for the child Amanda says she is too poor to have—and despite their similar status as squatters—Amanda discovers that Genevieve is bankrupt due to her husband's mania and that the stone house they are all staying in his sister's—the story's women never recognize themselves as kin. They are only "like" sisters. Solidarity, even in the "end of days" (126) and even among family and friends, remains impossible.[3]

Groff's most recent Florida fiction, "Dusk," published in an anthology of stories about climate change and inequality, again features the recurring narrator suffering from climate depression and foregrounds the lack of solidarity across class lines as well as with the nonhuman world. In this story, the narrator's double is not the homeless couple, who reflect her fear of vulnerability, but Dusk, a wealthy south Florida college student who mirrors her materialism. Moving into an identical house across the street, whose plans were "stolen" by "the sister of the woman who had built" the narrator's place, after which "the sisters never spoke again" (35), Dusk proceeds to party and to binge-buy goods from the internet, the boxes piling up on her front porch. Horrified by Dusk's hedonistic consumption, the narrator breaks down Dusk's boxes, neatly stacking them in the recycling bin, and stores Dusk's "unwanted things" in her garage, with a plan to donate them "one day" when she has the "courage" to rejoin "the world" (40). The story climaxes in two confrontations between the women. Dressed in a "white minimalist sheath" and a large skull necklace retrieved from one of the boxes, the narrator tries to "force the issue" by getting Dusk to see her own consumption on the "gallery wall" (42) of the narrator's body. Telling the narrator, "Wow! You look hot, sister" (42), Dusk does not recognize her own purchase, seeing her beauty rather than her complicity reflected back to her. In the second confrontation, the narrator, who Dusk says sounds like "[her] mom" (43), lectures Dusk on climate change. Spouting the selfish talking points characteristic of affluent youth—"it's my money," "we'll be dead before it matters," and "the people who are going to be hurt are the ones who aren't really contributing anyway" (44)—Dusk views her neighbor with contempt, not understanding. The narrator's failure with Dusk—and through her, the environment—exposes the limitations of her white middle-class politics: her focus on individual conversion rather than systemic change, her dwelling in dourness and dread (she is "grim and sure" [43] and loves the skull "almost too much" [41]), her understanding of feeling as action (she envisions Dusk's climate conversion as including tears and therapy), her lack of follow-through (Dusk's goods remain undistributed), and her white savior complex (the skull takes the place of a cross). Their break, which echoes that of the sisters who built the matching houses, underscores not just Dusk's blindness but the narrator's own. Rather than see Dusk as a sister, a daughter, a younger version of herself, or even a neighbor, she projects onto Dusk her own feelings of guilt and culpability. Envious of Dusk's wealth—the narrator hoards Dusk's things—and jealous of her youthful innocence—Dusk's lack of realization that she lives in a "house of disaster" (36) with termites teeming beneath its gentrified "skim of perfection" (34)—the narrator outsources her own reckoning with and responsibility for the climate crisis.

The narrator's refusal to face her complicity—repressing it as depression—and forge solidarity—if not with the human, then with the nonhuman world she claims to care about—is evident in her response to Dusk's adopted dog, a survivor of Hurricane Michael, who barks all day "in furious urgent need" (45). "Poor, small," "little" (42), and "homeless" (39), the dog insistently expresses the tsunami of suffering the nonhuman world is drowning beneath. The narrator wallows in her own climate grief—the absence of her beloved sandhill cranes, whose migration to the prairie has been derailed by hurricanes—rather than relieve or attend to the dog's distress. If the loss of the cranes and the natural "beauty" they convey through their "rubbery honks and metallic whirrs" (38) sends her into "the safety of [her] house" (34) at the beginning of the story, the dog's incessant barking, which vocalizes the nonhuman world's destruction from climate change, pushes her back out to the prairie at the end, where she picks up litter, calling the act "stupid" even as she claims she "is not doing nothing" (45). She may clean up some of the world's waste—the double negative describing this act emphasizes the difficulty of claiming its significance—but she actively runs away from the sound of nonhuman pain. Intent on lecturing Dusk, the narrator refuses to hear: she does not listen "hard enough" (45) or care enough to understand the climate trauma the dog is trying to transmit. Rationalizing her collusion in consumption through her responsible recycling and her righteous judgment of Dusk, the narrator runs from her recognition that it is she who wears the skull of death. Mired in her own goodness, her desire for beauty, and her refusal of suffering (except her own), the narrator is unable to confront her role in the dog's displacement. It is left to Groff as author, who bursts the bounds of the narrator's limited ability to listen or find the words to speak ("I had no words" [44]), to translate the dog's terrifying tale of death and displacement—"when he woke his whole world was gone" (46)—into language the reader can comprehend. Beginning the final paragraph with an address to the reader—"Perhaps he's telling us of that lost first life of his" (45)—Groff, through the expanded voice of the narrator's imaginings, discloses the dog's story, which he does not have the tongue to tell and the narrator does not have the "ears to hear" (46), to her reader. In doing so, she asks the reader to hear what the white middle-class narrator cannot bear.

Throughout her stories, Groff refuses her middle-class readers a "false catharsis" (Phillips). She confronts her readers with their vulnerability and culpability. She may offer moments of solace—a perfectly whole egg that survives a storm, a vegan buttercream cake left on a doorstep, birdsong—but no blanket of safety. As she states in an interview with Helen Phillips, "If you imagine the reader entering into this idea of climate change in a controlled space and by the end of the book" they "can walk away without feeling implicated," then "that's sending the reader down a false path and I think it's narratively corrupt in a lot of ways." Hence, her stories linger in darkness, occupying the space of climate dread without ever resolving it, and create damning doubles, the unnamed narrator as not just Groff's but also her white middle-class reader's mirror image. Her stories, like the narrator's gallery-wall body that displays the skull for Dusk's observation, are the artistic reflections in which readers might see the climate crisis as well as their own role in it. The narrator's realization in the collection's final story that "of all the places in the world, she belongs in Florida" (272)—accepting the state of homelessness as her new homeland—is the only resolution offered. Exposed on the beach at the end of the collection, too far from her son to help him "in a calamity," whether a "rogue wave" or "kidnapper," she "understands" (275) the unprotected position that she and her sons inhabit in the warming world. Similarly, Ange finds herself alone on the beach at night, unable to shake her climate dread or reach her sleeping daughter, "the darkness" sealing the gap between them, and the graduate student discovers herself alone on the prairie at night with "no relief in the sky" and "nobody to deliver her back to the solace of people" (203). Homelessness—the existential fear of being put out of doors and exiled from loved ones and humanity itself—is the state Groff's Florida characters come to occupy and accept. The question remains as to whether Groff's readers, who must dwell in this sinkhole space in the act of reading her Florida fiction, can learn to make their homes there as well.

NOTES

1. *Florida* won the Story Prize and was a finalist for the National Book Award. Groff's Florida stories written before 2018 were collected in *Florida*. Since then, she has written three additional stories, "Under the Wave" (2018), "Boca Raton" (2018), and "Dusk" (2020), which address similar themes and characters. Given that her Florida stories depict the same "psychogeographical" state of climate dread described in Waldman's analysis, I read them as a single, evolving oeuvre.

2. Schneider-Mayerson argues that contemporary climate fiction portrays "climatic destabilization primarily as a problem for white, wealthy, educated Americans" (945). Unlike the authors Schneider-Mayerson discusses, Groff attends to issues of climate justice and critiques the white middle class.

3. What little solidarity is available in these stories is found in the poor and working class. In "Above and Below," Eugene, a working class "brown man," offers the graduate student a job cleaning and calls her his "partner" (186). At the end of the story, the graduate student is welcomed into the Prairie House, a squat where

"everyone pulls their weight" (201) and occupants attempt to live outside of capitalism by cannibalizing its remains through reselling the university students' discarded items. In this communal space, a sinkhole becomes a swimming hole and a bonfire gleams in the dark.

WORKS CITED

Albrecht, Glenn. *Earth Emotions: New Words for a New World*. Cornell UP, 2019.
Ford, Richard. *Let Me Be Frank with You*. HarperCollins, 2014.
Groff, Lauren. "Boca Raton." *Warmer Collection*, vol. 2, Amazon, 2018. Kindle edition.
———. "Dusk." *Tales of Two Planets: Stories of Climate Change and Inequality in a Divided World*, edited by John Freeman, Penguin, 2020, pp. 33–46.
———. *Florida*. Riverhead Books, 2018.
———. "Under the Wave." *The New Yorker*, 2 July 2018. https://www.newyorker.com/magazine/2018/07/09/under-the-wave.
Kingsolver, Barbara. *Flight Behavior*. HarperCollins, 2012.
McCarthy, Cormac. *The Road*. Vintage, 2006.
Navakas, Michele Currie. *Liquid Landscape: Geography and Settlement at the Edge of Early America*. U of Pennsylvania P, 2018.
Nixon, Rob. "The Great Acceleration and the Great Divergence: Vulnerability in the Anthropocene." *MLA Profession*, March 2014. https://profession.mla.org/the-great-acceleration-and-the-great-divergence-vulnerability-in-the-anthropocene/.
Phillips, Helen. "Why All Fiction Should Be Climate Fiction: A Conversation with Lauren Groff." *Edge Effects*, 21 Aug. 2018. https://edgeeffects.net/lauren-groff/.
Schneider-Mayerson, Matthew. "Whose Odds? The Absence of Climate Justice in American Climate Fiction Novels." *Interdisciplinary Studies in Literature and the Environment*, vol. 26, no. 4, 2019, pp. 944–67.
Shofner, Jerrell H. "Forced Labor in the Florida Forests, 1880–1950." *Journal of Forest History*, vol. 25, no. 1, 1981, pp. 14–25.
Solnit, Rebecca. *A Paradise Built in Hell: The Extraordinary Communities That Arise in Disaster*. Penguin Books, 2009.
Waldman, Katy. "Lauren Groff's Stunning New Collection, 'Florida,' Unfolds 'In an Eden of Dangerous Things.'" *New Yorker*, 4 June 2018. https://www.newyorker.com/books/page-turner/lauren-groffs-stunning-new-collection-florida-unfolds-in-an-eden-of-dangerous-things.
Ward, Jesmyn. *Salvage the Bones*. Bloomsbury, 2011.

Epilogue
What Has Changed since Anthropocene Fictions?

ADAM TREXLER

Surveying the narratives discussed in *Cli-Fi and Class,* we can perhaps better understand this moment of climate fiction by differentiating it from the two decades that came before. Until roughly the 2010s, most cli-fi had a remarkably simplistic way of representing the temporality, politics, and economics of climate change. From the first novels in the early 1970s to around 2010, the vast majority of cli-fi understood global warming as a remote threat with a binary choice: humanity as a whole would either avert the crisis completely or suffer a dystopian or apocalyptic fate. Of course, this binary approach to a deferred climate change harbored significant conceptual errors, not least its presumption that the future would arrive as a disastrous moment rather than a long series of painful, unevenly distributed impacts. As my *Anthropocene Fictions* documents, the novels of the 1990s and the first decade of the 2000s almost universally compounded this geophysical oversimplification with an economic and political one, effectively representing the idea that "society should mass against the [capitalist] system, as the only hope of deferring an era of catastrophic climate change" (Trexler 198). As has often been noted, apocalyptic threats have spectacularly failed to marshal adequate emissions reductions; this rhetorical move must be judged an abysmal failure. Many serious thinkers continue to lay the fundamental responsibility for climate change at the feet of capitalism, and not without reason: it is undeniable that most greenhouse gas emissions have been produced by capitalist economies and that those economies have singularly failed to reduce fossil fuel use without strong government intervention into markets. Many climate critics believe emissions will only be addressed by a wholesale dismantling of the capitalist system, including severely curtailing individual consumption, reversing the fundamental economic goal of national growth, restructuring national and international monetary systems, all but eliminating global transportation and trade, and ending capitalistic organization of labor.

Even considering the potential merits of such a position, the novels of 1990–2010 tended to share a simplistic analysis of capitalism that was flawed in ways that limited meaningful political engagement. By arguing that climate change is an inevitable consequence of capitalism, they would defer specific and concrete action on myriad environmental problems until after total revolution or systemic collapse. Storm breaks, the blocking of oil pipelines, species protections, incremental battery development, a regional choice on coal versus wind power plants, and numerous other impactful but subsystemic interventions are pushed out of the political view. Just as problematically, the rhetoric of those novels cannot seriously contemplate a different future, because they are locked in a paradoxical nostalgia for the twentieth century: "If climate change presented a terrible threat to the future, writers could mount an impassioned paean to the preservation of the current order," an order dominated by capitalism (Trexler 199). This led most novels to elide the present while displaying a "deep nostalgia for the individual rights, safeties and comforts of late-twentieth-century capitalism" (199).

Indeed, perhaps the most serious charge against the novels of the 1990s and early 2000s is that they were structurally incapable of assembling a meaningful politics. The call for society to "mass against the system" presumes a social imaginary in which apocalyptic terror could erase all social difference, disregard culture, and force people to forget their material positions and look as one to the scientific and policy experts for new instruction on how to live and even, in some cases, how to depopulate without protest. Early thrillers imagined an elite group of scientists and officials saving the day by forcing draconian action. Later, novels like Kim Stanley Robinson's *Science in the Capital* trilogy explicitly imagined a politics whereby that elite group would dictate the entire transformation of society. The novels of this period rarely paid serious attention to the specific, uneven, and often catastrophic transformations that would be demanded of real groups of people, from coal miners, auto workers, and flight attendants, to car salespeople, farmers, and homebuilders, to Wall Street venture capitalists and the leaders of developing countries committed to decreasing poverty. Such a list could be expanded almost infinitely. The failure to give even a passing glance to those ways of life, as entrenched ways of producing the means of survival and deep identity, made for an impossibly dematerialized politics. Many more novels forewent politics entirely, simply portraying the dystopian threat as significant enough to "force change," without any reflection on who would be in a position to dictate that change, and who would passively and wholly receive that dictation.

Already as I was concluding the writing of *Anthropocene Fictions*, it was clear that more and more of the complexities of the late Anthropocene were finding their way into novels. Significant organizations were actively adapting to the discourse of climate change: energy and automotive corporations, insurers, government bureaucracies, charities, armies, voters, and artists reconfigured themselves to address their direct emissions and the politics of climate, with specific groups both pledging change and aligning in reaction. To take a schematic example, the Hummer line of extreme SUVs, which had become a familiar symbol of masculine status and climate villainy, was retired by GM in 2010. At the time of writing, the launch of a luxury electric car company has produced one of the wealthiest individuals in history, and even the Hummer mark now promises to be reintroduced as an all-electric platform. These changes are hardly indications of the collapse of the global economy, nor the elimination of global emissions, but they indicate complex reorganizations of capital in the Anthropocene. A novel like Bacigalupi's *The Windup Girl* (2009) could now describe how changed climate, risen seas, and energy constraints could force a diverse collection of agencies—businesses, governmental ministries, populations, storms, species, fuels—to reform each other. In Bacigalupi's imagined future, all class positions are similarly realigned: refugees and a criminal hierarchy are organized around scavenging fuel; sex work is exoticized to the point of profound unsustainability; mechanical labor is returned to genetically modified animals, while white-collar accountants must also use a foot treadle to run their computers; international capitalists practice cultural espionage in order to recreate biodiversity. This vision of the Anthropocene exemplifies a transformation of cli-fi, and it was driven by a growing cultural recognition that climate change's more extreme effects had begun to arrive.

As a matter of personal experience, when I began thinking about climate change and fiction in 2008, I viewed global warming as a vague but pervasive dread of the future and secretly hoped scientific warnings might be overblown. Without realizing the irony, I also believed climate science was finally forcing political discourse from denialism to serious bipartisan discussions of the best modes of emissions reductions. If anything, environmental dread seems more widespread now, and yet global warming politics in the United States have become even more entrenched in partisanship. Eleven years after turning my attention to cli-fi, as I sketched out a contribution to this volume, historically strong winds fanned the flames of wildfires that consumed the Pacific Northwest. A lifelong asthmatic, I found myself organizing the evacuation of two families from Portland to escape the smoke, our city's climate suddenly an immediate and personal crisis. To be sure, the ability to rely on credit cards and remote work, features of our class position, allowed us to find safety more easily, but it was flight nevertheless. In a very real way, then, my situated experience of thinking about climate fiction has shifted in the last twelve years, from a hope that we could imagine a future without or beyond the crisis, to an urgent, personal need to better understand the complex scene before me. This represents a fundamentally different temporal position, from futurity to contiguous present, and a concomitant shift from the Anthropocene totality to distributed agents, both human and nonhuman. In this moment, the urgent task is not just to avert but to better account for these unstable and conflicted systems, to better "imagine a way deeper into the crisis," in the words of Rosenthal and Molesky in the introduction. Perhaps the implied reader in the Anthropocene is undergoing a similar change, becoming more specifically located within geographic and ecological systems and more animated by their pluriform modes of making a living. In short, the idealized reader would seem to be undergoing an intersectional and material transformation toward ecological reading.

A transformation of this kind can certainly be seen in the climate fiction published after 2009 or so, possibly in relation to the global financial crisis. To be sure, there were earlier novels with compelling treatments of class. From a greater distance, T. C. Boyle's *A Friend of the Earth* (2000) deserves more praise as a visionary deconstruction, describing the collective dilapidation of domestic workers, upper-middle-class executives, and elite celebrities in California a quarter-century hence. So early, Boyle described how not one apocalypse but periodic floods, brownouts, forest fires, fish species die-outs, monoculture farm collapses, and the evaporation of government entitlements and insurance coverage would steadily corrode the elegant homes, careers, diets, and bodies of Californians of all classes. Across the novel's forty-year arc, Ty Tierwater narrates his class descent from inheritor of a strip mall fortune, to leader of an ecomovement, monkey-wrencher, political prisoner, animal caretaker, and finally climate refugee. From his vantage point, California's enviable glamour, safety, entitlement, and environmental idealism all melt under inescapable global heating.

During the writing of *Anthropocene Fictions*, it was clear to me that the impacts of climate change would be experienced economically, rather than solely as unmediated disaster. As *A Friend of the Earth* and *The Windup Girl* indicated, climate change already shapes supply-side facets like industrial regulation, global trade, fisheries, agricultural production, and labor, as well as demand-side considerations like how we eat, where we live, how we move, and even what options we have in a crisis. My thinking at the time was directed at how not to oversimplify the impacts and responses to global heating, dangers that were all too real in contemporary politics, fictions, and criticism alike. While that imperative remains, the essays in this volume incontrovertibly demonstrate what I could not see, that Anthropocene culture, in both the material and social meanings of "culture," is structured by class positions. Reading class in cli-fi is not a simple fixing of characters in static strata but rather involves closely observing how economies organize experience and choice in the material world. By its very premise, climate fiction rematerializes social narrative, drawing collections of characters into engagement with environmental forces beyond an individual's control, no matter their economic agency.

With the benefit of hindsight, I see that *Anthropocene Fictions* specifically neglected how class and climate change interface as two elements in the nonhuman gestalt that shapes character. An example can be instructive. In Barbara Kingsolver's *Flight Behavior*, the central conflict is over a wooded hill where butterflies have come to roost due to the changing climate. The hill is an ideal example of a boundary object: Dellarobia experiences it aesthetically and wishes it to remain intact for the safety of her domestic space; men in the family view its wood as a product (although erosion concerns could eliminate the value of surrounding farmland); scientists view the roosting site as a natural space productive of knowledge; activists want the hill to remain "natural." The entirety of this boundary object, however, is shaped by class: it is an argument over a place as productive capital, a sweated product, middle-class aesthetic experience, working-class precarity of home and safety, the intellectual class's privileged access to a field of study, a preacher's privileged ability to adjudicate family and moral imperatives in light of scriptural approaches to land, and middle-class environmentalists' assumptive assimilation of property. Kingsolver's design cannot be interpreted properly without diagramming class interests, which structure these incommensurable voices. *Flight Behavior* is extraordinary in its refusal to flatten these positions: all of them make moral and aesthetic claims that demand consideration in a polyphonic system.[1] Kingsolver's novel makes a compelling case that it is the incommensurability of these class interests that has doomed efforts by scientists, artists, and policymakers to form a unitary experience of climate change.

As has long been documented by critical theory, narrative strategies are rooted in class and social structures. The novel, as an artistic form, has been historically dependent on class-based narrative. If climate change is expressed through economic class, it follows that literary narrative also fragments along these lines. Homer, Crusoe, and Austen, or even a near-contemporary like Raymond Carver, developed archetypal narratives structured around social relations. Essays in this volume show that cli-fi continues to draw on these narratives: Odysseus's search for home, Crusoe's bourgeois fantasies of individual self-sufficiency, Austen's explorations of Victorian domesticity, and Raymond Carver's interrogations of suburban interiority. To take one through line, climate change is transforming "home" as a controlling narrative structure, as is made clear in the present volume when Horwitz foretells a time in which climate change's impacts will spread beyond poor communities and communities of color, or when Brown critiques climate fictions' nostalgia for partial ideals and patriarchal desires, or when Goddu argues that climate change physically and psychically dislocates home, lending a pervasive mood of dread that excludes simple class solidarity or middle-class community. These critical accounts document climate change's transformation of literary form, precisely because climate change is experienced in terms of class. The situating of character, place, dialogue and social interaction, character motivation, intertextual meaning-making, and even narrative hope and dread operate differently in the Anthropocene. These effects are of first importance for any account of the twenty-first-century novel, because the material foundations that underpin narrative are shifting with changing climatic systems. Numerous other narrative tropes are rooted in economic class, such as the rags-to-riches story, the bildungsroman, novels of decadence, science fiction entrepreneurialism, urban realism, and the numerous variations of romantic narrative. It seems inevitable that the class-based critiques of this volume will inspire further critical examinations of these and other narrative structures in climate fiction.

A serious failing of my *Anthropocene Fictions* is its failure to address intersectional aspects of class and specifically how the first several decades of climate fiction alternately caricatured and eliminated nonwhite points of view. As Schneider-Mayerson suggests in this collection, climate fiction's strong reliance on white characters evades consideration of poor and minority experiences of contemporary climate discourse and Anthropocene futurity. It would seem that the totalizing, planetary discourse of climate science and emissions rhetoric, a supposed system on behalf of "all," was too easily and too often mobilized by supremacist worldviews. So much climate fiction privileges a technocratic, hierarchical mode of emissions governance that would dictate access to energy and consumption, with little interrogation of its own values and a contempt for positions that would challenge it. Although I noticed at the time a true lack of nonwhite accounts of climate change, *Anthropocene Fictions* did not sufficiently interrogate the structural causes of this, nor the fundamental importance of centering the nonwhite narrative perspectives that had found their way to print. If climate fiction rematerializes social narrative, a pressing critical problem, as described by Bain in this book, is why Black structural positions have typically been figured as peripheral to saving a white, middle-class ideal that externalized emissions. "Reproducing and renewing Black people's (whether as body or flesh) structural relation to capitalism—as commodity, as means of production, as raw material for extraction" raises fundamental questions for how racialized class relations might be structurally inseparable from both carbon economies and supremacist modes of disaster amelioration.

Emerging, class-inflected interpretations of Black, postcolonial, and Indigenous climate narratives help address endemic weaknesses of climate critical theory. Indigenous technologies of adaptation, survival, and narrative decenter white dreams of technocratic, planetary harmony. Too often, other climate novels included Indigenous characters but excised their likely critiques of white culture, whether they are joyfully accepting repatriation into middle-class Virginia in Robinson's *Science in the Capital* trilogy or being portrayed as victims of the Anthropocene without any discussion of the traditional knowledge and "adaptive resiliency" that Jennifer Schell highlights in this volume. These silences deserve further critical interrogation. From another perspective, Black-centered, self-consciously postcolonial utopias call attention to a fundamental need for climate strategies that are not class-or race-"blind" but organize citizens in ways that attend to economic and climatic injustice. While deserving of critique, *Black Panther*'s box office success indicates the timeliness of nonwhite approaches to geoecological governance. This volume indicates that such Black and Indigenous climate narratives can expressly refuse assimilation, challenging climate politics to model nonunitary, inclusive, and locally controlled modes of enacting emissions reductions and impact amelioration. Without such explicit, conscious perspective-building, climate criticism seems doomed to continue in the inadequacy that has defined so much activism around global heating.

As this volume ably shows, mapping the material agencies that animate social classes is of first importance in organizing and rearticulating contemporary climate fiction. Novels have often sold the promise of a collective experience of climate change that would animate the disempowered and lead to unified, international action. Since the publication of *Anthropocene Fictions*, however, working-class political organization has just as often aligned in reaction *against* what have been perceived as elitist approaches to emissions reduction, from the *gilets jaunes* movement in France to the Rust Belt coal miners who became a central emblem of Trump's 2016 campaign. The persistence of "leave it in the ground" or attempts to tax industries out of work have shown the durability of class and material conditions as analytic categories, and the political futility of scientific and end-of-time environmental warnings. So too, middle-class voters have proved less enthusiastic about emissions reductions when the identifiers of class position—from cars to single-family homes—are threatened. Climate justice demands accounting for distributed impacts of unsustainable economic practices no less than failing environmental systems. Despite an unjust distribution of firefighters and disaster insurance, we have recently seen how megafires can obliterate the Malibu mansion, the Santa Rosa vineyard, and the Paradise community of fabricated homes, alike. One continues to hope that a plethora of asynchronous crises could finally help us abstract from the experience of personal vulnerability. A meaningful climate politics would seem to demand the equally distributed engagement of humans crossed and divided by their investments in material things, from jobs and fuel sources to identification with regions, races, histories, and biomes. Finding the common resonance in these polyphonic narratives is an epic critical task, one that has just begun.

NOTE

1. In this sense, Mikhail Bakhtin's critical theorization of polyphonic narrative as a plurality of voices that are irreducible to a single truth may deserve more examination, particularly as "voices" could be extended to describe the agency of nonhumans and humans, as well as points of view constructed by class.

WORKS CITED

Trexler, Adam. *Anthropocene Fictions: The Novel in a Time of Climate Change.* U of Virginia P, 2015.

Contributors

Kimberly Bain is Assistant Professor in the Department of English Language and Literatures at the University of British Columbia. Her forthcoming first book, entitled *On Black Breath*, traces a genealogy of breathing and Blackness in the United States.

Jeffrey M. Brown is Associate Professor of English in the Department of English, Writing, and Journalism at Saint Joseph's University. His work has recently appeared in *Modern Drama*, *Life Writing*, and *Text & Presentation*.

Jessica Cory teaches at Appalachian State University and is a PhD candidate specializing in Native American, African American, and environmental literature at the University of North Carolina, Greensboro. She is the editor of *Mountains Piled upon Mountains: Appalachian Nature Writing in the Anthropocene* (WVU Press, 2019) and the coeditor (with Laura Wright) of *Appalachian Ecocriticism and the Paradox of Place* (UGA Press, forthcoming 2023). Her creative and scholarly writings have been published in the *North Carolina Literary Review*, *North Dakota Quarterly*, *Northern Appalachia Review*, and other fine publications.

Teresa A. Goddu is Professor of English and American Studies at Vanderbilt University. She is the author of *Gothic America: Narrative, History, and Nation* (Columbia UP) and *Selling Antislavery: Abolition and Mass Media in Antebellum America* (U of Pennsylvania P). Her current research focuses on contemporary US climate fiction.

Jennifer Horwitz received her PhD in Literature from Tufts University and is a lecturer at the Rhode Island School of Design. Her research focuses on representations of education in multi-ethnic US literature that help us envision and enact the teaching needed in our time of climate crisis; her writing can be found in the journal *Multi-Ethnic Literature of the United States*.

Magdalena Mączyńska is Associate Professor of English and World Literature at Marymount Manhattan College, where she teaches courses on climate fiction and contemporary Anglophone literature. She is the author of *The Gospel According to the Novelist: Religious Scripture and Contemporary Fiction* (2015).

Andrew Milner is Emeritus Professor of English and Comparative Literature at Monash University in Melbourne, Australia. His recent publications include *Locating Science Fiction* (2012), *Again, Dangerous Visions: Essays in Cultural Materialism* (2018), *Science Fiction and Climate Change* (2020), and *Science Fiction and Narrative Form* (2023).

Jason de Lara Molesky is a postdoctoral fellow at Harvard's Mahindra Humanities Center, after which he will be assistant professor of English at Saint Louis University. He holds an MFA from the University of Mississippi and a PhD from Princeton University. Along with *Cli-Fi and Class*, he is also coediting *Teaching Energy Humanities* with Debra J. Rosenthal (forthcoming from MLA). His monograph in progress analyzes the artistic, activist, and environmental legacies of American company towns. His articles and essays can be found at jasonmolesky.com.

Lisa Ottum is Associate Professor of English at Xavier University in Cincinnati, Ohio. She is the coeditor of *Wordsworth and the Green Romantics: Affect and Ecology in the Nineteenth Century* (U of New Hampshire P, 2016).

Martín Premoli is Assistant Professor of English at Pepperdine University. His book project, *Global Fiction and Environmental Disaster*, is currently under contract with Bloomsbury Academic Press.

Debra J. Rosenthal is Professor of English at John Carroll University. She is the author of *Performatively Speaking: Speech and Action in Antebellum American Literature* (2015) and *Race Mixture in Nineteenth-Century US and Spanish American Fictions* (2004). She is the editor of *Teaching Climate Change Literature* (forthcoming from MLA) and *The Routledge Sourcebook on Uncle Tom's Cabin* (2003). Along with *Cli-Fi and Class*, she is also coediting *Teaching Energy*

Humanities with Jason Molesky (forthcoming from MLA). She is the coeditor with David S. Reynolds of *The Serpent in the Cup: Temperance in American Literature* (1997) and coeditor with Monika Kaup of *Mixing Race, Mixing Culture: Inter-American Literary Dialogues* (2002).

Jennifer Schell is Professor of English at the University of Alaska Fairbanks. Her specialties include North American literature, circumpolar writing, critical animal studies, and environmental humanities. After publishing *"A Bold and Hardy Race of Men": The Lives and Literature of American Whalemen* (2013), she authored numerous articles on ecogothic themes, most of which involve endangered or extinct species. She is currently working on her second book, *Ghost Species: North American Extinction Writing and the Ecogothic*.

Matthew Schneider-Mayerson is Associate Professor of English at Colby College and an affiliate in the Department of Environmental Studies. His research combines literary criticism, cultural studies, and sociology to examine the cultural dimensions of climate change, with a focus on climate justice. He is the author, editor, or coeditor of four books: *Peak Oil: Apocalyptic Environmentalism and Libertarian Political Culture, An Ecotopian Lexicon, Eating Chilli Crab in the Anthropocene: Environmental Perspectives on Life in Singapore,* and *Empirical Ecocriticism: Environmental Narratives for Social Change*.

B. Jamieson Stanley (Ben) is Assistant Professor of English at the University of Delaware. They work at the intersection of postcolonial studies, contemporary Global South literatures, the environmental humanities, and food studies, with a particular interest in how we narrate and understand relationships between globalization and environmental precarity. Ben's monograph, *Eating and the Global Environment: Narrating Precarity in Neoliberal India and South Africa*, is under contract with University of Minnesota Press.

Adam Trexler is the author of *Anthropocene Fictions: The Novel in a Time of Climate Change* and many essays on contemporary American fiction.

Index

abstraction, 2, 6–7, 134–35, 139–45, 171–72
abundance, 53–56. *See also* scarcity
Achebe, Chinua, 180
activism, 6–7, 10n1, 26–28, 40–43, 56, 93, 97n4, 106–8. *See also* justice
Adamson, Joni, 114n1
adaptation, 66, 93–94, 128, 154–56, 187–88, 190–91, 200, 241–42. *See also* resiliency
addiction, 38
adoption, 63–64, 129
affect, 68–70; American Dream, 195–96, 205, 209, 213–16, 218–19; climate change and, 85–86, 171–76, 180–82; climate fiction and, 87–88; knowledge and, 176; poverty and, 86–87. *See also individual affects by name*
Africanfuturism, 50–61
Afrofuturism, 47–50, 59–60; Africa and, 50–52, 54
agency, 18, 33–34, 180–81, 242; collective, 24–28, 30n7; distributed, 2, 15; knowledge and, 84–87, 173–74, 186; lateral, 38–39; nonhuman, 18, 24–26, 210–11; obscuring, 37–38; weak, 41–43. *See also* knowledge
air. *See* atmosphere
Akomfrah, John, 50
Alaimo, Stacy, 37–38
Alaska: Alaska natives, 118, 120–30, 130nn1–3, 130n5; climate change in, 117–18, 123–27; history of, 120–24; Land Claims Task Force, 121–22. *See also* Indigenous people

Alaska Federation of Natives (AFN), 121–22
Alaska Native Claims Settlement Act (ANCSA), 121–22, 130n6
Albrecht, Glenn, 221
almanacs, 134–35, 145–46
amnesia, 17–18, 23–26
anarcho-syndicalism, 20–21
Anderson, Gregers, 97n1
animacy, 18, 25–26
Anson, April, 118–20, 123–24
Anthropocene, 2, 16–18, 29, 42–43, 172–73, 181–82, 184; Black, 48–50; Indigenous knowledge and, 63–64, 66; literary modes of, 24–26; narratives of, 38; novels of, 34; racial capitalism and, 4; settler colonialism and, 76n3; sites of, 28; time and, 37–38
anxiety, 38, 168–69, 200, 205–6, 222–26; racial, 5
apocalypse, 59, 63–66, 68, 88–89, 118–20, 123–26, 128–29, 180, 206, 208, 211, 218, 235–36. *See also* catastrophe; crisis
Appalachia, 16, 29n2, 83–84
Aravamudan, Srinivas, 216–17
Arctic National Wildlife Refuge (ANWR), 117, 122–23
Arctic Slope Regional Corporation (ASRC), 123
art: Black traditions of, 134–35; climate change and, 21, 32–33, 184–85, 188; imaginative potential of, 15; proletarian traditions of, 24–28; ruins and, 209; trash and, 212–13. *See also* climate fiction

250 INDEX

assimilationism, 5, 67, 121–22, 124, 127, 241–42
atmosphere, 2–3, 15–16, 82–83, 133–37, 141, 145–46, 147n6, 193, 215. *See also* climate change; weather, weathering
Atwood, Margaret, 83–84; *Oryx and Crake*, 16, 19–20, 206–8, 210–13, 216–19

Baccolini, Raffaella, 156
Bacigalupi, Paolo: "The Calorie Man," 167–72, 174–75, 177–81; "The Tamarisk Hunter," 82, 87, 95–97; *Water Knife*, 207; *The Windup Girl*, 167–68, 237, 239
Bahng, Aimee, 134–35
Bang, Megan, 75
Bangladesh, 187, 201n5
Baucom, Ian, 143–44
Bellamy, Edward, *Looking Backward*, 162–63
Berger, Thomas R., 130n6
Bering, Vitus, Second Kamchatka Expedition, 120
Berlant, Lauren, 38–39
Berry, Wendell, 101
Best, Stephen, 44n3
Bilodeau, Chantal: *Forward*, 21; *Sila*, 21
bioderegulation, 35–36, 38–39, 42–43. *See also* deregulation
biodiversity, 52, 117, 186, 237
bioengineering, 192–93, 196–97, 206
biopolitics, 38, 120
Black Panther (dir. Coogler), 47–48, 50–51, 53–60, 241–42
Black radicalism, 4, 136–41, 145–46
Bloom, Dan, 47–48
body: class and, 4, 20, 35, 53; climate change and, 57–58, 64–65, 170–71; race and, 57–58, 134, 139–46, 195–96; theater and, 20–21
Bonds, Judy, 107–9
Bong Joon-ho, *Snowpiercer*, 15–16, 219n1
Boyle, T. C., *A Friend of the Earth*, 184–85, 238–39
Bragard, Véronique, 211–12, 219n3
Brand, Dionne, 76n5
breath, 136

Brecht, Bertolt, 22
Brennan, Teresa, 35
British Trades Union Congress, 164–65
Broadway, 17, 20, 28. *See also* theater
Bullard, Robert and Linda, 6–7, 11n7, 103–4
Burden-Stelly, Charisse, 139–40
Bureau of Indian Affairs, 121
burnout, 32–33, 43. *See also* exhaustion
Busch, Briton Cooper, 130n4
Butler, Octavia, *Parable of the Sower*, 15–16, 18–20, 47, 49, 102, 104–5, 109–14, 184–85, 207

Cajete, Gregory, 114n2
Campbell Memorial Award, 151–52
Camus, Albert, 27–28
Canavan, Gerry, 47, 59
capitalism, 8, 32–33, 117; anti-capitalism, 42–43, 63–64; biopolitical regime of, 38–39; boom-and-bust cycles of, 34–35; climate change and, 37–38, 63, 74–75, 117–18, 133–46, 157, 177–78, 180–81, 186–88, 205–19, 235–37; climate fiction and, 119–20, 124–30, 235–36; corporate, 121–22; decolonialism and, 67–68, 74–75; environmental degradation and, 36–37, 120–21; fossil, 3–5, 24–25, 28; global, 33–34, 36–37, 173–74; green, 3–4; origins of, 2–3; petro-, 47–52, 56–57; racial, 4–6, 11n4, 49, 51–52, 133–46, 146n2, 226–27, 241; resource extraction and, 55–57, 66–70, 126–28, 138–40, 144–45; speculation and, 134–35, 143–45; "24/7," 35–37. *See also* extraction; global, globalization; neoliberalism
Capitalocene, 2, 10n3, 37–38, 165n1
Caracciollo, Marco, 206
care, 39–40, 145–46
catachronism, 216–18. *See also* time, temporality
catastrophe, 7–8, 63, 74, 84–85, 88–89, 94, 97, 134–39, 144–45, 186, 200, 206–8, 216–17, 235–36. *See also* apocalypse; crisis

INDEX 251

causality, 6–7, 33–34, 37–41, 171–72
Center for the Study of Science Fiction, 151–52
ceremony, 72–74
Césaire, Aimé, 68–69
Chakrabarty, Dipesh, 181
character, 22–24, 63–64, 193–94; Indigenous representation, 86–87, 119–20, 126, 128–29
Chavkin, Rachel, 23
Chinese Communist Party (CCP), 160–61
Ciénaga, Colombia, 15–16. *See also* company towns
citation, 136
Clark, Timothy, 21, 85–86
class, 1–3, 8, 240; anxiety and, 222–26; climate change and, 1–9, 17–22, 29, 63, 65, 67–68, 81–97, 104–5, 109–13, 118, 168–75, 178–82, 205–6, 223, 232–33, 242; climate fiction and, 1, 3–4, 7–8, 15–18, 20–21, 24–29, 63–65, 81–97, 152, 163–65, 180–82, 185, 189–97, 205–9, 211–19, 221–33, 233n2, 237–42; colonialism and, 167–69; company towns and, 19–22, 28–29; energy economy and, 47–48, 52–60, 67–68; in environmental studies, 82–97; gender and, 229–30; genre and, 7–8; geophysical process of stratifying, 3–4, 9; global working class, 23; higher education and, 91–92, 102, 105–7; homelessness and, 222–27; Indigenous people and, 70–74; mobility and, 4–5, 109–13, 137–38; nature and, 2, 56–57; nostalgia and, 171–75, 177, 180–81; performativity and, 53; place and, 103–13, 115n3; race and racialization of, 4–6, 23, 64–65, 67–68, 103–4, 137–38, 146n2, 167–69, 215–18, 226–28, 241–42; reciprocity and, 63–64; socioeconomic justice and, 1–4, 6–8, 15–16, 24–29, 81–97; solidarity and, 229–32, 233n3; theater and, 20–21, 24–25, 27–28, 30n9; transnational operations of, 48–52, 54–57, 59–60
climate change, 2, 63, 205; affects of, 221–23, 233n1, 237–38; agency and, 180–81; in Alaska, 117–19, 123–27; capitalism and, 37–38, 63, 74–75, 117–18, 133–46, 157, 177–78, 180–81, 186–88, 205–19, 235–37; class and, 1–9, 17–22, 29, 63, 65, 67–68, 81–97, 104–5, 109–13, 118, 168–75, 178–82, 205–6, 223, 230–33, 242; colonialism and, 167–69, 186–87, 196–97; denial of, 198–99, 237–38; disease and, 94–97, 127–30; dystopia and, 47–50, 52–53, 57–60, 110, 156, 158, 197–98, 207–9, 218–19, 235–37; economy and, 37–38, 92–97, 103–5, 239; everyday and, 38; gender and, 93; global and, 19, 48, 193, 196–97, 201n4; higher education and, 101–2, 110–13; homelessness and, 221–25; humans and, 1, 6–7, 24–26, 35–38, 53, 64–66, 69–72, 74–75, 84–86, 102–3, 120–21, 142–43, 171–74, 180–82, 184–85, 205, 209–11, 215; Indigenous knowledge and, 63–68, 70, 74–75, 76n4; infrastructure and, 136–39; justice and, 1–9, 184–88, 194, 200; material culture and, 182n1; migration and, 113–14; mitigating, 152–57, 196–97; narrative and, 1, 6–7, 15–17, 20–24, 63, 168, 184–86, 200n1, 206, 240; nostalgia and, 168–81; policy and, 152–53; psychogeography of, 221–23, 233n1; race and, 4–6, 49–50, 63, 65, 104–5, 118, 133–46, 146n2, 205; responsibility and, 1–2, 180–81, 186–88, 230–33, 241; scale and, 6–7, 21, 37–38, 42–43, 84–88, 205; science of, 152–55; subjectivity and, 181; time and, 37–38, 85–86; utopia and, 47–50, 53–60, 151–53, 156–63, 217–18
climate fiction, 2, 6–7, 10n2, 32–33, 87–88, 97n1, 184–85; agency and, 84–86; apocalypse and, 235–36; capitalism and, 119–20, 124–30, 235–36; class and, 1, 3–4, 7–8, 15–18, 20–21, 24–29, 63–65, 81–97, 152, 163–65, 180–82, 185, 189–97, 205–9, 211–19, 221–33, 233n2, 237–42; colonialism and, 118–20, 124–30, 167–69; company towns in, 15–19, 23, 26–27, 29; criticism and, 38;

climate fiction (*continued*)
energy economy and, 47–52, 59–60; family and, 213–16; future and, 47–48, 83–84, 197–98, 209–11, 216–18, 236–38; gender and, 191, 195–96; genre and, 7–8, 87–88; global and, 199–200; history and, 209–11, 235–39; home and, 105–13, 168–71, 177, 180–82, 221–29, 232–33, 240; Indigenous people and, 63–65, 86–87, 119–20, 126, 128–29, 190, 241–42; justice and, 1, 48, 88–89, 185–86, 188, 191–200, 241–42; materiality and, 211–13, 216–18; normal and, 7–8, 206, 208–9, 212, 214, 218–19; pedagogies of, 114; politics of, 15, 188–200, 235–37; primitivism and, 154–55; race and, 63–65, 119–20, 129, 185, 189–98, 226–28, 233n2, 241–42; realism and, 152–56; settler colonialism and, 118–20, 124–30; time and, 3–4, 37–38, 43, 44n8, 85–86, 237–38; utopia and, 47, 59–60, 152–58, 160–65; "world without us" trope, 210–11

cloud, 135, 138–45

coal. *See* fossil fuels

Coates, Ta-Nehisi, 49

collectivity, 5, 17–29, 30n7, 51–52, 72, 108–9, 114, 181, 242

Collingwood, Luke, 144

colonialism, 48–49, 51–52, 55–56, 68–69; class and, 167–69; climate change and, 167–69, 186–87, 196–97; in climate fiction, 118–20, 124–30, 167–69; extraction and, 67–72; race and, 167–69; settler, 64–70, 73–75, 76n1, 76n3, 117–18, 120–30, 191–92; tropes of, 118–20, 124–26, 128–30

Columbia Exposition (1893), 16

commons, 2–3, 134–35, 158–59

community, 6–7, 20–21, 42–43, 66, 70–71, 74–75, 101–3, 112–13, 145–46, 229

company towns, 15–19, 22–23, 26–27, 29nn1–2; radical politics in, 19–20, 28–29

complexity, 2, 6–7, 15, 21, 37–40, 237

compulsion, 5–6, 38

Conrad, Joseph, *Heart of Darkness*, 168–69, 175–81

consumerism, 5, 91, 201n4, 205–6, 209, 212–19, 230–32

Coogler, Ryan, 47–48. *See also Black Panther*

COVID-19 pandemic, 32–33

Cox, Oliver, 11n4

Crane, Stephen, "In the Depths of a Coal Mine," 29n2

Crary, Jonathan, 35–36

crisis, 1–4, 6–10, 21, 47–48, 59, 66, 69–70, 134–35, 205–6, 213–14, 221–23, 237–39. *See also* apocalypse; catastrophe

criticism, critique, 2, 37–38, 84–85, 88, 97n4, 173–74, 201n3, 219n3; exhaustion of, 32–34; liberation and, 38–40; Marxist, 2; modes of deliberation, 33–34, 39–41, 43; postcritique, 44n3. *See also* ecocriticism; reading

Cronon, William, 102–3, 173–74

Crutzen, Paul, 172–73

Cussler, Clive, 184–85

cyberpunk, 15–16, 18–19

Cyberpunk 2077, 15–16

Dadaism, 212–13

Davis, Heather, 76n3

Davis, Rebecca Harding, 28–29, 30n12

Dawson, Ashley, 3–4, 20–21, 30n7

Day after Tomorrow, The (dir. Emmerich), 47

debris barricade, 213

de Brum, Tony, 194

debt, 34–35, 81–82, 90–91, 227–28

decay, 209–11, 214–15

decolonialism, 67–68, 73–74, 76n3. *See also* colonialism

Deloria, Vine, Jr., 114n1

democracy, 3–4, 28, 30n11, 49, 196–97

Demos, T. J., 49

Demuth, Bathsheba, 130n4

depression, 32, 200, 224, 230–32

deregulation, 32–34. *See also* bioderegulation

Dery, Mark, 50–51

Desai, Rehad, *Miners Shot Down*, 56

De Shields, André, 20
Desmond, Matthew, 83–84
Dhahran, Saudia Arabia, 15–16. *See also* company towns
Diaz, Junot, "Monstro," 82, 87, 94–95
digital, 138–43, 147n9. *See also* cloud
Dillon, Grace L., 129–30
Dimaline, Cherie, *The Marrow Thieves*, 64–75
Dimock, Wai Chee, 32–33
disease, 94–95, 120–21, 126–30, 187, 217–18. *See also* public health
displacement, 109–13
DNA, 71–73, 76n8
domesticity, 168–72, 205–6, 211–16, 218–19
Dominican Republic, 94–95
Donald, Gerald, 136
dread, 221–33, 233n1, 237–38
Drexciya, *The Quest*, 136
drilling, 33–37, 44n5, 49–50, 121–23. *See also* extraction
Du Bois, W. E. B., 11n4; *Black Reconstruction*, 6
dystopia, dystopian narratives, 47, 57–60, 156–58, 207–8, 218–19; "resource dystopia," 48, 52–53. *See also* utopia, utopian narratives

ecocriticism, 37–38, 87–88, 97n4, 102–3, 172–74, 211–12, 219n3. *See also* criticism, critique
ecofascism, 119–20
ecogothic. *See under* gothic
ecopoverty, 81–84, 87–88, 97n4
ecosocialism, 151–52, 159–62
education: climate change and, 101–2, 110–13; place-based pedagogy and, 101–14, 114n2
Ehrlich, Gretel, *In the Empire of Ice*, 117–18
Elder, John, 114n2
embodiment. *See* body
Emmerich, Roland, 47
empathy, 188, 197–200, 228–29
enclosure, 2–3, 158–59
energy economy, 3–4, 34–35, 47–48, 52–60, 67–68

Engels, Friedrich, 2
enslavement, 49, 51–52, 56–57, 139–41, 143–44, 215
environmentalism, 5–7, 11n7, 24, 30n8, 33–34, 39–42, 92, 97n4, 102–5, 173–74, 186
environmental justice, 6–7, 97n4, 104, 108, 126, 188
environmental studies. *See* ecocriticism
epic, 24–25
Erdrich, Louise, *Future Home of the Living God*, 63–64
estrangement, 221
ethics, 33–34, 39–40, 88, 185–86, 197; action and, 40–42; bioethics, 76n8; land ethic, 101–2
Evans, Mei Mei, 102–3
exhaustion, 32–33, 38–40, 43, 44n3. *See also* burnout
exploitation, 36–37
expropriation, 2–6, 22, 27, 36–37, 47, 51–53, 56–60, 67–68, 72, 74–75, 81–82, 119–23, 133–34, 177, 186–88, 218. *See also* capitalism
extraction, 2–8, 22, 28, 33–35, 37–38, 49–50, 64–67, 205, 210; global dynamics of, 48, 51–56, 59–60, 63; Indigenous people and, 67–72; resource, 69–72, 117, 120–24, 126–28, 138–40, 144–45. *See also* capitalism

family, 213–16, 230
famine, 128–29, 187
Fanon, Frantz, 68–69
fatigue, 32. *See also* burnout; exhaustion
Faulkner, William, 6
Felski, Rita, 44n3
FEMA (Federal Emergency Management Agency), 189–90
feminism, 67
Ferguson, James, 55–56
film, 47–48, 50
finance, 34–35, 133–35, 143–44, 189, 191–92, 208–9, 238–39
Firestone Tire and Rubber Company, 29n1

254 INDEX

Flaubert, Gustave, 7–8
floods, 9, 25–26, 96–97, 106, 136–37, 145, 147n8, 152–55, 158, 187, 189, 191–93, 213, 221, 238–39
Florida, 221–24. *See also* Groff, Lauren
Ford, Richard, *Let Me Be Frank with You*, 221
Fordism, 5
fossil fuels, 2–6, 8, 22, 28, 34–37, 47–50, 52–53, 55–56, 76n4, 91, 93, 104–5, 114, 123, 170, 187–88, 210. *See also* extraction
Foster, John Bellamy, 2–3
Fourth National Climate Assessment, 117
fracking, 6, 33–43
framing, 21, 85–86, 185–86, 200n1, 201n3
Fraser, Nancy, 2–3
frontline, 2–4, 32, 102, 107, 114, 208
future, futurity, 47–48, 50, 136, 142–43, 197–98, 209–11, 216–18, 236–38; imagining, 43; Indigenous thought and, 63–64, 73–75

Gaard, Greta, 93
Gabriel, Hayden, 84
Garner, John, 29n2
Garrard, Greg, 84
gaslighting, 38–39
Gee, Maggie, *The Ice People*, 206, 208, 210, 215–19
gender, 54; activism and, 28–29; class and, 229–30; climate change and, 63, 93; climate fiction and, 191, 195–96; labor and, 52–53; nature and, 24; performativity and, 53
genetic engineering, 177–79
genocide, 4, 59, 65, 68–71, 133–34
genre, 7–8, 205; of Anthropocene, 24–25; structural change and, 32–33; transnational operations of, 48–52, 54
gentrification, 208–9, 223, 226–27, 231
geoengineering (terraforming), 49, 67–68, 156–57, 196–97
geology, 34, 49
Ghosh, Amitav, 7–8, 120, 175–76, 205; "recognition," 24–25
Giardina, Denise, 28–29

Gibbs, Lois, 6–7
Gibson, William, *Neuromancer*, 18
Gikuyu and Mumbi myth, 51
global, globalization, 33–34, 36–38, 60, 87–88, 92–93, 103, 170–72, 180, 193, 196–97, 199–200
Global South, 1–2, 48, 51–52, 107, 133–34, 186
Goodbody, Axel, 91
gothic, 7–8, 37–38; ecogothic, 214–15
Great Acceleration, 5, 205, 223
greenhouse gases, 1–2, 5, 84–85, 92–93, 186–88, 198–99, 235–36
grief, 64–65, 231–32
Griffiths, Devin, 30n6
Groff, Lauren, 233nn1–2; "Boca Raton," 225–26; "Dusk," 230–33; *Florida*, 221–30, 232–33, 233n1
Gruenewald, David, 106–7, 114n2
Gulf War, 34–35
Gwich'in Steering Committee, 123
Gyasi, Yaa, *Homegoing*, 56

Haas, Toni, 115n5
Hades and Persephone myth, 21–24
Haigh, Jennifer, *Heat and Light*, 33–43
Hall, Stuart, 4
Hamming, Jeanne, 195–96
Haraway, Donna J., 33–34, 74–75, 77n11
Harbel, Liberia, 15–16, 29n1. *See also* company towns
Harrison, Tony, 30n9
Hartman, Saidiya, 28
Harvey, David, 2–3
haunted house, 214. *See also* gothic
health care workers, 32
Heise, Ursula, 103, 193
Hertel, Thomas, 83
history, 209–11; causality and, 37–41; geologic, 34
Hofrichter, Richard, 115n3
home, homelessness, 221, 224–29, 232–33, 240
Homestead, 15–16. *See also* company towns
hooks, bell, 114n1

hope, 68–70, 237–38
horror, 214–16
Huber, Matthew, 3–4, 17
Hugo Awards, 151–52
Hulme, Mike, 67–68, 186
humans, 6–7, 24–26, 35–38, 53, 64–66, 69–72, 74–75, 84–86, 102–3, 120–21, 142–43, 171–74, 180–82, 184–85, 205, 209–11, 215
Hummer (SUV), 237
Hunger Games, The, 15–16, 219n1
Hurley, Andrew, 11n7
hurricanes, 113–14, 136–38, 142, 144–45, 147nn7–8, 158, 189
hyperobjects, 15

Iheka, Cajetan, 53–54
imperialism, 4, 36–37, 58, 176–79. See also colonialism; global, globalization
Indian Child Welfare Act, 63–64
Indigenous people: Black indigenization and, 76n6; class and, 70–72, 74; climate change and, 63–65, 67–68, 74–75, 76n4, 118–20, 123–27, 129–30; in climate fiction, 190, 241–42; environmental justice and, 123, 129–30; erasure of, 117–20, 124–26; genocide of, 59, 69–71, 120–21; hope and, 68–69, 75; Indigenous knowledge, 63–70, 72–75, 114n2, 241–42; kinship and, 72–75; placemaking and, 73–75; racialization of, 70–74, 76n6, 76n8, 129; residential schools and, 69–70, 121; resiliency and, 123–24, 126–30; temporality and, 66
individualism, 63, 102–3, 112–13
industrialization, 1–2, 49, 186–87
infrastructure, 2–6, 136–39, 210–11
insurance, 143–45
International Trade Union Confederation, 164–65
Iñupiaq, 118, 122–30, 130n1, 130n5
Iranian Revolution, 36–37

Jackson, Shona, 76n6
Jamail, Dahr, *The End of Ice*, 117–18
James, C. L. R., 11n4

James, Henry, 7–8
Jameson, Fredric, 151–52
Jefferies, Richard, *After London; or, Wild England*, 210–11
Johnson, Hazel, 6–7
Jones, Gavin, 97n2
justice, 5–7, 97n4, 107–9, 115n3, 118, 123–24, 126–27, 129–30, 184–88, 191–200, 233n2, 241–42. See also under class; climate change

Kahiu, Wanuri, 47–48, 51
Kantner, Seth, *Swallowed by the Great Land*, 117–18
Keeling, Kra, 50
Kilgore, De Witt Douglas, 195–96
Kimmerer, Robin Wall, 63–66
Kingsnorth, Paul, 43
Kingsolver, Barbara, 184–85; *Flight Behavior*, 81–82, 87–94, 188, 198–99, 221, 239–40
kinship, 72–75. See also Indigenous people
Klare, Michael, 19
Klein, Naomi, 10n1, 20–21, 30n7, 129–30
Knadler, Stephen, 84–85
knowledge: action and, 84–87, 173–74, 186; affect and, 176; traditional, 241–42. See also Traditional Ecological Knowledge (TEK)
Kolbert, Elizabeth, 43; *Field Notes from a Catastrophe*, 117–18
Kurzweil, Ray, 142–43

labor, 2–4, 48, 52–53, 56–57, 152, 164–65; deregulation of, 35–36; extraction and, 22, 53, 59–60; precarious, 23. See also class
Ladino, Jennifer, 181
Lane-Zucker, Laurie, 101–2
Lanzendörfer, Tim, 190–91
Latour, Bruno, 21, 32–33; *Gaïa Global Circus*, 21, 30n8
Lebron, Christopher, 58
LeMenager, Stephanie, 38, 205
Lenin, Vladimir, 162–63
Lent, Peter C., 130n4

Levihn-Kutzler, Karsten, 124
Levine, Caroline, 44n3
Lewis, Simon L., 76n3
Leyshon, Cressiday, 95
liberalism, 49. *See also* neoliberalism
literary criticism. *See* criticism, critique
local, localism, 6, 58–59, 69–70, 73–74, 76n4, 87–88, 97n4, 101–5, 170–73, 176, 241–42. *See also* place
Lord, Nancy, *Early Warming*, 117–18
Lowe, Thomas D., 85–86
Lowenthal, David, 172
Ludlow, 15–16. *See also* company towns

machines, 22, 35–36, 87–88, 142–43. *See also* technology
Maldives, 193–94
Malm, Andreas, 3–4, 10n1
Mangharam, Mukti Lakhi, 53
Marches for Science, 152
Marcus, Sharon, 44n3
Marikana platinum mine massacre, 56
Marsh, G. P., 172–73
Marsh, John, 86–87, 98n8
Marshall Islands, 194
Marx, Karl, 2–3, 145
Marxism, 33–34, 53; analyses of ecological crisis, 2–4, 10n1; "hidden abode" of production, 2–3
Maslin, Mark A., 76n3
materialism, materiality, 15, 22–23, 37–38, 59–60, 103, 139, 171–72, 176–77, 182n2, 211–13, 216–18, 219n3
May, Theresa J., 21
Mayer, Sylvia, 87–88
McCarthy, Cormac, *The Road*, 206, 210–19, 221
McKittrick, Katherine, 76n5
media, 25–26, 89, 186, 188; media studies, 50, 201n3
Mehnart, Antonia, 87–88, 188
Melamed, Jodi, 145–46
melodrama, 20, 30n6. *See also* theater
memory, 171–77, 217
metonymy, 22–23, 206, 209, 211–12
Middle Passage, 136, 141

migrancy, migration, 23, 88, 93, 175, 202n10; race and, 5, 56, 133–34. *See also* refugees
military, militancy, 3–4, 16, 32, 63, 70, 180–81, 207
Miller, J. Hillis, 180
mines, mining, 2–3, 17–18, 28, 29n2, 30n11, 55–56, 127–28; class and, 3–4, 56–57; mountain-top removal, 6, 104–9; slavery and, 5–6
Mitchell, Anaïs, *Hadestown*, 17–18, 20–29
Mitchell, Audra, 68–69, 76n3
Mitchell, Donald Craig, 130n6
Mitchell, Timothy, 3–4, 28, 30n11
mobility, 109–13, 137–38
modernism, modernity, 21, 28, 53–54, 133–34, 139, 168–69, 176, 178–79
Molesky, Jason, 37–38
Monteverdi, Claudio, *L'Orfeo*, 30n10
Moore, Jason W., 10n3, 120–21, 165n1
morality, 40–43, 101, 185–86, 239–40
Moretti, Franco, 205
Morris, William, *News from Nowhere*, 162–63
Morson, Gary Sault, 7–8
Morton, Timothy, 97n3
Moylan, Tom, 156
Murphy, Patrick D., 91
myth, 20–26, 51

Nachtigal, Paul M., 115n5
Nance, Terence, *Random Acts of Flyness*, 135–46
Napoleon, Harold, 120–21
narrative, 2; of anticipation, 87–88; of catastrophe, 87–88, 94–95; class and, 240; climate change and, 63, 168, 184–86, 200n1, 206, 240; nostalgia and, 175–79, 181; scale and, 6–7
Nasheed, Mohamed, 194
nation: class and, 1–5, 56; globalization and, 36–37, 171–72; Indigenous people and, 76n4, 119–20; nationalization, 3–4, 159, 161, 164; parochialism and, 199–200; race and, 5, 51–52, 56; security and, 186
natural gas. *See* fossil fuels

naturalism, 15–16, 118
nature: appropriation of, 120–21; class and, 2, 52, 56–57, 65; gendering, 24; human and, 172–74, 209; as neutral, 102–3; nostalgia and, 180
Naydan, Liliana M., 91
Nebula Awards, 151–52
Needham, Andrew, 5–6
Nelson, Edward, 128–29
neoliberalism, 23, 25–26, 32–33, 42–43, 58, 63, 121–22, 164, 171–72, 178–79, 205. *See also* capitalism; global, globalization
Newitz, Annalee, 191
Nixon, Rob, 39–40, 77n9, 84–86, 107, 199–200, 223
Noblezada, Eva Maria, 23
nostalgia, 168–82, 209, 214, 217–18, 236. *See also* solastalgia
novel, 7–8, 15, 33–39, 44n8, 84–86, 153–54, 184–86, 188, 205, 209, 211–13, 218, 240–41

Occupy movement, 229
ocean, 136, 140–41, 143–45
oil. *See* fossil fuels
Okorafor, Nnedi, 50–51; *Shuri: The Search for Black Panther,* 54
Okri, Ben, 51
Old Socialist Labor Party Hall (Barre, Vermont), 20–21, 26
Olsen, Tillie, 28–29, 30n12
Organization for Economic Co-operation and Development, 83
Orpheus and Eurydice myth, 17, 21–27, 30n10
Orr, David, 103–4, 114n2

Pan-Africanism, 54
Pancake, Ann, *Strange as This Weather Has Been,* 102, 104–9, 114
pandemics. *See* disease
paranoia, 32–33, 42
Parenti, Christian, 19, 63, 74
pedagogy, 84–87; place and, 101–14. *See also* education

performativity, 53
Peri, Jacopo, 30n10
peripheries, 2–3
petrocapitalism. *See under* capitalism
petroculture, 56–57
petroleum. *See* fossil fuels
Phillips, Helen, 232–33
Pierrot, Briggetta, 63–64, 118–20
Piketty, Thomas, 164
pipelines, 2–3, 121–22, 236
place: attachment to, 101–2; care for, 108–9; class and, 103–4, 106–13; erasure of, 114n1, 115n5; globalization and, 103; Indigenous knowledge of, 114n2; as neutral and universal, 102–3; place-based education, 101–14, 114n2, 115n5; placemaking, 63–66, 73–75; time and, 108–9
plantation, 2–4, 6, 11n5, 56–57; Plantationocene, 11n5
pollution, 1–2, 5–6, 37–40, 201n4, 207
postcolonialism, 54, 180, 241–42. *See also* colonialism
postmodernism, 164, 171–72
poverty studies, 81–84, 86–87, 95–97, 98n5; lived experience and, 87–88, 92; regionalism and, 87. *See also* class
Powell, Dana E., 77n9
power plants, 2–3, 161–62, 236
precarity, 17–18, 23, 56–57, 125–27, 221–22, 224–27
production, 2–4, 30n7, 33–35, 52–53, 98n7, 143, 157, 171–72, 201n4, 239, 241
protest, 1–4, 6–7, 15, 28–29, 93, 123
public health, 32, 125, 186–87
Pullman, 15–16. *See also* company towns
Pumzi (dir. Kahiu), 47–48, 51–53, 57–60

queerness, queer studies, 44n3, 65
Quesada, Sarah, 95

race, racialization, 2–3; abstraction and, 134–35, 139–45; Anthropocene and, 48–50, 59; anti-Blackness, 49, 59, 70–71, 76nn5–6, 133–46, 146n2; capitalism and, 4–6, 11n4, 49, 51–52, 133–46,

race (*continued*)
146n2, 226–27, 241; class and, 4–6, 23, 64–65, 67–68, 103–4, 137–38, 146n2, 167–69, 215–18, 226–28, 241–42; climate change and, 4–6, 49–50, 63, 65, 104–5, 118, 133–46, 146n2, 205; climate fiction and, 63–65, 119–20, 129, 185, 189–98, 226–28, 233n2, 241–42; embodiment and, 139–45; energy extraction and, 59–60; futurity and, 136, 142–43; Indigenous people and, 70–74, 76n6, 76n8, 129; mobility and, 137–38; speculative fiction and, 134–46; transnational operations of, 48–52, 56, 59–60; utopia and, 241–42; whiteness, white supremacy, 4–6, 49, 51–52, 56, 64–66, 68–72, 74, 90, 102–3, 118–20, 125–30, 137–38, 140–42, 146n2, 171–72, 185, 191–200, 213–15, 217–18, 221–33, 241–42

reading: causality and, 37–41; modest forms of, 44n3; paranoid, 42; reparative, 32–33, 42–43; speculative, 134–35. *See also* criticism, critique

realism, 7–8, 152–56, 174–77, 190–91, 205, 218–19

Rearden, Don, *The Raven's Gift*, 118–19, 126–30

reciprocity, 63–64, 72, 75

refugees, 89–91, 93, 109–14, 187, 193–95, 197–98, 202n10, 208

resiliency, 123–24, 126–28, 194–95, 241–42. *See also under* Indigenous people

Rich, Nathaniel, *Odds against Tomorrow*, 185–86, 188–92, 200, 201n2, 213

Rickford, Russell, 58

Rifkin, Mark, 76n7

Robinson, Cedric, 4, 11n4

Robinson, Kim Stanley, 151–52, 162–65, 184–85; *Aurora*, 156–57; *Fifty Degrees Below*, 152–53, 192, 194–96; *Forty Signs of Rain*, 152–53, 192; *Green Earth*, 152–56, 159; *The Ministry for the Future*, 161–62; *New York 2140*, 158–60, 213; *Red Moon*, 160–61; *Science in the Capital* trilogy, 185–86, 192–97, 200, 201n2, 236–37, 241–42; *Sixty Days and Counting*, 152–53, 155–56, 192, 196–97; *2312*, 156–57

Romanticism, 102–3, 173–74, 219n3

Rosch, Stephanie, 83

Ross, Andrew, 92–93

ruins, 47, 205–6, 209–11, 216–17, 219n2

Rushkoff, Douglas, 30n4

Saffir-Simpson scale, 136–37. *See also* hurricanes

Saint-Amour, Paul, 42–43

Samatar, Sofia, 51

Sanders, Scott Russell, 106–7

Santesso, Aaron, 175–76

satire, 190–91

Sayles, John, *Matewan*, 25–28

scale, 2, 6–7, 15; "scale framing," 21, 85–86. *See also under* climate change

scarcity, 48, 52–53, 69–70, 113, 128–29. *See also* abundance

Schenkkan, Robert, 30n9

Schilling, Dan, 74–75

Schneider-Mayerson, Matthew, 1–2, 233n2

science, 71–72, 103, 151–53, 161–62, 172–73, 192–93, 237–38, 241; Indigenous thought and, 63–66, 76n8; labor and, 152–53; uncertainty and, 184, 186. *See also* Traditional Ecological Knowledge (TEK)

science fiction, 7–8, 18–19, 119, 151–52, 192–93, 201n2, 205–6, 240. *See also* climate fiction

Science Fiction and Fantasy Writers of America, 151–52

Scranton, Roy, *Learning to Die in the Anthropocene*, 47

Sedgwick, Eve Kosofsky, 44n3

self-reliance, 102–3

service learning, 86–87. *See also* education

Seymour, Nicole, 63–64, 118–20

Sharpe, Christina, 49, 133–34

shock, 85–86, 96–97, 168–69

Simpson, Leanne Betasamosake, 67, 77n10

Sinclair, Upton, *The Jungle*, 27–28

singularity, 142–43

Sirius B (planet), 51

slavery. *See* enslavement
Smedley, Agnes, 28–29
Smith, Kimberly, 172
Sobel, David, 103, 114n2
solastalgia, 64–65, 69–70, 73–74, 221
solidarity, 23–24, 229–32, 233n3
Solnit, Rebecca, 229
sovereignty: agency and, 38; tribal, 63–64, 71–72, 74–75
space, 21, 48–49, 51, 157; domesticity and, 211–13, 215–16, 218–19, 226–27; Indigenous thought and, 72; pedagogy and, 114; race and, 138–43; regionalism and, 87; of utopia, 54–56. *See also* place
speculative fiction, 48, 134–46. *See also* climate fiction; science fiction
Spillers, Hortense, 139–41
Stegner, Wallace, 115n4
Stewart, Kathleen, 40–41
Stinson, James, 136
Stombeck, Andrew, 208–9
Stoppani, Antonio, 172–73
strikes, 2–4, 16, 25, 56, 159, 163–64
strong theory, 32–34. *See also* criticism, critique; reading
Stuelke, Patricia, 44n3
subjectivity, 180–81, 195–96
sublime, 102–3
subsistence, 123–24
survival, survivance, 38, 64–65, 68–69, 74–75, 108–14, 123–24, 129–30, 138–39
sustainability, 3–4, 47, 52–53, 67
Svoboda, Michael, 47–48
Syrian war, 113–14
Sze, Julie, 11n7
Szeman, Imre, 59

TallBear, Kim, 71, 76n8
Tantaquidgeon Zobel, Melissa, *Oracles*, 63–64
Taylor, Dorceta E., 77n9, 115n3
technology, 50; climate rhetoric and, 63, 65; Indigenous thought and, 63–75; utopia and, 54–57, 59. *See also* machines; science
terraforming. *See* geoengineering

theater, 17, 20; class and, 20–21, 24–25, 27–28, 30n9; energy regimes of, 20, 30n6; myth in, 21–26
Theroux, Marcel, *Far North*, 188, 197–98
Thomashow, Mitchell, 114n2
Thompson, E. P., 4
Thoreau, Henry David, *Walden*, 102–3
Three Mile Island disaster, 34, 36–39
Tidwell, TiaAnna, 126–27
time, temporality: Anthropocene and, 37–38; climate change and, 37–38, 43, 44n8; climate fiction and, 83–86; deep time, 34; of deregulation, 35–36; of fossil fuel extraction, 34–35; future and, 216–18, 237–38; Indigenous, 66; of justice, 43; novel and, 37–38; place and, 108–9; poverty and, 83–84; present and, 3–4
Todd, Zoe, 73, 76n3
Tony Awards, 23
tourism, 117, 207
toxic waste sites, 102, 106–8, 115n3
Trade Unions for Energy Democracy, 164–65
Traditional Ecological Knowledge (TEK), 63–68, 70, 72–75. *See also* Indigenous people
Trans-Alaska Pipeline System (TAPS), 122
Transcendentalism, 102–3
trauma, 32, 121, 161–62, 169, 181, 216, 221, 231–32
Trexler, Adam, 10, 91, 124, 213–14, 217–18; *Anthropocene Fictions*, 197–98, 235–36
Tropical Storm Elsa, 136–37
Tsing, Anna, 103
Tuana, Nancy, 4–6, 205
Tuck, Eve, 130n6
Turner, George, *Sea and Summer*, 207
Tuvalu, 193–94
two-spirit, 65
Tyndall Centre for Climate Change Research, 85–86

uncertainty, 168–69, 186
urban, 2–3, 28, 75, 124, 210–11, 218–19; utopia and, 54–55

utopia, utopian narratives, 47, 50, 57–60, 152–65, 192–95, 218–19; race and, 241–42; "resource utopia," 48, 53–54, 56–57, 59; revolution and, 152–53, 158–64; technology and, 50, 54–57, 59; urban space of, 54–55. *See also* dystopia, dystopian narratives
Utopian Studies (journal), 151–52

vagrancy laws, 5–6
vibranium. See *Black Panther*
Vidal, Gore, 159–60
violence, 2–3, 8, 169, 197–98, 209, 214–15; racial, 49, 56, 133–34, 139–40, 145, 176–79; settler colonial, 28, 49, 68–69, 71, 74–75, 76n1; "slow violence," 37–40, 84–86, 214; utopia and, 59–60
Vizenor, Gerald, 123–24
von Mossner, Alexa, 87–88
Voyles, Traci Brynne, 77n9

Wagner-Martin, Linda, 93–94
Wakanda. See *Black Panther*
Waldman, Katy, 221–22
war, warfare, 32, 34–35, 52, 58–59, 113–14, 120, 164, 194
Ward, Jesmyn, *Salvage the Bones*, 221
Warmer Collection (Amazon), 225–26
waste, 211–13
water, 40, 52–53, 95–97, 136. *See also* ocean; scarcity

Waters, Susannah, *Cold Comfort*, 118, 124–26
weak theory, 32–34, 38, 40–43, 44n3. *See also* criticism, critique; reading
weather, weathering, 133–45, 146n1
Weisman, Alain, *The World without Us*, 210–11
Whitehead, Colson, *Zone One*, 206, 208–9, 211, 213, 215–19
whiteness, white supremacy. *See under* race, racialization
Whyte, Kyle Powys, 63–64, 66–68, 76n4, 119, 123–24
Wildcat, Daniel, 114n1
wilderness, 102–3, 122–23, 173–74
wildfires, 32–33, 43–44nn1–2, 113–14
Willers, Bill, 173–74
Williams, Eric, 11n4
Wilson, Robert Charles, *Julian Comstock*, 197–98
Wohlforth, Charles, *The Whale and the Supercomputer*, 117–18
Womack, Ytasha, 50–51
working class. *See* class
World Health Organization, 32–33
World Science Fiction Society, 151–52
Wright, Alexis, *The Swan Book*, 63–64

Yusoff, Kathryn, 4, 49

Zola, Émile, *Germinal*, 17–18, 27
zombies, 206, 208–9, 213, 215–16
Zong (slave ship), 144

Recent books in the series
UNDER THE SIGN OF NATURE: EXPLORATIONS IN ENVIRONMENTAL HUMANITIES

James Perrin Warren • *Thoreau's Botany: Thinking and Writing with Plants*

Katherine Cox • *Climate Change and Original Sin: The Moral Ecology of John Milton's Poetry*

Jeremy Chow • *The Queerness of Water: Troubled Ecologies in the Eighteenth Century*

Monica Seger • *Toxic Matters: Narrating Italy's Dioxin*

Taylor A. Eggan • *Unsettling Nature: Ecology, Phenomenology, and the Settler Colonial Imagination*

Samuel Amago • *Basura: Cultures of Waste in Contemporary Spain*

Marco Caracciolo • *Narrating the Mesh: Form and Story in the Anthropocene*

Tom Nurmi • *Magnificent Decay: Melville and Ecology*

Elizabeth Callaway • *Eden's Endemics: Narratives of Biodiversity on Earth and Beyond*

Alicia Carroll • *New Woman Ecologies: From Arts and Crafts to the Great War and Beyond*

Emily McGiffin • *Of Land, Bones, and Money: Toward a South African Ecopoetics*

Elizabeth Hope Chang • *Novel Cultivations: Plants in British Literature of the Global Nineteenth Century*

Christopher Abram • *Evergreen Ash: Ecology and Catastrophe in Old Norse Myth and Literature*

Serenella Iovino, Enrico Cesaretti, and Elena Past, editors • *Italy and the Environmental Humanities: Landscapes, Natures, Ecologies*

Julia E. Daniel • *Building Natures: Modern American Poetry, Landscape Architecture, and City Planning*

Lynn Keller • *Recomposing Ecopoetics: North American Poetry of the Self-Conscious Anthropocene*

Michael P. Branch and Clinton Mohs, editors • *"The Best Read Naturalist": Nature Writings of Ralph Waldo Emerson*

Jesse Oak Taylor • *The Sky of Our Manufacture: The London Fog in British Fiction from Dickens to Woolf*

Eric Gidal • *Ossianic Unconformities: Bardic Poetry in the Industrial Age*

Adam Trexler • *Anthropocene Fictions: The Novel in a Time of Climate Change*

Kate Rigby • *Dancing with Disaster: Environmental Histories, Narratives, and Ethics for Perilous Times*

Byron Caminero-Santangelo • *Different Shades of Green: African Literature, Environmental Justice, and Political Ecology*

Jennifer K. Ladino • *Reclaiming Nostalgia: Longing for Nature in American Literature*

Dan Brayton • *Shakespeare's Ocean: An Ecocritical Exploration*

Scott Hess • *William Wordsworth and the Ecology of Authorship: The Roots of Environmentalism in Nineteenth-Century Culture*

Axel Goodbody and Kate Rigby, editors • *Ecocritical Theory: New European Approaches*

Deborah Bird Rose • *Wild Dog Dreaming: Love and Extinction*

Paula Willoquet-Maricondi, editor • *Framing the World: Explorations in Ecocriticism and Film*

Bonnie Roos and Alex Hunt, editors • *Postcolonial Green: Environmental Politics and World Narratives*

Rinda West • *Out of the Shadow: Ecopsychology, Story, and Encounters with the Land*

Mary Ellen Bellanca • *Daybooks of Discovery: Nature Diaries in Britain, 1770–1870*

John Elder • *Pilgrimage to Vallombrosa: From Vermont to Italy in the Footsteps of George Perkins Marsh*

Alan Williamson • *Westernness: A Meditation*

Kate Rigby • *Topographies of the Sacred: The Poetics of Place in European Romanticism*

Mark Allister, editor • *Eco-Man: New Perspectives on Masculinity and Nature*

Heike Schaefer • *Mary Austin's Regionalism: Reflections on Gender, Genre, and Geography*

Scott Herring • *Lines on the Land: Writers, Art, and the National Parks*

www.ingramcontent.com/pod-product-compliance
Lightning Source LLC
Chambersburg PA
CBHW021659230426
43668CB00008B/667